Hack

Home Truths About Foreign News

Ed Harriman

Zed Books Ltd.
London and New Jersey

Hack was first published by Zed Books Ltd., 57 Caledonian Road,
London N1 9BU, UK, and 171 First Avenue, Atlantic Highlands,
New Jersey 07716, USA, in 1987.

Cover illustration by Christopher Hobbs
Printed and bound in the United Kingdom
by Billings & Sons Ltd., Worcester.

British Library Cataloguing in Publication Data

Harriman, Ed
    Hack! : home truths about foreign news.
    1. Foreign news
    I. Title
    070.4'33   PN4784.F6

    ISBN 0-86232-704-0
    ISBN 0-86232-705-9 Pbk

Library of Congress Cataloging-in-Publication Data

Harriman, Ed.
    Hack! : home truths about foreign news.

    Includes index.
    1. Foreign news. 2. Foreign correspondents—United
States—History. 3. War correspondents—United States
—History. 4. Reporters and reporting—United States.
I. Title.
PN4784.F6H36 1987   070.4'33   87-13812
ISBN 0-86232-704-0
ISBN 0-86232-705-9 (pbk.)

Contents

Nel mezzo del cammin di nostra vita
  mi ritrovari per una selva oscura
  che la diritta via era smarrita.
Ah quanto a dir qual era è cosa dura
  esta selva selvaggia e aspra e forte
  che nel pensier rinova la paura!
Tant' è amara che poco è più morte;
  ma per trattar del ben ch'io vi trovai,
  dirò dell'altre cose ch'i' v'ho scorte.

Dante Alighieri, *La Divina Commedia*, 'Inferno', Canto I.

for my children
. . . and their mother

Introduction

THIS BOOK IS about HACKS—journalists, the men and women who fly into famines and wars and in a few days churn out stories telling the world, or at least their newspapers' readers, what's been going on. The result can be fine, sustained journalism, but sometimes the hacks never find out. Sometimes they lie. And sometimes their editors take what they have dutifully written and torture it until it's incomprehensible. Sometimes editors just throw it out.

This book is about how HACKS work—how they have covered some of the big news stories and festering hidden wars of the past decade. The Vietnamese Boat People. El Salvador. The Fall of Idi Amin. Guatemalan massacres. Czechoslovakia's brave human rights movement. It's also about how one HACK—the author—thinks; how he has picked his way through the political minefield of journalism and survived, so far at least, with only the loss of a few stories chopped, a few others consigned to the waste bin.

HACK is also about 'newspeak' and double talk, the phoney language newspapers and television commentators often use to square what's actually happening in some forlorn or war-torn land with the comfortable complacencies their organisations are promoting at home. This book is about how journalists carry on regardless.

If there is one theme to what follows it is that what's going on 'out there', no matter whether it's in Hong Kong's quarantined warehouses or behind a Saharan sand dune, is by no means half as difficult to understand as many newspapers seem to make out. People are remarkably similar the world over.

And if journalists and editors wrote about them in more down-to-earth terms, and dropped their cliches and—all too often—their clapped out Cold War rhetoric, then people who depend on newspapers and television for their news would be a lot less confused, a lot less intimidated about the rest of the world, and a lot better informed.

1

It's been my pleasure to work with several journalists, cameramen, sound recordists and photographers who sincerely believe this, and who fight tenaciously to keep what they report from being hideously warped, repackaged or coolly defused. They cause a good deal of trouble to governments, police forces, even their bosses. But the press would not be worth reading, and current affairs television not worth watching without them.

I would particularly like to thank Granada Television and my colleagues on *World in Action*, especially those with whom I worked making films about atrocities in El Salvador and Argentina and covering the plight of the Vietnamese Boat People, which are among the stories described in this book.

I hope my television and newspaper colleagues, and anyone interested in finding out something about journalism today will enjoy HACK and find it worthwhile.

Ed Harriman
1987

1
El Salvador

HE'S SITTING UNCOMFORTABLY on the edge of a deck chair. El Presidente. Jefe Supremo as his bodyguards might know him. They're standing around us, arms folded, heavy bulges under some of their close-wrapped grey suits, just under their left armpits. This guy is the last hope for democracy left in the country, the American ambassador said. But then American ambassadors are always saying that.

I'm sweating. El Presidente is looking somewhat uncomfortable himself. Two questions he said. Two tries at nailing him to the coffins of some of the 30,000 dead we've seen picked up out of the dirt, blood all over them, and slung into the back of pickup trucks; who we've seen lying bloated, dead, the knuckles of their toes picked clean to the bone by the country's only reliable witnesses—the vultures. Have you seen the lava flow at La Plyon, Señor El Presidente? Have you seen the skulls the birds leave there, the school cards of 14-year-old boys left blowing on the coarse basalt, school identification cards each with a photograph of a clean young boy wearing a necktie, smiling as their mothers would want them to? You'll find them there on the lava, discarded just as are their rib cages and the few rags of their trousers. The vultures prefer flesh. So too, it seems, Señor El Presidente, do your soldiers. Young boys would be proud to be called guerrillas in a country like this. It is September 1981.

The sunlight reflecting off the hotel swimming pool makes me squint. Jefe Supremo adjusts himself in his chair. Around us now are half-a-dozen local journalists from the country's remaining press. Ah, yes, there could be a story here . . . but rather one for them to whisper over beers than splash on the front pages, I fear.

Mr. Presidente is waiting. Effortlessly, he had just polished off the man from the BBC. A good man, a bit overweight perhaps, whose home is in the London studio interviewing the Chancellor about the bankrate. That's where he's expected to be, maybe that's

3

where he should be. But he is here.

"And tell me, Mr. President," the BBC man had said, "how can you account for all the murders and deaths in your country if many of them are carried out by the security forces and you are the man in charge?"

El Presidente moved, almost imperceptibly, but he moved nonetheless, like a large trout gulps a fly and returns to the bottom to rest, like a bored businessman plucks the maraschino cherry from his fifth Manhattan in a hotel bar. As if the question was entirely inconsequential . . .

"And you tell me," El Presidente replied, "what about Northern Ireland, how do you explain the killings there?"

To be fair to the man from the BBC, there is an issue of degree, of scale involved here. And El Presidente is supposed to be a civilised man dedicated to democracy, as in Britain for example. He shouldn't be answering that way.

But he does. They don't play fair here, Mr. BBC. Or perhaps the BBC man has got El Presidente wrong, perhaps he's not just acting querulously on a sweltering afternoon, perhaps he's presiding wittingly, knowingly over a government up to its eyeballs in blood watching the American-financed and managed massacre of his country. It's not a nice thought. But it's happened before.

The man from the BBC has no answer. Sweating, as we all are by the swimming pool, he tells me it's my turn.

Two years before I had asked the same question. Next door—in Guatemala—and I'd learned. El Presidente there was a fullblown military tinpot, a man who had stepped on the epaulettes of his rivals and who was said to sleep on a cot in his office rather than dare go home at night, a man who got rich on oil, who spoke the local Indian dialect, a man who saw massacred those Indians who stood in his way.

"And what about the Yorkshire Ripper?" this particular Caligula's adviser replied. "Doesn't every country have its own level of violence?"

In Britain the police were trying to catch the Ripper, not doing the killings themselves. Nonetheless the reply was not without some tacky elegance in that presidential drawing room. The mood was different in a chicken coop just outside town where an Indian man lay shivering, hidden, for daring to challenge the oil pipeline being laid across his jungle clearing. Also in the local barracks when the soldiers returned, in the early morning, their guns dirty, their trousers caked and spattered with blood.

No, today by the pool with the sun and palms and grey-suited bodyguards, I wasn't going to ask that question again. We wanted something more specific, something frankly that would test Señor El Presidente's mettle. We wanted to ask him about someone he knew.

"Mr. President, what can you tell us about the disappearance of René Machón?"

"I don't know anything about him, he disappeared, we tried to look for him, we don't know what happened to him."

Now that was an excellent reply. We were going to get on just fine. The grey-suited thugs and local hacks are looking blankly about. They don't know what we're talking about. But El Presidente does. We saw it. And when we look at the film later back in England, in slow motion, his face sets, his jaw hardens, his eyes glaze over as if he's taken a stomach punch. When people watch it on television they say he looks more like a *mafioso* than a head of state.

But we know something else. We know he's lying.

El Presidente starts to talk, as if he hadn't quite said enough.

"He was a very bright man, he's a very hard-working man and he was trying to do the best to solve the very difficult problems of coffee in the world, and for our country. So I believe that he was working hard and we really miss him because he was doing his job."

With that his mouth sets. He breathes deeply through his nose, his eyes casting back and forth, probing the faces of the men circled around us, demanding obedience, searching for doubts. I can't see the thugs. I'm only aware of the swimming pool, the warm air and the tropical plants. It's a real tourist brochure setting, and one René Machón would have enjoyed. What better place to ask a few questions? The problem is that the president would clearly like to consider the matter closed, whereas we have just begun.

★ ★ ★

A year before, René Machón had simply been a name in a brief Reuters report, a four-inch story buried in the more inconsequential pages of the financial press. Dated 17 December 1980, it read:

GUNMEN KIDNAP EL SALVADOR COFFEE INSTITUTE PRESIDENT

San Salvador: The president of the national coffee institute, INCAFE, René Machón, was kidnapped by a group of gunmen, police said.

Machón was snatched when the group intercepted his car as he was returning to his home, they added.

INCAFE is a semi-official company which has controlled the

5

production and marketing of coffee in El Salvador since early this year after the civilian-military junta decreed the nationalisation of the country's foreign trade.

I had cut it out and thumbtacked it to the office wall. Within weeks it had begun to turn yellow. And within those weeks René Machón began to become interesting, began to become a person to us. More than that, he became someone we wanted to find out about. That, after all, was the job.

Machón was in charge of selling El Salvador's coffee on the world market, a lot of coffee, worth some $500 million a year. On the face of it that was a motive for kidnapping, and murder as well.

So we began a carousel of assignations in the City of London where most of the world's coffee is bought and sold; phone calls to harassed buyers on the coffee exchange, cool meetings in deep-pile, leather-upholstered executive suites high above the Thames, and three-hour credit card lunches in mock Tudor restaurants where the waiters offered asparagus, strawberries and château-bottled wine.

"Did you know René Machón?"

"Sure," a coffee-broker replied.

"What sort of person was he?"

"Well . . . He liked to have a good time. He was always joking, saying don't worry about him. He was good at his business, knew how to sell coffee . . ."

"What were his politics?"

"Well, he was a sort of liberal. He wanted the money from the coffee sales to go back to El Salvador, instead of into private Swiss bank accounts . . ."

"So why do you think he was kidnapped?"

"You must understand El Salvador is a strange country. I must be going now . . ."

The same questions, over and over again to different men in pin-stripe suits. Each answer the same, but different; another facet cut into our particular prism. But the centre was still opaque. The City of London is full of whispers, but in confidence whole choruses of voices can be heard.

"I'll help you," one informant said "but you mustn't mention my name. We could lose all our business . . ."

"Yes, sure," said another. "There are certain people who certainly had reason to hate him. Let me tell you something about who owns the coffee mills in El Salvador . . ."

"No, I don't think he was worried." We were talking to another man. "Now wait, the last time he was here he mentioned something about a bomb . . ."

"When was that?"

"December . . . December . . . 12th, December 12th or 13th . . ."

"Only days before he disappeared?"

"Yes . . . Yes . . . Now that you put it like that, it must have been . . ."

Anonymous men told the story of the coffee trade, of Salvadorian connections, and for some of them their friend. The rules of the game despite the French waiters and Savile Row suits were straightforward and crude. No names. And no quotes. That suited us fine. Eventually some of them changed their minds, as people often do when they realise that for some crazy reason you're not going to give up or, for that matter, let them down.

For their part Machón's friends could be a bit rough, even on a friend who might well have been dead. René Machón wasn't always a nice guy. He could be loud-mouthed and pushy. He knew what he wanted. And it made sense. Bring the money from the sale of coffee back to El Salvador, deduct the taxes owed on it and give them to the national bank to finance land reform, and then, and only then, dish out the profits to the owners of the large estates. To Machón that seemed better than letting the growers stash the profits in Swiss bank accounts and then turn out empty pockets back home when the government asked for its dues. That had been going on for years, which was why the Salvadorian government was perpetually near bankruptcy while rich Salvadorian planters bought condominiums and office blocks in Miami and New Orleans.

But there was one question we couldn't answer. Why hadn't the Salvadorian government, or El Presidente himself, who after all was being sold to the world as an untiring democrat, said anything about the disappearance of René Machón?

Wasn't René Machón one of El Salvador's top civil servants? Didn't he control most of the country's foreign wealth? Wasn't he in charge of the country's main industry—coffee? In Britain it was inconceivable that the government would say nothing, let alone not mount a major search and enquiry if such a man had been kidnapped on his way home.

We combed the newspapers. But there was nothing. We phoned contacts in El Salvador. But there hadn't been a word. So we decided to go to El Salvador and look for ourselves.

★ ★ ★

Widows cry, yet they seem to cry a lot less, if that seems possible, than wives who don't know for sure whether their husbands are still alive, or dead. Today, hundreds of thousands of women share that sorrow, from Uganda to El Salvador. But because it's considered lousy newspaper copy, it hardly ever makes the world's press, let alone the action-man thrillers sold on railway and airport news stands.

Widows also know that there is little more that can happen, except to themselves. Anxious wives, on the other hand, sense that anything they might say could lead to their husbands' death. Behind most "disappeared" persons in the world today there is a wife, mother or friend; whole families encapsulated in a private hell. It's one of the unstudied phenomena of what sociologists call social control, and its real name is terror. Not the spectacular airline hijack kind of terror but the more down-to-earth sort, the sort found in homes.

René Machón's wife talked to us. She was young and afraid. She wanted to know. She talked to us because Machón had friends in London who wanted to help.

By the same poolside where El Presidente was to deny knowing anything about her husband's disappearance, the same bright sky, the same bartenders bringing tall cool drinks, while the hotel parrot kept chewing its cage, she recalled how her husband was already home from London taking a shower when she got back that Saturday evening in December. They went to the beach the next day with friends, the black volcanic Pacific beaches where El Salvador's rich keep cottages and air-conditioned second homes.

It was a fine day. But he said something strange. He said he had made out a will. And he gave her a necklace, for Christmas two weeks away, just in case he couldn't give it to her then himself.

"Why could that be?" she had asked him.

"Oh, you never can tell," was all he replied.

Three days after they went to the beach Machón disappeared.

By the swimming pool Machón's wife kept knotting a small white handkerchief, rubbing her wrists as she spoke. She showed us a picture she kept of him, a black and white passport size snapshot, nothing special in more ordinary times, now a stubborn fact that said that René Machón did exist. She carried that weight in her handbag, clutching the memory of a man who, more likely than not, was a corpse.

Later we learned that El Presidente had summoned her and Machón's parents to his office soon after the kidnapping. The heads of the security services were all sitting there, the army, the police and the National Guard. Did they know anything, El Presidente asked each of them in turn. No, they had all made enquiries and, sadly, there was nothing to report. It would be best, they agreed, not to take the matter further in public at least. Everyone there understood.

Later when we returned to El Salvador to film there it proved impossible to find René Machón's wife. She too had disappeared, of her own volition and for her own peace of mind, I hope.

★ ★ ★

In happier times someone seems to have had a vision of San Salvador, the country's capital, as a little piece of suburban America nestled under a volcano—McDonald's hamburger stands, Coca-Cola billboards, and air-conditioned shopping malls. If you kept your eyes closed and turned up the car stereo when driving through the slums you'd believe you were closer to Los Angeles than Mexico. Sure, there may be smatterings of gunfire most evenings before curfew. But what the hell, this is South of the Border. What do you expect anyhow?

Life became a bit more serious after the guerrillas blew up the power station, plunging the city into darkness for the better part of a week. Nonetheless there was still "Noche Mexicano" at the hotel for the young at heart. Every Wednesday evening middle-aged couples shuffled past oysters, spareribs and meatballs at the poolside buffet, toasting each other with Pina Coladas, dancing tired rumbas and tense tangos, if not with the gusto of bygone times, at least just glad to be alive. At 9:30 the waiters fished crumpled paper napkins out of the swimming pool and the Cinderallas hurried home. The streets were then empty but for stray dogs rooting through garbage and the National Guard on patrol. Then the killing began.

We saw bodies on the rubbish tips in the early mornings. Men and women with blood caked on their torn trousers and ripped dresses, dirt from the roadside in their hair. Many of them had their thumbs tied behind their backs.

Everyone in El Salvador knows the bodies are dumped on rubbish tips so it's easier for the undertakers—doleful men who have somehow managed to get hold of a pick-up truck and the ear of the local police—to find them. Everyone knows the National Guard ties people's thumbs together before torturing and killing them.

Few of the corpses are guerrillas. There are too many for that. And there are too many testimonies by parents and friends who have come, distraught, to the churches the mornings after their husbands and children have been hauled out of bed and "disappeared".

Everyone knows that too. But in a country fighting an heroic war against communism and chaos, anyone shot by the security forces is officially suspected of having, at least, guerrilla sympathies. It's a big lie. The lies often are. And more often than not they work.

Nonetheless the National Guard was upset. We'd gone to army headquarters and signed for security passes. The colonel was drunk. He squinted and said he thought he'd seen me somewhere before. He was also known to be partial to a bottle of Scotch. So soon we were sitting in another anteroom, sweating and swatting flies, waiting for an audience with General Carlos Eugenio Vides Casanova, Director of the National Guard.

René Machón had had a helicopter—it went with his job—to fly to coffee estates chopped out of El Salvador's jungle-wrapped countryside. His pilot was close to the military. We had discovered that shortly after Machón disappeared, this pilot had pulled aside one of Machón's few friends in the government and said, 'Don't be afraid. They have him. The National Guard have him. They are going to free him in a few days so you don't have anything to fear."

That friend, Carlos Paredes, who had been El Salvador's Minister of Planning, told us more. He said that Machón told him that he had had a phone call. It was the morning before he was kidnapped. He was told he would be killed, nothing more. So Machon told Paredes he was going to see the Director of the National Guard.

"Why?" I had asked. "Was he going to ask for protection?"

"No, he was just trying to figure out what the problem was. He thought the head of the National Guard would probably know why he'd been threatened."

Paredes paused. "He didn't make it."

Shortly after Machón was kidnapped Paredes resigned in disgust and fled the country.

Outside the National Guard headquarters green recruits were drilling on a soccer field which doubles as a parade ground. Sitting, watching by a clutch of battered pick-up trucks with the casual, tired nonchalance of men relaxing after a hard night's work were men in the dark sunglasses, their paunches drooping heavily out of their golf shirts over revolvers tucked into wide cowboy-style leather belts. "I can assure you that the relationship between the security forces and the death squads is one of the things that concerns us," the American ambassador, Deane Hinton had said. My director—John Blake of Granada Television—and I were a little concerned too.

The door to the office opens. We jump up. Out he comes. But it's not the commander. No, instead it's a fat man in a black cassock, crucifix dangling on his chest and a string of rosary beads from his waist. Even the National Guard it seems has its own bishop. This one has gold teeth, a wide beaming smile, a pudgy handshake and he slaps me on the back.

"You like our country?"

"Yes, well . . ." I'm mumbling.

"You're from England. I have a cousin in England. She is in Doncaster. Do you know Doncaster?" He's laughing.

"Yes, um . . ."

"You come and see me sometime while you are here in El Salvador . . . Yes? . . . Good . . . Welcome."

And he's off. We slouch back in our chairs. Sweat a bit more. Crack a few jokes that catch the dryness in our mouths. An aide tells us that Vides Casanova is busy. But a major will see us. Would we like that? Yes. Would we like a Coke? Yes.

"You see, we've been having trouble with journalists. Not all journalists, but some." The major begins. "The National Guard is an elite proud of its honour and traditions. Some journalists don't want to know that. They just tell lies."

It's our turn. "Yes, well," we answer, "we only want to film the parade ground, and perhaps a patrol."

"I think you should film the flag raising ceremony."

The major clearly knows what he wants.

"Yes, of course we'll film the flag raising ceremony as well . . . First if you like . . ."

"You see, some journalists just tell lies. They say we are killers, that we kill innocent women and children."

The major is getting into his stride.

"The Germans, that German magazine, they said we toss babies into the air and then catch them on the ends of our bayonets."

"Oh?"

"That is not true."

"Oh?"

"No. You know why it is not true? It is not true because our men do not have bayonets."

"Pretty convincing proof one would have thought," we reply. We'll give him that. "But what about all the other stories, and the bodies?" we ask.

"They are lies. We are fighting communism. We've had only one really good TV crew here, the Japanese. They seem to understand that."

"Yes, well, if we could just get on and film your men, and the flag ceremony . . ."

And we did. With the sunglassed pistoleros skulking around us

11

and one particular National Guard soldier glowering at us we carefully, deliberately, filmed his uniform from his helmet to his boots, and back again.

Had we sold out? Lied by omission to the earnest major? That's something the holy father might console them about. We got what we wanted, and got out.

Over the next few days we had a package tour of the war. We were taken to an unfinished church basement where hundreds of refugees were in hiding—the remains of a village the army had pacified. There was little fresh air, less light. Squalling babies wriggled fitfully on makeshift hammocks. Little girls and boys squatted in the corners, bare-bottomed, squirting out streams of pale green dysentery shit. Their mothers kept scrubbing the rough cement floor. Others were cooking endlessly upstairs, stirring massive blackened cauldrons of beans, slapping tortillas between their hands. We choked on the smoke. Their eyes were reddened and wet. These people ate one orange each a week. Tuberculosis, dysentery, conjunctivitis and bronchitis were comfortably festering there. So too was fear.

In a small room was an eleven-year-old boy, his leg paralysed, his eyes glazed over, almost inconsolable with pain. He had a bullet in his spine. The National Guard had shot him as he ran away. They had killed his father and brothers. Several doctors had been asked to come and examine the wound. They had all refused. A fine edge of bitterness crept over the voice of the young Catholic priest who had taken us to the church as he spoke.

"You see the bullet holes. Here on the wall. We try to put pictures over the worst ones," he said.

The pictures were pages torn from the local weekly TV magazine, of ski slopes, yachts, fast cars—icons from the world these people were supposed to crave for, and to have threatened as well.

Twice the army had come, searching for weapons they said, upturning hammocks, slashing grain sacks, smashing boxes. Twice foreign television crews had arrived just as the army had tried to march away suspects at the end of bayonets. Faced with television cameras, the army released its hostages. Such is the usefulness occasionally of television – ersatz international protection racket without guns.

Other refugees weren't so lucky or well served. Living in the countryside far from the international hotels, the video units and overseas telephones, running from their villages which had been burned, they had become strangers in their own land. Running, they had to draw on other, unknown villagers' compassion, careful, anxious not to arouse suspicion or fall foul of the National Guard. Such is the logic of war in El Salvador that safety lay for many only in areas the guerrillas controlled.

We saw a young man, an ordinary kid, come to an undertaker's parlour—a crude shop with cheap wooden coffins stacked like cordwood inside—to identify the corpses of a man and a woman lying stiff and blood-soaked on the cement floor. Yes, it was his brother Jauquin, and his brother's wife. Yes, he knew they never got home last night. No, they had nothing to do with the guerrillas or politics of any sort. Yes, he would tell his mother. They could afford a burial, but it would have to be cheap.

"That's luck," he said. "It can happen to you. It can happen to me. It can happen to anyone here."

Two days later we saw their graves, rough-hewn white crosses and a few bouquets of fast fading flowers tossed on two dirt mounds among hundreds of graves, dozens of them fresh, in a roadside vacant lot. Mongrel dogs were scavenging as we left.

★ ★ ★

The woman at the national library lugged out a heavy stack of old newspapers. It was hot. The building's few fans hardly moved the air, let alone dealt with the sweat on our own, and it seemed everyone else's faces. The papers were already yellowing, sticky to the touch. We found a large table and laid them out.

El Diario de Hoy, jueves 18 de diciembre de 1980. Page one dealt with the previous night's bombing of the Bank of America office. Page two: the faces of five people, four men and a girl, stare out of the paper. They had been murdered by unknown assassins. Like most days. Page three: "Sequestran al Presidente del INCAFE." This was it. Tucked in the corner was a picture of René Machón in shirtsleeves, pens in his breast pocket looking every bit the government technocrat that he was. The report said he had been kidnapped between 7 and 8 o'clock two nights before by a group of unknown armed men. His vehicle had been found later near the national stadium. There were no signs of a struggle. The keys were in the dashboard.

Then there was nothing. Not another mention of René Machón in El Salvador's press. Yet he was responsible for running the country's entire coffee industry, earning El Salvador's life blood in foreign exchange.

Except for one day. *La Prensa Gráfica*, miercoles 1 de abril de 1981. Buried away on page 20, a privately placed advertisement. It read:

13

PLEASE LISTEN TO ME!
With an afflicted heart and praying with the deepest faith in
God, to those who hold my husband captive
RENE ALEJANDRO MACHON RIVERA
I ASK:
Let him send me news,
don't hurt him and
return him as soon as possible to his family.
FREE RENE ALEJANDRO
who has been in captivity close to four months. To his captors,
whom I beseech in the name of his parents, brothers and friends,
send him back to me quickly.
San Salvador, 31 de marzo de 1981.
HIS WIFE

She was in hiding now.

A few days later we visited the neighbourhood where Machón
lived. Children stood staring at us, dogs barked and sniffed at our
feet, the neighbours said nothing. No, they saw nothing. No, they
knew nothing. We talked to several others. They refused to help us
openly. But they gave us clues. Eventually we found a person who
admitted to us that she had seen Machón's kidnapping.

She was frightened. How could she be sure they would not kill
her? She couldn't. How could she know we were to be trusted? She
had to make up her own mind about that. We had little to offer
except an enormous risk and a chance to tell the truth. It's not a lot,
but she wanted to talk.

She had been on her way shopping when she saw men with rifles
stop Machón's Cherokee land cruiser in front of a small shop close
to his home. Machón's driver was taken out, pushed into the back
of a waiting red pick-up truck and beaten. Machón was bundled
into the front seat of the pick-up, and it and the Cherokee were
driven away. The whole incident had taken less than five minutes.

The men who kidnapped Machón wore green uniforms, black
helmets and boots up to their knees, she said. They were National
Guard. She was in no doubt about that. She agreed to film an
interview describing what she had seen with her back to the
camera.

Back at the hotel El Presidente, Señor José Napoleón Duarte had
been lunching with businessmen. They wanted reassurances as to
how he was going to protect them against communism. As they
tucked into their fruit compôtes and ice creams he rose to speak.
There was muffled applause. For the most part they hated him. He
was soft. But the American ambassador was there, breezily puffing

14

a fat cigar, wearing a tropical seersucker suit. Today El Presidente would be shown some modest respect.

He began to speak. Then the lights went out. The businessmen started murmuring, anxiously twisting in their chairs. Had the power station been sabotaged again? The lights came on. The audience seemed relieved, some of them running fingers under their collars looking towards the door for fresh air. Over the distorted public address system El Presidente was lambasting Nicaragua.

". . . A hotbed of revolution . . . El Salvador will not be friends with Cuban clowns . . . We will protect what is dear to us . . ."

Duarte droned on. He was drum thumping. It didn't work. The businessmen were tired, grown impatient. All they wanted was an election, guaranteed by the army to get their own man in. And the American ambassador, puffing so firmly on his fine cigar, promised a vote.

It was at the poolside, immediately following the business lunch that we confronted El Presidente about René Machón.

"Would you be surprised to know that eye witnesses say that the National Guard was involved in his disappearance?" I asked.

"Then I would say that if it is true," he replied, "tell this witness to go to the judge and say so, and if he does that then we'll have the basis to start looking around."

"But isn't it a fact in this country that people are afraid to come to the officials in cases of crimes where security forces may have been involved?"

"That is not always the truth," he said.

"In this case people are frightened to tell what they saw," I explained.

"I don't know," Duarte answered. But he was stumbling. "If you have information," he said, "if you have names I'll be delighted to have them in order to tell the attorney general to call upon them and to investigate directly. But give me the names."

We wouldn't. Duarte was stumbling as he was beginning to so often now. Only a week before on America's "Meet the Press" programme interviewers said to him, "Mr. President, we are asking you questions. We expect answers and you're giving us speeches." That was an insult. The press attaché at the American embassy had told us how carefully his office had planned that trip for El Presidente to the United States. And how badly it had gone. Now El Presidente was temporising in front of us. On film.

Duarte was a man who ten years before had been elected president of El Salvador only to have the office snatched from him by the military in a fraudulent vote count; a man who was said to have been imprisoned and tortured in his time, saved by the intercession of Catholics around the world. Once he had been a democrat. Now he was one of those rare uncomfortable beasts, a political pachyderm, fed for years on meagre grants and kept on a short political lead in exile until such time as his masters had use for him. For Duarte this meant putting a democratic smile and some last vestiges of respect on the face of a hideous war scarred by midnight murders and unspeakable atrocities.

The American embassy made no secret that it was they who were keeping Duarte in power. As the ambassador put it, "I mean what more can the United States ask for, a reform government pledged to bring democracy to its country that is fighting against externally supported terrorist groups. The junta looks to us like the best thing in Central America for many years."

Ambassadors are paid to talk like that. And this one was a good talker. But the embassy's hardbitten analysis also knew about the nightly killings. In cold military textbook terms terror was the only way to keep the guerrillas out of the capital. Arbitrary murder cannot be left out of the equation of kill ratios and fire power in dirty backyard wars. Such is the efficacy of fear.

★ ★ ★

The highway to the airport from San Salvador snakes through green hills dripping lush jungle and banana groves. Small pillows of mist lie in the valleys, burning off under the morning sun. We pass small boys prodding their families' cows along the roadside; gangs of men, barebacked and bronzed, digging culverts, occasionally straightening up and mopping their brows—beasts of burden harnessed to government projects now.

The airport gift shop sells Japanese radios, silk scarves and brightly coloured beach towels. Businessmen hug their children as their flights are called. When we arrive in Miami the people meeting us are wearing shorts and T-shirts. They're munching enormous hamburgers washed down with soda pop and milk shakes. The air is salty and hot. Our rent-a-car is air-conditioned. We head for our bayside hotel.

The newspapers speak of the continued communist threat in El Salvador. Communism here is about as welcome as botulism in a tin of baked beans. Several times a day government health warnings are repeated on the radio and TV.

But there are also a lot of Vietnam veterans about. Many people are sceptical, they don't want another war. More just don't want to know. On weekends the football stadiums are full while those at home settle down in front of televisions with six-packs of beer.

16

Into this gridiron culture, church and human rights groups try to explain what is happening in El Salvador. The news is hard to swallow, yet perhaps it's a taste that should be acquired.

Miami is also the playground for El Salvador's rich on the run. Some are content to get on with life, drive their Cadillacs, send their kids to private schools. For others it's a more serious affair. Protected by tax loopholes, attorneys and fat bank accounts they set about buying their way into Washington, rubbing shoulders with the new breed of stalwarts in the Reagan administration. But why, they ask, has Reagan been so slow to take up their cause?

Over cocktails and bar snacks in steak houses and on the verandas of elegant Biscayne Bay bungalows we are earnestly and passionately told about the "communist menace", about how their families' coffee estates were taken over during El Salvador's brief spurt of land reform, about René Machón. He is either spoken of with a venom that would make a cobra wince, or portrayed as an insignificant fool.

Late one night after endless whiskies, awash with mock camaraderie, I am shown a video film taken the day one of the estates was occupied by its workers. "Isn't it outrageous," my host demands, "how can people take away what my father and his father before him so carefully built? . . . Here, I will show you some other pictures . . ."

We look at snapshots spread over the kitchen table, of coffee bushes, tractors, drying and processing mills. There are no pictures of the workers' dwellings, crude cement cubicles with dim lightbulbs dangling from exposed wires, with no toilets, no running water. My host doesn't mention that his family had helped finance the local National Guard post. Nor does he mention that René Machón had gone to the estate to be there the day it was officially occupied as part of the land reform programme. My host's Biscayne Bay neighbour told us that over cocktails another evening just before he and his wife went out to dinner. "Perhaps you would like to join us later," she said as she put her husband's .45 automatic pistol into her handbag. "Oh that," she explained, "I don't like to carry it, but you can't take too many precautions here."

★ ★ ★

Duarte's time was soon up. The men in Miami wanted their man in power and the American embassy had promised an election. The problem was that their man, Major Roberto 'Bob' D'Aubuisson had a warrant outstanding for his arrest in El Salvador in connection with the assassination of the country's prelate, Archbishop Oscar Romero.

Romero had been shot in San Salvador's cathedral the year before. D'Aubuisson's assistant had been captured shortly afterwards and was found to be carrying a coded diary giving details of this and several other clandestine terrorist acts.

Written on a page close to the date of the archbishop's murder, 24 March 1980, the diary read:

Equipment
Operation Pina

1. Starlight
1. 257 - Roberts'
4. Automatics
   Grenades

1. Driver
2. Marksman
3. Security

"Pina" is Spanish for pineapple. "Starlight" is the name of a special telescopic sight. "257 – Roberts'" refers to the same type of rifle said to have been used in the assassination. Written in the back of the diary were names of men who'd contributed money, intelligence, political muscle and arms to D'Aubuisson. Many of them were now driving Cadillacs along Biscayne Boulevard. We knew. We'd been drinking with them.

"D'Aubuisson is a pathological killer," the previous American ambassador to El Salvador, Robert White, had said. But White was one of Jimmy Carter's liberals and what he said didn't matter much now. The details of the diary were not given much coverage in the American press, even though they had been read into the report of the Senate Foreign Relations Committee's hearings on El Salvador. D'Aubuisson had been intelligence chief of the National Guard. He was also widely said to be the leader of El Salvador's most ghoulish death squad. But that didn't seem to matter either.

"I am an anti-communist," Major Bob told the editor of the *News-Gazette*, El Salvador's fiercely pro-American free enterprise English language tabloid. "And so are most Americans. Therefore if I am an extreme right, so are most Americans," he said. His logic was inexorable.

On 28 March 1982, El Salvador's peasants trooped past soldiers into fortified polling stations to have their hands stamped as proof that they had availed themselves of the democratic choice which is rightfully theirs. The guerrillas tried to disrupt the voting, and those who didn't vote were answerable to the National Guard. Hundreds were shot. D'Aubuisson's party formed a majority coalition and he became president of the National Assembly. El Presidente Duarte was president no more. The American ambassador is reported to have said, "This is truly a day for democracy and I think democracy is strengthened by this."

It wasn't. Ronald Reagan pumped more and more military aid into El Salvador to keep its stumbling army, if not properly trained, at least equipped to fight more losing battles in an ever-escalating guerrilla war. "El Salvador is nearer to Texas than Texas is to Massachusetts," he told a joint session of Congress in April 1983. "El Salvador has continued to strive toward an orderly and democratic society," he said asking for more money for more rifles, helicopter gunships and grenades.

At the same time in El Salvador General Vides Casanova was promoted from Director of the National Guard to Minister of Defence. His predecessor, it seems, "suffered from the far right after he came out in support of land reform." Or so said the *New York Times* on 24 April. The newspaper described Casanova as "a soft-spoken, amiable man who had a reputation as an excellent administrator. General Vides', the paper continued, "has not had much actual field experience in guerrilla warfare, but he is well read on the subject." Such is the curious manner in which the American press described a commander whose men at night dragged people from their beds, tied their thumbs behind their backs, tortured, mutilated and killed them, leaving their corpses by roadsides to rot.

Behind the elections and the American embassy's public relations campaign El Salvador had experienced an internal coup. Men like Roberto D'Aubuisson and Vides Casanova formed the Salvadorian government. And it became even more difficult to disentangle the activity of the official security forces from the death squads. The men in Miami were happy. It was their money and lobbying in Washington that helped pass El Salvador's government over to such profoundly unattractive thugs.

The *Wall Street Journal* positively purred with satisfaction at the turn of events. Business confidence was damaged by "reforms", one of the paper's deputy editors explained (6 January 1983). The new government has been "trying to remedy this strong sense of alienation among some of the country's most able citizens by bringing private sector people onto the boards of the central bank and the coffee export agency."

So much for René Machón. Few people by then talked of him. His memory was soon smothered by official silence, his coffee reforms buried under the rhetoric of anti-communism and patriotic war.

But René Machón was found. Shortly after his story was televised in Britain a woman phoned. She was from El Salvador. Her name was Marianella García Villas' and she was president of El Salvador's Commission on Human Rights. In exile then, she had recognised the face on television, in the black and white snapshot Machón's wife had carried and let us photograph. It was the face of a man Marianella had seen in another photograph—of a man lying on a heap of dead bodies in one of San Salvador's morgues. The dates roughly corresponded. "What struck me about the picture from the morgue," Marianella said, "was that this man was wearing good clothes, slacks and a sportshirt. He was well groomed, that's why I noticed him lying with the others who were peasants, without shoes, wearing rags."

I thanked her. We would try somehow to tell his wife. One thing began to seem more certain. Had René Machón turned up in that morgue, the government would likely have been informed.

Our investigation was closed. But the war carried on. A year after our programme was broadcast, on 18 March 1983, the British press carried a small news item. A woman named Marianella García Villas had been killed in El Salvador, it said. Shortly afterwards José Napoleón Duarte was again elected president, victor of an election desperately needed by the Reagan administration to show a cleaner face to the American Congress before it was prepared to vote yet more funds for the war. For some time to come young boys will be proud to be called guerrillas in El Salvador.

2
Portugal

MY WIFE WAS off to New York to spend the summer with her uncle, or so she said. The suitcases bursting with sweaters and rolled up panti-hose seemed a lot for summer in the city. But I took little notice at the time.

"See you in the autumn, darling."

"Sure, love."

We tossed each other kisses, and set off. Such was to be the end of married life. We were both in a hurry; she to a new life—a dreamed of house and shaggy dog with kids' toys on the stairs paid for by someone who could afford it. And I . . . well, I was off to become a journalist, whatever that would involve. I may have been naive.

But I had thirty quid, the price of a sleeper ticket to Aberdeen. And Aberdeen, from what I had read at least, was the Klondike of the North Sea oil boom. Thousands of millions of pounds were sloshing about there, spent on offshore rigs, supply tugs, diving bells and beefed-up wage packets, the strong steady scent that drew Texas oilmen, Irish navvies and hustlers from everywhere. On the other hand Aberdeen is a city so dour that when the cold salt spray blows off the reckless sea, local folks tend to screw up their eyes when passing strangers, mutter under their breath, and pass on. It was as good a place as any to start. I also knew I could manage a small town. And that's what Aberdeen is . . . a special, peculiar sort of town, "peculiar" being a word they don't mind up there.

From the train station in the early morning haze, along cobbled streets down to the wharf where fishermen were slapping crates of wet cod, mackerel and herring on coarse pallets to be weighed, gulls soaring overhead, I saw the Aberdeen of last year's tourist brochure. The sturdy dying industry of earnest men, unshaven, filling the markets of London, fine stores, and neighbourhood fish stalls. Wholesome enterprise tinctured with a whiff of poverty, so much of what in Britain is regarded with fondness, like a last slow pint of beer in a pub before closing time, a lukewarm slightly bitter

21

draught laced with melancholy.

The piercing shrieks of the gulls, the hammering grate of the winches, the slow thud of tugs dragging out to sea: Aberdeen was waking up. By ten o'clock the wharves were silent but for lone men hosing down the piers under a slowly burning sun. By noon it was blistering.

I made my way to the trade union club up a steep cobbled back street for lunch. Then the surprise. There was a queue outside, women and children waiting quietly dressed in clothes off market stalls and hand-me-downs; ill-shaped dresses, cheap jumpers, broken scuffed shoes. Aberdeen was supposed to be the new Mecca of untold oil wealth. But this, by any description, was a soup kitchen. Pie and mashed potatoes and a glutinous treacly pudding scooped on to battered plates for fifteen pence a serving. It's a fair price for a hot meal. If you're poor.

The families waited patiently at the window, took their meals to sit at long tables, hardly talking as they ate. Were these the wives and children of the trade union barons, the ones who were holding the American drilling companies to ransom over unionisation and exorbitant pay claims on the North Sea rigs? That's what the London papers said. Were these their families? Queueing for meat pies?

Obviously something was amiss in Aberdeen; and it wasn't just a concern of anxious mothers trying to keep their daughters in at night, hoping against hope as more squalling babies were born out of Friday night pay packets, whisky and beers and gropings outside dance-halls with men seen once who said they came from somewhere near Cork, which as any mother knows is far away.

After the pubs closed, middle-aged voyeurs paraded their dogs up and down George Street, watching couples waiting for late night buses. While their hounds squatted at the curbside these mock guardians of high street morality loitered by couples embracing, some rubbing quietly, rhythmically against each other by lamp posts. Yes, Aberdeen is a small town.

"It's nice when the sun shines," they say. But then it would have to be. Most of the year the slate grey skies are pierced only by the grey spires of grim kirks standing stolidly between blocks of saddened grey terraces. The oil rig workers knew nothing and cared less for Aberdeen's tired attractions. They were getting drunk in the hotel bar. So was I.

Drunken conversations are usually unusually boring. That night was no exception, except for one diver, a thin young Frenchman who couldn't understand why the oil company's doctor refused to listen to his chest during his last medical examination. The young

Frenchman had just surfaced after working 14 days from a diving bell more than 500 feet down in the sea. The more whisky the less the Frenchman understood. The oil company must care for his safety. "It must," he said. But now he had doubts, serious unsettling doubts, and with each whisky he clutched for reassurance he only found frayed nerves.

"In France such a doctor would be fired immediately," he said. I nodded.

"You know he was smoking a cigarette, he didn't even seem to care."

Two years later the same young Frenchman knocked at my door in London. He was drained, spent. Did I want to buy his Porsche he asked. And he gave me the keys. He was going back to France. Three days previously his friend had passed out somewhere on the bottom, hundreds of feet from the diving bell and the drilling rig. The man died. Twenty divers were killed in the North Sea between 1973 and 1979, according to the British Department of Energy.

Back in the hotel bar huge American oilmen boasted of swimming pools somewhere back in Texas. The talk turned to overbearing bosses, then to Aberdeen women with big tits, the biggest tits this side of the Clyde. So big you could stick your . . .

The next morning I went looking for a story.

The first stop, the Aberdeen office of the Scottish Development Agency, the offices of the local planners whose job it is to see that North Sea oil benefits rather than destroys their fair little corner of sea coast and gorse. These are the men with the briefcases, with an eye to their community's interests, not to say the main chance, Aberdeen's own negotiators staring eyeball to eyeball, or did they rub shoulders . . . with the ministry men from London and the jet set lawyers of the American oil moguls. It's this relationship I wanted to explore.

'I understand the American companies have been buying large tracts of commercial and residential property around here," I began.

"Indeed they have. There's a future here and they want to expand with it," the agency official replied.

Early in the morning there is nothing I like better than a man in a positive frame of mind.

"You wouldn't say they were out to corner the property market?" I suggested.

"My goodness, no. That would be going much too far."

The interview followed a predictable course. And as invariably happens in government offices the secretary arrived with tea. It's an underrated and important ritual. I said no thank you to sugar, and

23

trying to collect the crumbs from my custard cream biscuit, proceeded.

"I also understand that some of the local planners have taken jobs with the oil firms. . ."

"Yes, indeed," he replied. "A man must move with the times." He was still fresh as a daisy that morning, my interviewee.

"And these would be men who had access to land registry and local authority files, who could take with them unparalleled expertise in matters of land sales?"

"Well, yes." My host was looking a little less pleased. "Now look here," he said. "I don't think you want to get this one out of perspective . . ."

His smile turned sour and we talked on, about Mr. S and Mr. T in particular. It wasn't bad for a first morning's work. Out on the street I went to a call box. Pushing tuppences into it as if stuffing geese I contacted the gentlemen in question, neither of whom wanted to take the matter further.

Pity. I had neither the time nor funds to spend the next three months rummaging through land registry files, tracking down vacant lots studded with "For Sale" signs. There were others in Aberdeen who had been doing that well. Instead I found the American oil men at the country-clubbish Treetops Hotel. After all, I'm an American myself. What did they think of the people in Aberdeen?

The result appeared in *The Guardian*. It began: "'These Scots are the laziest bastards I've ever seen. I'd rather work with niggers anywhere – Filipinos, Spaniards, Indonesians – than with Caucasians. They don't complain.' So confided a Texan oilman in an Aberdeen bar. If he and his buddies don't soon shut up, they will be shipped back to the Gulf of Mexico . . ."

The cheque was for £35. Journalism worked.

★ ★ ★

Coming back to London on the sleeper I shared a compartment with a square-jawed smooth shaven man in his early forties, an officer of one of Her Majesty's nuclear powered submarines. He'd been to Aberdeen. It was all somewhat hush hush, he said. "You can imagine what could happen to those North Sea oil fields during a war. Havoc," he said. Then he explained what he said wasn't classified. "Mustn't forget the strategic dimension . . ." he added.

Indeed not. Later in the night I heard a strange yet familiar sound, an echo from boys' camp years ago. I leaned over to see my naval friend busy stroking himself under the sheet reading *Playboy* magazine.

"You don't mind, do you?" he asked. "You do a lot of this on submarines."

No, I didn't mind. I was thinking of the strategic dimension, listening to the click of the rails, pleased to be on a train screaming towards London through the night.

It was at about this time that I too started having dreams. I saw Henry Kissinger as a prima donna of the trapeze. He was naked, grinning, walking a tightrope high above a three ring circus. Without a dinner jacket Henry's tummy stuck out. His toes curled around the tightrope and he held a long balancing baton in his pudgy hands. Off the ends of the baton drooping like baubles were cold, grey 500-pound bombs. When they fell they blew the white circus horses and dancing zebras to smithereens. And Henry continued his dance on the trapeze.

It was absurd. Clearly what I had been reading in the newspapers was beginning to have a curious effect on me. At the time Kissinger was trying to convince the world that the secret bombing of rice paddies and forests in Cambodia could have won the war in neighbouring Vietnam. The question was who would believe him? The American Congress certainly didn't, that is after they found out. Several journalists set about unstitching Mr. Kissinger's secret war, and indeed, made their reputations on it. I was more interested in the place nearer to home which he forgot all about—Portugal. To give Kissinger his due, it seemed such an unlikely place for a coup.

★ ★ ★

The romantic heart of Europe, of plaintive fado music, eucalyptus, port wine and sardines – Portugal was a docile sleepy ally until the morning of 25 April 1974, when the people of Lisbon woke to find soldiers in the streets who laughed when they put red carnations in the barrels of the carbines. This little European oversight in the mega-world plan unleashed whirlwinds throughout Africa that Kissinger and his colleagues had not anticipated and are still trying to contain now, more than a decade later. With one stroke, the ability covertly to feed NATO weapons into Portugal's rickety colonies to fight leftist guerrillas—in Mozambique, Guinea Bissau and Angola—was in ruins.

The Portuguese troops, weary from fighting bush wars they couldn't win, and led by their officers, had turned their guns on the country's septuagenarian dictator, Marcelo Caetano. When the people of Lisbon awoke that 25 April, soldiers were already

25

bundling away PIDE agents, the secret police. Within days Senhor Caetano, who only a few months before had dined at Buckingham Palace, was in exile in Brazil. It was the first and so far only successful leftist coup in Western Europe since the end of the Second World War. To make matters worse for Kissinger and his colleagues, the majority of Portuguese not only saw it as a revolution and gave their support, they began taking matters into their own hands. People occupied factories and farms where they worked, demanded electricity and public sanitation for their shacks, set up councils to get their old bosses sacked. The process was called *"saneamento"*—sanitisation. The word had an awesome resonance in a country where it was estimated there had been over 3,000 police spies.

For a would-be journalist with £35 in the summer of 1974, Portugal looked like the place to be. It also proved an introduction to the international press menagerie.

✷ ✷ ✷

Maurice was first. He didn't look like Virgil. And I certainly was no Dante. Nonetheless, he had taken it upon himself to show me around. Maurice wore loose shirts and baggy trousers and read inordinately long daily dispatches to the BBC. He was the journalistic equivalent of an Austin A40 motor car; middle-aged, reliable, with a few idiosyncrasies that meant he had to be British. His glasses were so thick I was never sure how much he could see. Maurice was also a very nice guy.

I met him, or more correctly he met me, on the sun-scorched esplanade in front of the new, revolutionary Portuguese government's press office on Lisbon's grand Avenida da Liberdade. In a trice we were out of the sun, having pushed aside two glass bead curtains, said hello to several well-powdered plumpish middle-aged women, and plopped ourselves down on the faded and red velvet cushions of two wrought iron bar stools. We were the only customers in this little hideaway, one of Maurice's favourites which, as he pointed out, was less than two minutes' walk from the government telex machines. We started with whisky, I think.

By the time we emerged he had told me about the old, now out of favour and even on-the-run politicians and business fixers who frequented the bar. The place seems to have been a watering hole for the has-beens of the old regime, a fact confirmed by various ladies who drifted over to renew acquaintance from time to time.

Maurice was a friend. In that musty bar he unlocked a fair number of skeletons in some of Lisbon's more well-heeled closets. The trouble was that when we emerged the sun was still beating

26

down on the tiles of the esplanade and my head felt like a Scottish bog.

The next newly found colleague to size me up was Chris, a punchy Fleet Street pro who had stepped on too many editors' toes and as eternal penance was filing stories for *The Guardian* whenever its rambunctious young reporters got bored or skived off to the Portuguese countryside with their leggy girlfriends. Chris's tactic was remarkably effective and blunt. It's called grappa; Italian grape pomace liqueur drunk with coffee, before coffee, in coffee, after coffee or by itself. There was always one more bar—usually a hole in the wall lit by a paraffin lamp—down some garbage strewn cobbled street after the last bar had closed where bums like us could get a drink. Chris must have thought I was a liar because I really had no idea then which London journalists were stabbing which other London journalists in the back. For my part, I was never quite sure whether the retribution he so determinedly sought was being wrought on Fleet Street or himself.

After a few grappa expeditions, drinks on *The Sunday Times* in Lisbon's Tivoli Hotel—deep pile lobby carpets, bell hops and marble everywhere—were child's play. I began to have a sense of what I could manage to write about. The Prime Minister's office wasn't terribly impressed phoning back to the pay phone of my back street pension. On the other hand there were a lot of British in Portugal. And a lot of them wanted to unburden themselves of their own versions of what the coup was "really" about, with and without embellishments.

Even before Wellington set out to drive Napoleon's troops from the Iberian peninsula, Portugal had been on its way to becoming a de facto British fiefdom. In 1703, John Methuen, the son of a wealthy Bradford cloth manufacturer, negotiated a treaty with a Portuguese wine producer which effectively destroyed the Portuguese textile industry and assured Britain cheap agricultural products and port wine ever since. Everything from trolley cars and elevators in Lisbon, to the grapes, cork and eucalyptus in the countryside came within the British maw.

The Royal British Club on Rua da Estrela in one of Lisbon's more comfortable residential areas is not particularly impressive, even if it was a favourite of Edward VII. Nor is the curry they serve once a week for lunch. Nonetheless it was a good talking shop.

"I'm afraid we're a bit short of staff," my host, a British businessman and long-term Portuguese resident, explained. "They've asked for a raise and I'm afraid we just can't afford it, and frankly we don't want to give it in any case."

That didn't matter. I was unashamedly more interested in the gossip. And there was plenty of that.

"I was talking with the ambassador yesterday and he says . . ."

"Yes, it probably was a bit hasty of X to fly off to Brazil with his golf bags stuffed with money. But then, you know, the missus has already packed the china and sent the paintings back to London . . ."

We finished the curry and tucked into the sweet, blobs of vanilla ice cream with wafers, the sort served at school dinners and church fêtes. A large stand of eucalyptus had recently been burned to the ground on one of the member's estates. Had the culprits been found?

"No," said the owner, "but you can be damned sure that the insurance is going to pay. And they're going to do it into a London account too . . ."

It proved easy to be an attentive guest. Yet I couldn't help feeling that for one lunchtime, for Englishmen, despite the old school ties and the slightly raffish manner, my hosts managed to lick an awful lot of sore wounds. It seemed as if the discomforts and irritations they were each experiencing amounted to an unpardonable affront by the great Portuguese unwashed, a collective slap in the face of British aplomb. For some it was more than that, it was an historic betrayal of trust.

The question which interested me was whether these men were out simply to look after their own interests in the Portuguese turmoil, or were they contemplating going further, getting involved in economic sabotage?

It's not the sort of question British expatriates like having put, nor for that matter is it always easy to ask. In troubled times a friendly face who speaks the same language is supposed to be on "our side". To have cast doubts on that assumption can be seen as a perfidious and near traitorous act. Yet Portugal's revolution, if it was a revolution, was not just a comic opera of parades and waving flags, aborted midnight plots and diplomatic deals. It was hundreds of mini-revolutions as well, many of them taking place on the farms and in the factories owned by the men who sat down to curry at the Royal British Club.

If your family has been doing nicely out of Portugal for at least five generations, then you're not about to leave in a hurry if it can at all be helped. On the other hand, if you've been scraping dirt all your life and you're worried that your kids don't have shoes, then if the owner skives off to Lisbon with his wife and the silverware you might feel inclined to take over his manor house. There was a possibly irreconcilable conflict of interests here. And it is in this rich social humus of personal ambition, resentment and fear, that determination to get what you want, or to hold on to what you see as yours gets honed to the bone. Within six months of the coup while farmworkers were holding meetings in tomato fields the patrons were reaching for their cheque books, looking for men to sort matters out.

There were plenty of mercenaries about. PIDE agents who had fled to Spain returned, raising havoc throughout the mountainous north, burning farms, beating students, later bombing Communist Party offices. The Catholic church, the Archbishop of Braga particularly, spoke out against political sinners. Priests intoned against the communist anti-Christ. They warned peasants against the unnaturalness of women who wore trousers—university students who had flocked to the villages as part of a leftist literacy campaign.

More sinisterly, a group of Portuguese fascists and international hit men began organising what was to become the ELP, a secret right-wing army hiding just across the border from Portugal in Spain. Among those to become involved was a freelance American terrorist, who two years later was to end up in an Algerian jail for some bombings in Algiers.

Only one person had been killed the day of the coup, hit by a stray bullet outside the PIDE headquarters. There had already been three governments in the space of five months. Left-wing mini-parties had spread like a rash, but they seemed to be most effective digging into each others' throats. Kissinger, never short of an answer, saw the American ambassador sacked and a four man investigative team dispatched to see how the United States could keep the revolution under control. Portugal was denied access to NATO strategic briefings. American military assistance was embargoed. Also drafted in were several additional CIA spies who spoke fluent Portuguese and/or were experienced in coups. Rooms in the Sheraton Hotel were booked for men in dark glasses who didn't smile. There were even whisperings that General Antonio de Spinola, the disillusioned figurehead of the 25 April coup, was eager to march down Lisbon's Avenida da Liberdade, declare a state of siege and usurp all powers for himself, a Lusitanian Charles de Gaulle.

One thing seemed clear. The men at the Royal British Club had, for the most part, decided to see the revolution out. As yet they saw no reason to relinquish their grip on the chunks of Portugal they controlled. I was curious to see what this would involve. They were also curious as to what I would do.

★ ★ ★

29

The first to be seen was a young man, the scion of one of the oldest British families in the Portuguese cork trade. His office was in the company warehouse in the Lisbon docks. The business had run as smoothly as skittles on grease. To the warehouse came the bark stripped from thousands of trees, left bare in the fields, along roadsides, covering whole hillsides looking like the torsos of anguished contorted dancers abandoned across Portugal. From the warehouse cork went to plug wine bottles, supply floor tiles and bulletin boards around the world. The man was obviously fit, industrious and rich. He was also sharp witted.

"No, we've had no trouble here," he said. "The boys were a bit excited at first. They wanted to talk about a few changes. Obviously I obliged. But it's back to normal now . . ."

"That was odd," I replied. "The commercial attaché at the embassy told me that your mother kept phoning him up."

"Well, you know what mothers are like," he offered.

"He says you were held hostage here for over a day."

"Look, if you're not going to help, why don't you piss off."

Short, splenetic and to the point. I could understand that. I also came soon to understand that he could dish out stronger medicine as well. Unless it was hands off the family business, the government had been told, then there would be precious little cork export for a while, no foreign currency coming into the bank. Nor would his firm be buying bark from the countryside. Those workers who had so cavalierly taken over the estates of the owners who had sold to his family for years would be without a buyer, short of cash and left with piles of cork that would soon rot.

"Serves them right," my informant, a British businessman told me over whisky and olives in the Tivoli bar. The economic counter-offensive had begun.

The next stop was the Timex factory across the Tagus estuary from Lisbon. More cheap watches were said to be made there than anywhere else in Western Europe. The company is based in Dundee, the profits come from Portugal. In the staff changing room the workers' committee described how they caught the manager slipping out of a back door during what were supposed to be negotiations, how he had been surrounded in his Rover 2000 automobile for three hours until he agreed to talk, how later he had been locked in with the workers' committee for two days until an agreement was reached. High on the workers' list was their insistence that the foremen stop touching up the girls. Was it true that they had been?

There was a knock on the changing room door. The manager wanted to talk. Now. He was a Scot. Upstairs in his office there were no pleasantries. No cup of tea.

"What are you doing here?"

"Talking to your employees."

"Why didn't you ask my permission first?"

"Is that really necessary?"

"This is a private firm."

We were getting nowhere, so I plunged in. "How long have your foremen been touching up the girls?"

"I don't expect journalists to . . ."

"They tell me that you have to sleep with one of the bosses to get a promotion."

"I don't expect journalists to come busting in here . . ."

He was fairly sputtering now.

"But you don't deny it, do you?"

"Look here," he roared, "We've got enough problems as it is without your type nosing about."

It was an utterly thuggish approach, truculent, heavy on candour, devoid of finesse. Later, driving back into Lisbon in the company car he confided that he suspected the allegations about some of the foremen were true. He would rather that it wasn't written about though. He wanted to stay in Portugal. The climate and the seafood were wonderful. He believed that the unions sincerely wanted to do business. If only a few of the hotheads could be sorted out . . .

"But didn't you have PIDE agents in the factory before?" I asked.

"There might have been, from time to time," he replied vaguely.

"Well?"

"It wasn't just us. A lot of firms did. Sometimes they came in and took people away, and O.K., sometimes we all used to look the other way."

We stopped for a coffee and grappa. The Timex man was talking about his kids' school. I interrupted. Frankly, I said, I couldn't see there was much for him to worry about. He only had to begin handling industrial relations in a sensible manner. After all, surely Timex in Dundee didn't call in the Special Branch every time workers complained. We paid and went our own ways.

★ ★ ★

The carefully whitewashed houses of Casa Branca shimmer in the sun. Their portals are freshly painted blue, green, a few are pink, signatures of local housewives. Dogs lie in the dust under eucalyptus trees. Old men sit more or less motionless on a rough wooden bench outside the bar.

Casa Branca is a postcard village on the northern edge of the

Alentejo, Portugal's great blistered central plain, a 100-kilometre wide swathe of scorched grain fields and cattle ranching cut across Portugal's belly. It's a region of huge latifundia and smatterings of small villages. Casa Branca is one of them.

Most of the adults in the town work, when there is work, on the 2,000-acre estate of Dr. Albert "Bouncer" Reynolds, "The Englishman" they call him, who's in Lisbon now. "He didn't spend much time here anyhow," one of the men outside the bar wants known. "When the revolution came we went to him, we got together and we said that this year when we cut the cork we want 180 escudos a day." That was three pounds.

"And what were you getting last year?" I asked.

"120 escudos. That's not enough."

"And what did he say?"

"He said no, not until he saw the government decree saying he had to pay us more."

So the workers took over the estate. Now they were running the place but they couldn't find a buyer for the year's cork harvest, and "Bouncer", who also had a law practice in Lisbon, had refused to help them on their terms.

"He says there's not such a good market for cork now," one of the men explained.

"Well?"

"That's just not true. We know he could sell it. He just doesn't want to."

The logic was simple and blunt to the workers in Casa Branca; no markets, no income, no food. The men were sullen, fed up. They cut thick slices of dried sausage with crude knives as they talked and drank wine. Everywhere there were flies. Only a whisper of a breeze caught the curling eucalyptus leaves and gently shook the trees.

In the dry fields of another, nearby estate women washed the dirt off their hands with squashed tomatos. They sat chatting under a makeshift awning waiting for the tractor to collect them, keeping out of the sun. Some of them had children and infants. They were passing around pieces of melon.

"What were the English owners like?" I asked.

"The English one, what do you want me to say?" A young woman with two kids playing around her skirts, eating melon, was talking. "Every time she come back from Lisbon in that fine car, there was never anything for us. Just if once there had been something for the children to play with . . ."

The women nearby nodded. They either agreed or were keeping their thoughts to themselves, as if to say, what do you expect us to tell a journalist from Britain. The kids began throwing dirt at each other and slipped out from under the awning into the blistering sun.

"Bouncer" Reynolds would probably have understood. Over cocktails in Lisbon he'd told me that he didn't expect much from his farm now. The wife was a bit upset. "I mean, after all those years." But there was no sense in giving up. "Sit tight. That's what we've got to do. It's bound to improve." He talked like a man capable of considerable feeling and compassion whose nerves had been suddenly cauterised. It probably was best that he didn't try to return to his estate then. He wasn't welcome.

His big house was set on a small hillock surrounded by eucalyptus groves deep in the centre of the estate at the end of a long twisting dirt track which crossed streams and cut around piles of cork. It was a fine home, full of fine fabrics and china, built to catch the cool evening breezes after days sweltering in the Alentejo, an ideal place to have friends for the weekend.

I had heard children in the master bedroom, snotty nosed, good humoured and in rags. Their mothers had discovered the bath. Behind the house, on the fringes of the dirt yard where a few mongrels skulked and chickens pecked in the dust, were the workers' shacks, threadbare but for dangling light bulbs and cold water taps.

The men told me they only wanted some justice. Instead they were broke. The estate was piled high with unsold cork and there was no credit forthcoming from the bank. We had a few drinks. They called it absurd.

In *The Sunday Times* I wrote: "the haze of privilege is passing slowly . . . 'The cook listens to the communist radio all day,' one executive's wife complained. 'She says she hates it but she won't turn it off.' " That was one side of the story; of brashness, audacity and pleasure many ordinary Portuguese were gulping down in large draughts for the first time.

There was, though, another story which also needed to be told. The villagers of Casa Branca had found that there is more to revolution than just demanding a fair price and occupying factories and estates. So too did the farmers of the Douro Valley who grow the grapes for port wine.

It was there that the British community dealt its sharpest, most devastating and crippling blow.

★ ★ ★

Port is made by allowing grapes to ferment into what is called "must", and then adding *eau de vie*, a clear brandy distilled from the previous year's must, to stop fermentation and fortify the wine. The chemistry is simple and traditional. The peasant farmers who cultivate the steep rocky hillsides of the Douro valley utterly depend on it. Not only must they sell their grapes. Most of them must also sell modest, yet to them crucial, quantities of the must, which they have stored in vats on their farms, if they are to see the winters through.

Late every summer, when the purchasing agents from the port firms climb the twisting road from Oporto along the cataracts of the Douro River, peasants throughout the region know that their families' livelihoods for the next year will be determined by the quantities purchased and the prices struck. Unsold grapes taste as good as any others. But to people who need to buy shoes, calicos and hoes they are as worthless as yesterday's news. Leftover must can't even be used for pig swill.

The port firms have always done well. And yet a whiff of scandal hung over the trade. Only the finest *eau de vie* from the best Douro grapes goes into creating the finest ports, sold at king's ransom prices in *haute cuisine* restaurants and club bars. Connoisseurs don't expect plonk. Why then had bulk shipments of cheap Yugoslav and French *eau de vie* gone into some of the previous year's port? The reputations of all the port firms, including the well-known British ones—Cockburns, Sandemans, Warres—even if they weren't involved, stood to be compromised if news of this adulteration spread.

Yet inspectors at the Instituto Vinho do Porto ruefully admitted it was true. And they knew, though they wouldn't say, which firms were involved. All day they held up to the light, tasted and then spat out and graded every batch of port coming from the companies' lodges in Vila Nova de Gaia across the river from Oporto. The foreign purchase seemed a risky cost-cutting ruse. Possibly it was part of a commercial squeeze, so as to buy less from the Douro farmers as well. But why should the port firms do that? For generations they had comfortably held the Douro peasants, tied to interminable mortgages, by the throat.

The answer lay in the factories of France and to a lesser extent Germany, Belgium and the Netherlands. The sons of Douro farmers returned from them in the summers driving new Peugeots, their heads full of plans, their pockets full of cash—not a lot, but enough, so many of them felt, to buy their families out of port wine servitude. Perhaps it was only a matter of time before a persuasive entrepreneur, a man who talked fast and made sense and said he had a way with the banks, suggested that he take their money, buy up the harvest, hold it, and then force the port firms to buy from him, for once at reasonable prices.

That happened the year before the coup. And not surprisingly the port firms felt burned. They had contracts to meet. So they paid the new, what they considered to be extortionate prices. But at meetings of the Gremio, their trade association, they vowed it would never happen again. From Lisbon I telephoned the manager of one of the British firms.

"Sure, love to talk," he answered. "But there's a bit of a problem just at the moment. The workers' committee has come into the office and, well . . . they're carrying guns."

Nonetheless he seemed remarkably confident. I promised to phone back. Two days later we met in the company's offices behind gigantic wooden casks stacked in caves by the river in Vila Nova de Gaia.

"Sorry about that," he said. "You see, we're in a bit of a spot and these fellows don't seem to understand."

In fact they did, all too well. One of Cockburns' executives told me that for the second year running Cockburns were buying no port at all from the farmers and only small quantities of must. Sandemans man in Oporto said its policy was similar, and that much of theirs was purchased from the estates of absentee landlords residing in Lisbon, Oporto and overseas. Other firms were doing the same. The peasants were flattened.

For the next two days one of the British firms' Portuguese buyers drove me about the Douro, pointing out farms, explaining how port was made, showing me his company's new stainless steel vats. He was casual, nonchalant. He also talked about the need for order, the loss of faith by the farmers, the spread of communism. He advocated drastic steps. Yes, he had heard about the demonstrating workers who had been beaten in Oporto. But then, that's what they should expect. He was a good employee, a god-fearing citizen, a capable man who clearly liked wearing a suit and driving the company car. His political views were tailored to match. I left him in Regua, the small market town where the farmers had gathered to sell their harvest. The best meal to be had was sardines and potato soup.

As I was eating I began thinking about sensibilities, those of the men in Oporto with whom I could discuss cricket scores, my driver who had been eager to please but also, like myself, a bit bored, and the men across the wooden table in the Regua cafe. I had shared meals with all of them. Yet only in Regua did I know that there was really no other choice. You took what you were served, you paid, and you got out knowing for certain that your next meal would have to be at home. Because as far as selling grapes was concerned,

35

there were no buyers to be found.

The explanation was pinned to the notice board outside the municipal office. Most of the firms had made most of their purchases privately. Farmers who had taken part in the previous year's unusual marketing scheme would have to fend for themselves. Such was the stuff of which life in Portugal five months after the coup was made. The British were playing their part.

★ ★ ★

Lisbon was in turmoil. Rumours from the São Bento and Belem palaces spread like rats through the bars and cafes, among the barrios and into the anterooms of banks. During the day everyone sweated as Lisbon sweltered under a suffocating sun. At night gangs were out with aerosol spray paint, buckets and clubs splashing new slogans and warnings across walls and on the streets. The mood was unsettled. The holiday resorts were almost empty. The tourists were keeping away. Something ugly was about to happen. But what?

The men at the Royal British Club had their suspicions, but kept them to themselves. The *Daily Telegraph's* correspondent was soon to spell out the situation. "The communists continue to show themselves far and away the best organised and most astute of the political parties," he wrote. "There are those who believe that if the communists maintain their present performance they are bound to win the 'free and democratic' elections for the constituent assembly promised for March next year. . . . President Spinola is deeply preoccupied by this prospect."

But the communists, whose leader Alvaro Cunhal held a seat in the cabinet, said they were acting within the principles set down by the coordinating committee of the Armed Forces Movement. And it was this committee made up of a couple of dozen predominantly young officers which effectively ruled Portugal.

On 10 September, aloof, monocled President General Antonio de Spinola made a speech calling for the "silent majority" to "wake up and defend yourselves actively against totalitarian extremists at work in the shadows." Soon after, a new poster appeared throughout Lisbon calling on the "Silent Majority" to take to the streets on 28 September. To the officers of the coordinating committee this looked like a thinly disguised call for a right-wing putsch.

By early morning on the 28th the roads leading into the capital were blocked by troops turning back would-be enthusiasts for the general to assume extraordinary powers. By midday Spinola himself issued this brief communique: "In view of the changed state of public order which arose in the early hours of today, His Excellency the President of the Republic considers it inappropriate that the rally announced for this afternoon in the Parca do Imperio should take place, in order to avoid possible confrontation." Spinola had lost, and resigned. He had tried to command the army over the heads of the Armed Forces Movement and failed.

Six months later, on 11 March 1975, his supporters tried again, mounting a comic-opera coup from the air force base at Tancos north of Lisbon. For his part Spinola was supposed to rendezvous outside the capital wearing false whiskers in a hired Mercedes before being driven triumphantly to assume his historic role. But that was not to be. Troops having yet again failed to rally to his call, Spinola, his wife and a handful of officers ignominiously fled by helicopter across the border to Spain, whence into exile in Brazil.

Yet again the Portuguese "revolution" had, if not been saved, at least not been overthrown. Nonetheless, shrewder minds appreciated that if General Spinola was not to be the man of the hour, then someone else had to be groomed to assume the anti-communist mantle.

In June 1976, Mario Soares, leader of the Socialist Party took office as Portugal's first elected Prime Minister since the 25 April coup two years before, setting Portugal firmly back in the Western alliance. There were more than a few bumps along that road.

★ ★ ★

July 14th, 1975. Rio Major, a small town some 60 miles north of Lisbon. Farmers sack the Communist Party's headquarters.
July 20th. Communist headquarters are burnt to the ground in Valença, a small northern town near the Spanish border, and in Matosinhos, a fishing port near Oporto. Fourteen people are reported injured.
July 21st. Again communist headquarters are attacked; in Castelo Branco, Minde and Val de Cambra. The next day two people are wounded as the same happens in Alcobaça.

Throughout July and August communist offices in northern Portugal are attacked by mobs brandishing stones, broken bottles, rifles, grenades and petrol bombs. Filing cabinets and papers are thrown out of the windows, furniture is smashed, the buildings are gutted by fire. Scores of party members and their attackers are injured in the biggest wave of violence since the coup. Party workers' homes are also sacked and put to the torch.

Mario Soares is coincidentally outside the country when the violence begins, conferring with his European allies. In

Minneapolis, Minnesota, United States President Gerald Ford delivers a bullish speech telling the Russians to keep "hands off" Portugal. *The Times* correspondent writes, on 18 August, "Portugal's Communist Party is today facing the prospect of no longer being able to operate openly as a legitimate political force in the face of mob violence and the failure of the military government to impose elementary protective security."

Portugal's communists had become the target of a classic destabilisation campaign. Emboldened by the violence condoned around them, landowners in the Alentejo tried to grab back their expropriated farms. But the farm workers were having none of it. When a car full of dispossessed owners turned up at an estate near to "Bouncer" Reynolds' they were set upon with rakes and hoes. Women were in the forefront screaming abuse. When landowners confiscated some cattle from an estate which had been expropriated near the town of Chança, farm-workers from the entire neighbourhood occupied the town where the herd was being held until the cattle were returned. But these were small skirmishes.

During the year 1975 virtually the entire Western media set out to bolster the anti-communist movement in Portugal. Millions of dollars were poured into the Portuguese Socialist Party and other political organisations by the United States and other NATO governments and parties. As Henry Kissinger told *Time* magazine that October, "During the summer the West Europeans came to the same conclusions we had earlier reached: namely, that pluralism had to be actively encouraged." The Portuguese communists responded by shrinking back into their narrow sectarian habits, adopting formulas and tactics known only too well to their adversaries. These were trite refuges which, nonetheless, the communists thought they could trust. When the National Assembly elections were held the next spring the socialists won comfortably. Portugal was back in the western fold.

Yet a price had been paid, something had been lost during that "pluralist" crusade, as Henry Kissinger had called it. In the campaign to stymie the communists even liberal papers such as the *New Statesman* fell into step. The feelings of the peasants, the workers and just possibly of British and other landowners were pushed out of sight. And yet, it was a time full of genuine passions as well as high political intrigue. For their part the British could only look backwards and try to abort what was happening around them. The Portuguese who had worked for them, however, were seeing their dreams unfurling before them for the first time in their lives. To take a bath in the landowners' house, to set the price for the port grapes that determined their lives, to run a factory without

38

secret police intimidation: these were wonderful moments. Compared with such inspiration the men at the Royal British Club had little to offer, and more than once I sensed that they felt cheated because there was so little around for which they could muster enthusiasm.

Since then the Portuguese people have found that life can be very complicated if not dispiriting. Cork and grapes are worthless if no one will buy them. You can't manage estates and factories without bank loans and other credits. Land deeds are mere fictions if government agencies refuse to acknowledge them.

Portugal has now returned to the sunny pages of tourist brochures. The secret police, by and large, are gone. So too is the bankrupt African empire. Some changes from the days of the coup have endured. But today many Portuguese are still among the poorest people in Europe, forced to live on a diet of potatoes and sardines.

3

The Spanish Sahara

IT BEGAN IN the editor's offce with the *Times Atlas* open to the plates for the Sahara desert, little but brownish peppery patches denoting sand dunes and arid waste from one edge of the volume to the other.

"Where did you say they were?"

"Here."

I pointed vaguely to a spot about 500 miles south of the Mediterranean, south of Morocco's Great Atlas mountains, deep in the desert about 150 miles east of the sand dune coast where Africa's hump pushes into the Atlantic.

"That's where the refugee camps are. It's also from where, as I understand it, they set off at night in stolen Land Rovers to ambush Moroccan troops."

"How many are there?"

I didn't know.

"What do they call themselves?"

"POLISARIO." He obviously already knew.

"Go on," he said.

I explained that POLISARIO was the acronym for the political movement of the tribes which lived in the Spanish Sahara and who'd just seen their stomping ground handed over by Spain to be carved up and incorporated into Morocco and Mauritania. It was February 1976.

"O.K., that's enough." I'd passed the first test. "How are you going to get there?" he asked.

"The Algerian army," I replied. "It's the only way."

We were looking at a dot on the map, just inside the Algerian border near where Algeria, Morocco and what was labelled the Spanish Sahara meet. The dot's name was Tindouf. Once it was a French Foreign Legion outpost. Now it was an Algerian garrison town.

The editor said nothing, thought, then looked up.

"O.K.," he finally said. "Find out how many there are, who they

40

are, what they want. I want to know if they're an Algerian front, Algerian troops got up as desert tribesmen to have a bash at the Moroccans."

"They're supposed to be refugees," I said. We had had these conversations before. "You know," I went on, "refugees with no food and sick kids living in moth-eaten tents . . . "

"Sure, sure. Off you go, and don't forget . . . "

I waited.

"All refugees are the same."

Why do the world's cynics sit behind newsdesks?

★ ★ ★

The contact was in Paris. The cafe was like hundreds of others, and presumably in them also strangers met to arrange matters they would rather other people, particularly the police, knew nothing about. Such I'd always assumed was Paris, the city which year after year has more political bombings and assassinations than any other capital of Europe.

We drank bitter coffee. Smoked Gauloises. And I listened while the two men, both young, black and very thin, gaunt, explained how they'd been betrayed, yet again by the Spaniards.

Apparently their semi-nomadic tribes, a few hundred thousand people in all, had for hundreds of years migrated back and forth from the cold Atlas foothills of Morocco south to the salt mines of Mauritania, and further south into Senegal. They traded salt, slaves, sugar and tea. But mostly they lived off their herds of sheep, goats and camels, carrying their firewood with them, surviving on couscous, milk and occasionally onions and tomatoes. They knew every wadi and desert ridge in the area on the map politicians and cartographers referred to as the Spanish Sahara.

In June 1970, there were reportedly ten casualties after a demonstration calling for self-determination in the colonial capital, the coastal town of El Aaiún. It was the first public act which led, three years later, to the formation of a national liberation army, the Popular Front for the Liberation of Seguiet el Hamra and Rio de Oro—POLISARIO—demanding independence and willing to fight for it. Since then there had been trouble.

Europeans had written off the region as worthless until 1947 when some 1.7 billion tons of phosphate, the basic material of many fertilisers, was found lying indecently near the surface at a place called Bu Craa. Bu Craa soon became one of the largest phosphate mines in the world. Spanish Foreign Legionnaires guarded the 100 kilometer conveyor belt that carried the rock to the coast. A Spanish consortium and French financiers took much of the profits.

41

On 20 November 1975, Generalissimo Francisco Franco died in Madrid after a team of Spain's best surgeons had worked for over a month to keep him alive. The Spanish army had all but withdrawn from the Sahara, leaving only Legionnaires along the conveyor belt and in isolated garrison outposts. The young men of POLISARIO felt that independence should have been near at hand. Yet the International Court of Justice in The Hague, on reviewing their case for self-determination, had given a judgment which seemed deliberately vague. More to the point, neither the Parisian bankers nor the Spanish Foreign Ministry were willing to concede the income from at least 10 million tons of phosphate a year—enough to challenge control of the world market—to a bunch of nomads of uncertain political pedigree.

Instead they drew a line through the middle of the map. The southern sector of the Spanish Sahara went to Mauritania, which as a poor, weak country couldn't easily argue that it was getting the short end of the deal. The north, with the phosphate mine, went to King Hassan to become part of "Le Grand Maroc". Within days of the partition Hassan's air force began bombing the nomads as they fled towards safety over the border in Algeria. They in turn blew up the conveyor belt from Bu Craa to the sea, hijacked lorries and Land Rovers and began fighting back.

There could be little question of the depth of feeling of my POLISARIO contacts in that Paris cafe. They were on the run, without proper papers. "You see, the French too are making it hard for us," they said. I believed them. I also believed that they genuinely felt they were fighting a just war. But for the moment that wasn't really at issue. My editor wanted to know if they were a front, a puppet show propped up in the desert to attract journalists while a sleight of hand was being worked by, who knows, Algeria, Libya, the Soviet Union. Crudely, I was being sent to discover whether they were yet another African proxy in the tired Cold War, or people with genuinely independent emotions and views.

As we left the cafe the two men said they would be in touch with people in Algiers whom I must contact. And yes, they would be in Paris when I returned. We shook hands. Then one of them asked if I could do him a favour. Could I take a letter to his wife? She was a nurse in the refugee camp, or at least she was the last time he had heard from her.

★ ★ ★

Algiers is one of those Mediterranean cities—Marseille, Haifa and Tangiers are others—where whitewashed buildings cascade down from a corniche on to grey railway yards and piers which alone seem to keep them from plunging into the sea. Hugging the

42

shoreline is the boulevard, a promenade of palms and tropical shrubs along which boys polish shoes and peddle ice cream. Up the hill are the government buildings, the grand hotels, the elegant shops and cafes. Below are the slums, in Algiers the casbah where, in 1957, General Jacques Massu and his torturers of the elite 10th paratroop division set out to exterminate the Algerian independence movement, the FLN, and failed.

Both the hill and the casbah were then social ghettos, each with its own clear manner and style, its own poets and illusions. The European colonialists claimed the hill as their own with its wide avenues and the fragrance of orange blossom and jasmine at dusk. Albert Camus was their most enlightened spokesman. Frantz Fanon, the physician turned guerrilla tactician spoke for and to the people of the casbah. "At the level of individuals, violence is a cleansing force," he wrote in *Wretched of the Earth,* reflecting on the Algerian war. "It frees the native from his inferiority complex and from his despair and inaction, it makes him fearless and restores his self respect." Over a million Algerians were killed during the war, many of them summarily executed, or first tortured then butchered to death at the height of Massu's terror.

Those were heady, momentous times, which brought Charles de Gaulle to power in France and gave birth to the idea of "the third world". Today they are the stuff of the sensible, literate world of cinema, lost illusions and literary reviews. Between the hill and the casbah today lie seedy hotels, threadbare offices, and shops selling third rate shoes. That's the centre of Algiers now. It's dirty, noisy, and garbage piles up on the streets. The people are harassed, worn down, querulous from the struggle of daily existence, yet they seem proud to be Algerian. Algiers has become an ordinary place. On the other hand to those who know its history it will never quite be just pedestrian.

My POLISARIO contacts' friends were staying in a fleabag hotel used by Bulgarian engineers and East German surveyors. The mattresses were sacks of lumps, the water was off during the day and the electricity—what there was of it—gave a dim glow to 15 watt light bulbs. Algiers and Algeria are overwhelmingly poor, nonetheless the city still has political pace and sophistication.

Somewhere in the city Eldridge Cleaver, the American Black Panther, had been holed up with a few associates, one of dozens of exile groups from spent and lost causes to have found meagre refuge there. Elsewhere in town Henry Kissinger's Assistant Secretary of State for Middle Eastern Affairs was negotiating a natural gas deal. The cinemas were showing a short film about a group of terrorists who had smuggled bombs in from Marseille and then blew up the offices of Algeria's semi-official newspaper,

El-Moudjahid, in early January. It looked remarkably lifelike. On 4 March, *El-Moudjahid* gave over several pages to the trial of the very same men. Three of the seven defendants had been given death sentences. One of these was Jay Sablonski, the American from Philadelphia who the year before was reported to have been involved with Portuguese fascists.

I was incredulous. "How," I asked the newspaper's editor, "did you get the accused to play their own parts in a film which could only lead to their convictions?"

"Maybe they were promised some mitigation," he replied.

"But they were given death sentences."

"So," came his laconic reply, "they haven't been executed yet."

Algiers was fraught with infuriating ambiguities, and I had to find a way out to the desert. The first meeting was with POLISARIO'S representatives, not the young men sharing the fleas with me in the cheap hotel, but the slightly older, better dressed spokesmen, many of whom had been educated in Paris, now holding court at the Hotel St. Georges, a repository of bygone French elegance.

While the Algerian government picked up the tab they argued their cause, sipping coffee on the terrace surrounded by rhododendrons. It was undeniably pleasant. But by then the arguments seemed all too familiar and well rehearsed. One question remained. What was happening in the desert?

★ ★ ★

"Trained him myself."

"What did you say?" I found myself yelling. The Mercedes in which we were sitting careened around another corner just missing yet another pedestrian.

"I said I trained him myself."

"I thought as much."

Harold Edelstam was the Swedish ambassador, an errant aristocrat who obviously hated the pomp and restraints of his job. In Chile during the 1973 coup he had taken dozens of refugees into the embassy and then personally escorted them to the airport and safety in his limousine. His Algerian driver seemed to have caught on. We were literally crashing through the streets. Maybe Edelstam was bored with Algiers. Maybe he had reason to rush.

"If anyone tells you those refugees don't need any help, they're lying. They need blankets and food. We're sending tents from Sweden. But it's not enough. It's terrible what's happening out there."

"But they're supposed to be revolutionaries," I reminded him.

"Who cares?"

If he was correct there were a lot of liars among the NATO states' diplomatic community in Algiers. The American attaché had been most frank. "Look," he said, after punching the code into the electronic lock of the door that led to his office. "You know what I do here so let's not beat about the bush." I didn't know as a matter of fact. I only suspected he was a spook. He then gave me a resumé as to why POLISARIO, decent people though they might be, would not get American support.

Morocco was America's natural ally in the region, controlling the southern shore of the Straits of Gibraltar with harbours on both the Atlantic and Mediterranean. The king had allowed the country to be used for American air bases, which had become doubly important since the Yom Kippur war in the Middle East and the uncertainties following the Portuguese coup. Hassan was a friend of America. The Algerians, on the other hand, were shrewd and unpredictable. They were tough and worthwhile business partners, and while socialist, knew how to look the other way when it came to making a good deal. But friendship between the two countries didn't go much further than that. Algeria supported POLISARIO. The worthwhile portion of the Spanish Sahara had been ceded to Morocco. Simply put, there was no room for the desert tribesmen and their national liberation movement, let alone their refugee families, on the State Department's geopolitical map. "It's tough," he said, "but that's it."

The Swedish ambassador understood that. He didn't like it, but it made a coarse kind of sense.

The British diplomat was another matter.

"Going out there, huh?" He was looking me over very closely, having offered a sherry before sitting down on his office settee.

I said nothing.

"Empty you know."

"Oh?" I said.

"Yes, nothing in those tents. Nothing. Nobody. It's all part of a bloody propaganda exercise."

His argument, if brief, was nonetheless breathtaking in its simplicity.

"So you think I'm wasting my time going out there?" I said.

"Not for me to say. It's all been set up for you press Johnnies."

"Oh yes. How can you be so sure?"

"Just count the tents. Then go look inside. See how many have people in them. Bloody few I'll tell you."

"I might drop in when I get back."

"Do that," he said. "Now goodbye."

There was nothing more to add. He was a wet cod, bored by me, possibly bored by his job, posturing over a glass of sherry. Back at

45

the hotel there was a message. I was to be picked up in the morning. I went to the casbah to buy a pair of boots.

★ ★ ★

The desert runway was made of prefabricated corrugated metal sections laid on the sand. When the wheels touched down the plane vibrated as if skidding across a washboard. We counted the MiGs camouflaged behind sandbags along the runway. "Five, six, seven . . . How many on your side?"

I was travelling with a Swedish journalist and the Algerian army. He said he's one of the world's leading slum pornographers. "I take the pictures of starving babies that make people in Stockholm phone up and ask where to send their money," he said. There must be worse jobs.

Tindouf—what could be seen of it—is one main street of squat palms and low red stucco buildings. By noon the wind was already whipping up gussets of sand, pushing drifts across the street, biting everywhere and into everything. The sun was a faint yellow glow in a grey haze swallowed up by the sand, like a massive swarm of flies stinging your eyes, invading your mouth as you speak. There was only one place in town to eat according to the somewhat fanciful hoarding outside the restaurant.

Inside, the slow, revolving fan hardly disturbed the flies flitting off soft drink bottles and half eaten plates of couscous. Humphrey Bogart might have recognised the place. Our interpreter, Ahmed, introduced himself. If we could just make sure that he accompanied us whenever we wanted to talk to people, then we would get on fine . . . He was middle-aged, a bit fat, a decent guy who obviously would rather have been home in Algiers, or asleep.

In the small hospital the slum pornographer photographed several refugee children with gauze wrapped around stumps where their arms and legs should have been. They were the casualties of bombing raids. They stared at us with limpid brown eyes, hardly crying. Some of them had severe burns, but it didn't look like napalm.

South of Tindouf the desert is harsh yellow crust, caked over baked hillocks and parched pebbled wastes remorselessly scoured by sharp winds and sand. After an hour's drive we came across tents, hundreds of tents, everywhere, huge billowing white and black canopies anchored around one miserable spot because of its solitary water tap, enough to be marked as an oasis on maps. It's called Hassi Robinet.

Women in indigo scavenged for stray twigs in the sand. Their faces were blue from the cloth of their garments. Other women were squatting over small fires brewing bitter green tea. Children were running about everywhere. These were nomads. The tents were well staked, but even so the fierce wind ripped corners away. Under the tarpaulins sitting on rough handwoven rugs mothers suckled their infants while their daughters monotonously picked stones out of shallow dishes of couscous. Outside the sand piled against the canvas.

It could have been a normal encampment except that there were too few men about. I went looking for the nurse whose husband had given me a letter in Paris.

She was young, wearing a dirty white doctor's smock examining babies in a small makeshift hospital tent.

"Where are the men?" I asked.

"Fighting."

"Why don't I see many old people?"

"Most of them have died."

Tuberculosis was rife. She explained that there were few medicines aside from a small quantity of aspirin. The children had bronchitis and dysentery. They needed sweaters for the cold desert nights. They had fled their homes in a hurry leaving most of their possessions and clothing behind. There were said to be over 40,000 refugees in the vicinity. The British diplomat's admonition seemed woefully out of place.

Ahmed was anxious to deliver us to a mud-walled building, four rooms with only a few straw thatchings for a roof. Once it had been a French Foreign Legion outpost. Now it was our guest house. Leaning against one of the door frames and looking every bit like T.E. Lawrence, badly in need of a shave and utterly fed-up, was the Reuters man I'd last seen in Lisbon.

"Been here long?" I asked.

"Don't ask." He was in no mood for teasing.

"Come on."

"Two weeks."

"And?"

"They won't let us go to the fighting."

That was the rub. I had heard that the day POLISARIO declared itself an independent Saharan Arab Democratic Republic a fortnight previously, a handpicked clutch of journalists had been driven around in the dark for a few hours, then informed they were well within what used to be the Spanish Sahara and told to watch a flag-raising ceremony by moonlight. Reuters men expect more than that. So do I.

We waited. At night we were served endless small cups of green tea by a young boy in a long, grey burnous. The tea came on a brass tray. Between each cup we talked, then the boy added more sugar and boiling water. They have a saying: "The first cup is sweet like

47

youth. The second cup is smooth like love. The third cup is bitter like death." Several old men, sheikhs, told us stories about life under the Spanish, why they had encouraged their sons to join POLISARIO, why they had recently fled. Our hosts were genuinely friendly. Outside, a young POLISARIO fighter kept guard, rubbing his hands together to keep warm under a deep desert sky pitted with stars.

During the days we played an adult version of cat and mouse. While Ahmed slept we wandered off to the tents where the women served us tea and talked about their men. The children were being taught the alphabet using rough slates and chalk in a dugout bomb-proof school room. They also learned how to march. Shortly Ahmed would come running across the sands, his turban half unwound, screaming at us not to talk, complaining wildly, sure he would lose his job should his boss find out. The women found him amusing. We did too, but we were also getting fed up.

In the evenings we were presented with a large round plate of couscous. There was always one tomato set on top. We ate slowly, looking at the tomato but leaving it there, our only daily meal, chewing well, spitting out stones. The plate was then taken away to feed those in the tents. Hunger was soon gnawing in my stomach like a small rat. How did the children fare? They ate less than us.

On the third day the fighters arrived, churning up the desert in Land Rovers, tearing through the camp. That night there was meat in the couscous. It was tough. After we chewed we put it back. The only camel I'd seen, a shaggy old bull which seemed ceaselessly to chew its cud had been slaughtered for the occasion by an old man in a loincloth using a stone knife.

The POLISARIO commanders wanted to talk. They were like most decent fighting men anywhere: tough, prepared to cooperate, and frank. They clearly weren't rapists or looters, and they had none of the crazed arrogance common to psychopaths—both black and white—then marauding in uniform elsewhere in Africa.

There was only one problem. There were few vehicles. They were hard pressed. All of them were needed for the fighting. There was only room for two journalists. The Reuters man and his colleague got in; they had waited the longest.

A few hours later they were back. The Land Rover reeked of petrol leaking out of a 50-gallon oil drum in the back. The windows were completely caked with sand. They had been riding blind in a petrol bomb. One of the journalists had hurt his back. No one doubted him. It's often a fine line between faint hearts and good sense.

That evening the POLISARIO men held a conference. The next

morning they explained. They had only been fighting a few weeks. There were military objectives to be met. No, they weren't saying that journalists were too much of a bother. But any more trips, well . . . they would have to wait. Several months later other journalists were to report eye-witness accounts of hair-raising ambushes and desperate escapes in those Land Rovers. But that came later. I had to find answers to some straightforward questions, not least for an editor in London, and I had to find them then.

The slum pornographer was sitting just inside the doorway of our derelict Foreign Legion pension taking pictures of children and a group of old men sitting by goats about a hundred yards away. He was using a 500mm lens on a camera with a motor drive. With that he hardly needed to get up. "Don't worry," he said. "You know these guys aren't Algerian. Look at those women and the suffering they've had to put up with."

I knew that. But who was really doing the fighting? I sat down with the POLISARIO men. While they cleaned their Kalashnikov rifles we talked, about El Aaiún, the coastal town which for many of them was once home and now was the objective of midnight raids. And where is the post office? I see, and how did you get from there to the lorry depot? Is that a dirt or macadam road?

While they told their stories I wrote down details, details to be checked in London. Details which proved to be true.

And wasn't the conveyor belt from Bu Craa sabotaged? Several times? Couldn't have been easy, that one . . .

They were remarkably patient. A picture of their desert war began to emerge, of night attacks on isolated Moroccan outposts, mad highspeed drives across the desert reaches, ambushes from behind barren ridges, relentlessly pursued by Moroccan jets. These men in brown khaki and canvas boots, with Kalashnikovs, small mortars and RPG anti-tank rockets piled into the back of a handful of Land Rovers, were beginning to tie down nearly 100,000 of King Hassan's best troops. I didn't doubt that they were doing the fighting. But weren't the Algerians out there too?

Silence.

"No," came a solitary reply.

"But they're helping you?" Alas, it's not always pleasant to interrogate one's hosts.

More silence. "No. They don't do the fighting. They don't cross the border."

"But do they come to your help if you need them?" I asked.

"No. Once we're there, we're on our own."

That was their story and they were sticking to it. It was one of those situations in which you have to ask yourself how you can be sure. The answer is that you can't. The refugee camp held many truths; the nomads were suffering and their men were certainly fighting a war they felt was just. But there still could have been an Algerian tank regiment over the next sand dune. I wasn't to find out. Neither, so I understand, did any of the journalists who followed, even those who accompanied the Land Rovers attacking across the desert. To be fair, it was a question which prejudiced its own answer. Seeing the Algerians would have been conclusive in one respect but not seeing them was no evidence that they weren't elsewhere. Nonetheless it had to be asked.

★ ★ ★

The next day the refugees held a fête. Children paraded across the dunes carrying green and white POLISARIO flags singing heartily and marching with sticks for rifles on their shoulders. There was goats' milk, camel meat in the couscous and a treacly pudding with endless cups of green tea. It was a feast, sitting on ornate rugs patterned with vegetable dyes under a broad, low-slung canopy. The people were laughing. The nurse was sullen. More elderly people had died during the night. Could the Red Crescent be informed that they needed sweaters for the children? I said I'd do what I could.

Back in Tindouf we went to the hospital again. Just to check. There were POLISARIO fighters there. And yes, they had shrapnel and bullet wounds.

In Algiers I decided to forgo the British diplomat well-pickled in Her Majesty's official formaldehyde. I went looking for Antonio Cubillo, "The Voice of the Free Canaries" instead. Every evening the women at Hassi Robinet had tuned their battered portable radios to Cubillo's programme. It was a heady concoction of staccato news, rasping music and endless exhortations to the brave POLISARIO freedom fighters calling for self-determination for the Sahara and Spain's Canary Islands lying just off the African coast. The women in the desert loved it. Who was this man who never seemed to stop speaking, whose enthusiasm seemed never to waver, who castigated the Moroccans and Americans without respite?

His battered Volkswagen Beetle drew up, sputtered and jerked to a halt. A little boy and a dog hopped out. Then Cubillo, a thin man in his forties, pushed open his door which was buckled from at least one of several apparent collisions, stuffed a pile of newspapers under one arm, scooped up some books with his free hand and kicked the door shut with his foot. The kid by this time had bounded up the stairs to the office of the Movement for Self-determination and Independence of the Canary Archipelago, MPAIAC. Cubillo shook hands trying to keep the papers from spilling over the street. I helped him pick them up.

The "office" looked like a student flat after a police raid—shambolic, from the Che Guevara poster to the unwashed coffee cups.

"Please sit down, I'll just be a minute," he said.

With that he started rooting through a pile of newspapers, returning triumphantly clutching a Spanish gazette.

"See that?" Cubillo thrust a page into my hands.

"Yes."

"You know what it means?"

"Yes," I said.

"Well, what? Here was a man who could combine friendship with impatience.

It was a report of engineering works on airstrips on Grand Canary Island.

"It looks like the Americans are getting it ready to handle heavy aircraft."

"Right."

I'd said as much as I was supposed to, it seemed. Cubillo then explained that the concrete on the runways, which were over two miles long, had been laid over 30 inches deep, and that new radar had been installed providing an electronic net covering the whole of what had been the Spanish Sahara. Already the United States had extensive anti-submarine sonar equipment and a spy satellite communications centre in the Canaries, making the islands among America's most formidable strategic installations in the Atlantic.

"And Hassan?" I asked.

"He's just a dupe, their pawn," he spat.

He then recounted how as a teenager he had carried out petty sabotage against the Spanish in Tenerife, his home town; how he'd gone to Moscow; where he became fed up; went to Paris and then came to Algiers. He was dedicated and full of enthusiasm. Now POLISARIO needed his support against Morocco; he said. Perhaps he exaggerated. Perhaps he owed a few political debts I knew nothing about. In any case his spirit was undiminished. Two years later he narrowly survived an attack at his home, stabbed in the chest and back by Spanish would-be assassins.

★ ★ ★

A few months later I was lunching at Wheeler's Braganza restaurant in Frith Street in London's Soho. It could hardly have been further from the desert wastes of the Sahara. White tablecloths, wine waiters, and fresh asparagus and oysters when in season, a restaurant where well-fed well-heeled professional men flatter each other with expense account lunches. My guest was an executive of an exclusive public relations agency with offices in Knightsbridge's Sloane Street. It held the publicity account for the Moroccan government. He was an old hand at Arab affairs, having previously been in the Foreign Office where he'd done a stint in Baghdad.

"They always suspected I was the MI6 man when I was in Iraq," he told me. "But it wasn't me. It was the fellow at the next desk." He seemed amused by his private joke, though the Iraqis must have long ago figured that out for themselves.

The agency was doing well. It acted as consultants for Oman, where British mercenaries and the SAS were busy putting down a guerrilla uprising in the mountains, Bahrain, and the Organisation of Arab Petroleum Exporting Countries (OAPEC). The Moroccan brief was tricky, but by no means impossible. There was the usual tourist bumph. And then there was the question of the Spanish Sahara, of POLISARIO.

My guest was confident. Soon there was to be a conference of the non-aligned nations in Colombo, Sri Lanka. Algeria would again raise the question of recognising POLISARIO as the sole legitimate heir to the region. My guest's task was to help frustrate that, and make sure that the issue didn't come up for formal discussion, let alone a vote. He'd had prepared a hefty briefing package which put the Moroccan government's case. Others in the agency had just returned from Rabat where they'd been collecting material from their client.

"And did your people go down into the desert into what used to be the Spanish Sahara?" I asked. It seemed an eminently fair question.

"No," he said, as if it was difficult to imagine why anyone should care to ask.

"Well, did they go to El Aaiún, the capital of the region?"

They hadn't done that either. All the agency would be doing was rewriting into credible English and putting a gloss on Moroccan Ministry of Information handouts. They would talk to several well-chosen delegates at the conference as well.

The conference took place. The issue didn't come to a vote, because even to have discussed it could cause "irreparable damage" to the non-aligned movement, or so said the organisers. At several subsequent conferences the reaction has been much the same. In effect, Morocco has repeatedly threatened to walk out. And the war goes on.

In November 1975, King Hassan had called for his famous "Green March" to reclaim the desert. Some 350,000 Moroccan volunteers, mostly students and the unemployed, hiked or were driven into the Spanish Sahara. By most accounts they had a wonderful time, singing, talking uninhibitedly, many for the first time, and making friends. But the Moroccan "Woodstock" had to end as Hassan could neither adequately feed nor defend them. Nonetheless, the march effectively quashed hopes of a United Nations-supervised plebiscite on the future of the region and proved the direct cause of the current war.

Today, Morocco has reverted to more conventional means to exercise sovereignty: French F-1 Mirage and United States F-5 jet fighters fitted with Magic and Sidewinder missiles, counter-insurgency aircraft and Puma helicopters, tanks, armoured cars and heavy artillery. Over 100,000 Moroccan troops have been deployed at a cost estimated at over $1 billion a year. More than $350 million has come from the United States with another $500 million reputedly from Saudi Arabia recently. In all, it has cost nearly as much to keep the Moroccan army in the field as the Israelis spent on the Yom Kippur War. And to have achieved what?

The Bu Craa mine is producing at far from full capacity. POLISARIO units have attacked garrisons in Southern Morocco and repeatedly breached a 300-mile long earthwork perimeter complete with barbed wire, mines and sophisticated radar built to defend the phosphate mines. Yet the war has been almost forgotten by the Western press. The side that's getting paid can't seem to win. So perhaps, it seems, news of it is best lost among the desert wastes and diplomatic conference corridors.

Yet for the women in indigo robes brewing bitter tea at Hassi Robinet, and their husbands with their battered Land Rovers, the war wears on. When I joined them they were just getting used to new routines. The men were away in the desert for weeks at a time ambushing Moroccan columns, scrambling over sand dunes and rocky wadis, sapping supply lines. The women sat in their tents—the huge black canvases flapping in the interminable sand storms—picking stones out of couscous, suckling babies, Cubillo's tirades crackling over their portable radios. The children, like all refugee children, played soldiers, marching between the tents carrying sticks for rifles, the older ones shouting mercilessly at their younger brothers and sisters to stay in line. Then one of the older men would grab them and drag them off by the ear to a shallow dugout bunker they used as a schoolroom. There the kids sang rousing anthems no doubt as many refugee children do, and shouted the alphabet and numbers in unison as in many refugee camps elsewhere.

For them the days were fun. The nights were their killers. Huddling against their mothers in the tents, shivering, with only thin jumpers to shield them from the desert's bitter chill, many of them perished. They had too little nourishment, few clothes, nowhere warm to escape to. The sky was pure, dark ultramarine blue, studded with stars, as diamonds are scattered across the vaults of sultans tombs. It was silent. Small bundles were taken silently from some of the tents at dawn.

That was what amounted to life a little bit below Tindouf, a speck on the *Times Atlas* to which I had pointed with the editor weeks before. To one way of thinking there wasn't a story there.

But then, if that was the case, there wasn't a story either in the bunkered Saharan garrison towns where Moroccan conscripts themselves find refuge from the blistering sun, biting sands and **POLISARIO**'s savage attacks. They too have had no choice but to fight. And today they too are paying with their lives, so that King Hassan's territorial ambitions and United States strategic priorities are maintained. It can't be much fun for those draftees, sweating in the Sahara far from their home, men also about whom almost nothing is ever written and little is known.

4

Czechoslovakia

THE TRAIN WHICH usually leaves from Vienna's
Florisdorf station at 09:20, arriving in Prague at 14:51, leaves that
day from Mitte station instead. At 11:30 it stops at Gmünd on the
Austrian side of the border, a small country town among tall pines.
At 11:45 the train slowly crosses the half mile no-man's-land to the
Czech control post at České Velenice. Soldiers carrying machine
guns take up positions at either end of the train. Two more with
Alsatian dogs slowly walk along the platform, the dogs sniffing the
undercarriages. Inside, the border guards begin working their way
down the compartments demanding papers, searching baggage,
unscrewing the carriage seats and interior panels looking for
contraband and For the next half hour the air is static but for the
buzzing of flies, the heat shimmering off the rails and the faint
odour of pines. There are five of us in the compartment.

The middle-aged man with the Tyrolean hat and the faded tan
suit has said nothing for the whole journey. His suit doesn't fit.
One shoulder seems higher than the other. Maybe that's because of
the way he's sitting, crumpled against the compartment window
next to the corridor. He had an Austrian newspaper earlier. That's
disappeared.

The woman in the flowered dress and her prim eight-year-old
daughter have their passports out, right side up, holding them
starchily in their laps. They were eating sandwiches which have
now been carefully wrapped and put away. So, too, have the paper
napkins with which she kept wiping her kid's fingers and lips.

There are two other passengers in the compartment: a gregarious
blond in her late fifties whose dress has ridden up above her knees,
who's a bit fat and obviously loves to eat, rummaging in her straw
carrier bag every few minutes in search of another fruit, and I.
We're friends.

I'm dressed as a student in dirty dungarees on a modest touring
holiday. She's a grandmother and she's just been to see her

daughter who lives in Zurich with her husband, who's a doctor, and their infant son. I've looked at the snapshots, I've said no to a second peach and we were just discussing which Czech spas are best for dealing with liver complaints. She's visited all the well known ones: Karlovy Vary, Mariánské Lázně, Františkovy Lázně . . . "It's so refreshing to get out of Prague for a couple of weeks," she said, tossing her head back and sighing. I'll bet.

She flounces her bosoms and combs her hair, squinting into a small red-rimmed pocket mirror. I'm just sitting there looking dumb.

While one of the jackbooted guards attacks the panel over my seat with a screwdriver, poking his head and flashlight behind, his colleague takes our passports and retreats to the aisle.

"Where are you going?" He's talking to me.

"Prague, then Budapest and Istanbul."

He flips through the passport again.

"I'm on holiday."

"Okay."

So much for stage one.

He wants to see into the blond's straw bag. She lifts it to her lap, and while he bends over to look inside she gives a little wiggle, gently but firmly pushing her breasts into his face. He's young. He's a bit embarrassed. He's also a bit annoyed. She smiles. Then he has a cursory glance in my bag.

"Cameras?"

"One."

"Show it to me."

I take out a cheap instamatic and begin to open its case.

"Okay. Okay . . ."

Then he goes away. It was, as the expression goes, a piece of cake. No one says anything for another quarter of an hour. Then the train gives a jerk and we are soon rolling through well-kept pine forests and rich alpines past the brightly painted story-book houses of Bohemia. My friend leans forward, motioning for me to bend nearer.

"They're so stupid," she says in her hoarse whisper. "They never find anything. Look."

With that she opens her straw bag, and under a newspaper pulls out a handful of *Reader's Digests*. It's a real prize catch and illegal in Czechoslovakia. She's beaming with pride. I know how she feels. I'm carrying a detailed letter of introduction to Charter 77, the outlawed Czechoslovak human rights movement and an embarrassingly large quantity of unexposed television film.

★ ★ ★

It is July 1977, seven months after 239 Czech and Slovak workers, ex-politicians, actors and intellectuals had signed a decree demanding full restoration of human rights in their country in line with their government's official agreement to be bound by an International Covenant linked to the so-called Helsinki Final Act signed by the United States and the USSR. Since then many of them had been shaken from their beds and frog-marched from their homes at night, interrogated and thrown in gaol. Several television crews had tried to make programmes with the Chartists. One crew returned with one out-of-focus filmed interview, a qualified success. The others had failed. It was our turn. John Pilger would be arriving with a crew in a few days for filming. I was there to set it up.

There was no question but that the Chartists' initial declaration was heady stuff. "Tens of thousands of our citizens are prevented from working in their own fields for the sole reason that they hold views differing from official ones," they claimed. "Hundreds of thousands of other citizens are being condemned to live in constant danger of unemployment or other penalties if they voice their opinions."

Doubtless this was true, but in Czechoslovakia it was incautious, at best, to say as much. Later, one of the Chartist spokesmen said, "We are not aiming at constitutional change but at the just application of existing Czech law." It was not an organisation, "it has no rules, permanent bodies or formal membership. It embraces everyone who agrees with its ideals, participates in its work and supports it . . . It does not form the basis for any oppositional political activity." Oh no? To anyone in the Czech government the Chartists must have looked like a troupe of wild dreamers or a band of insurrectionists. "It wishes," the Chartist document went on, "only to conduct a constructive dialogue with the political and state authorities." The government could oblige them in that respect.

Within days of the Charter's appearance *Rudé Právo*, the official newspaper of the Czechoslovak Communist Party thundered back. The Charter, it said, was "commissioned by anti-communist and Zionist centres," signed by "political and social shipwrecks". It was "a reactionary and shameful document". That went without saying in the workers' state. "Those who place hurdles in the path of socialism and infringe the laws of the socialist state must expect to face the consequences." They need hardly have been warned.

The hotel's a dump on a drab working-class street with a streetcar stop nearby. The young girl behind the wooden counter flirts as she pushes across the well-thumbed hotel register to be

57

signed. How long will I be staying? Well, as long as it takes to tour the baroque churches. I study architecture you see, and perhaps she knew where to find good pilsen beer and cheap meals.

The room's on the fifth floor. There's little space to hide anything outside on the window ledge, the bed frame is hollow but pretty obvious as well so the film stock has to stay in my bag, there for anyone to steal or inspect. Washed and changed I leave for the first rendezvous.

The flat was in a post-war council block some distance out of town. The taxi had stopped several streets away. There was no one behind, and no one on the landing so I rang the bell. A woman opened the door. She had a handkerchief in her hand. She looked rattled, pale. The handkerchief shot to her mouth.

"I've come from friends," I began to say in English.

She waved her hand vigorously. Did she want me to go away? No, that wasn't it. She wanted me to be quiet. And she pulled me inside.

"Are you from London?"

"Yes."

"You were to meet X?"

"That's right." The flat was dark. A gentle breeze was coming through the drawn shutters, but the rest was cossetted, hushed, as if someone had a serious illness inside. She then summoned up what I later discovered to be an enormous well of good sense, composure and courage.

"I'll explain later," she said. "We'll meet tomorrow at 9 a.m. outside the Lenin Museum. Don't say hello. Just follow me."

Did I know where the museum was? I'd find it. If there were any problems we agreed that she would be carrying her shopping bag in her left hand. I left, walked several blocks and took a streetcar into downtown Prague.

The streets were uniformly dreary, grey flat facades looking out on to cobbled streets where people in commonplace clothes queued impatiently at tram stops or loitered at kiosks buying newspapers and cheap cigarettes. It was a part of Europe which seemed not to have brightened up since the end of the Second World War. And yet that wasn't so.

Prague hadn't been bombed, though some areas had been damaged in the fighting during the closing stages of the war. These had been quickly repaired. Huge council estates had shot up to house workers for Prague's engineering, electronics and auto-mobile industries. Yet all had been done according to the Comecon plan.

Czechoslovakia's vigorous factories and mills were forced to produce entire new factories to be exported to the country's fraternal war-torn Eastern Bloc neighbours which lacked significant industries of their own. The Soviet Union monopolised the country's rich uranium deposits, and traditional light industries in which Czechoslovakia had excelled, such as china and glass making and precision instruments, were largely ignored. Centralised planners moulded the economy simply by setting quotas and issuing decrees to whose conditions it was difficult to object.

During the Prague Spring of 1968, people tried to shake off this dross. They took to the streets. The party leader, Alexander Dubček, shared podiums with students. Those free-spirited times were not just an attempt to put a smile on the face of a communist state. The Czechoslovak politbureau was pressing for more favourable terms with the Soviet Union and the other Comecon states.

The combination, of course, proved intolerable. A whole nation had let its hair down and has been paying the price ever since. When Warsaw Pact troops crossed Czechoslovakia's borders the night of 21 August 1968, it was the beginning of the largest purge in Eastern Europe since Stalin's death. Alexander Dubček was thrown into exile miles from Prague, given a job as a clerk in the forestry department in Bratislava. Dr. František Kriegel, a tough Jew who had fought in the Spanish Civil War, lost his place on the presidium and returned to private life. Jiří Hájek, Czechoslovakia's foreign minister, was forced to retire. Altogether some 500,000 party members—school teachers, trade unionists, office clerks as well as managers and bosses—lost their jobs, pensions and school places for their kids. Political life was "normalised", and after the purge the economy was "stabilised". For the next ten years production made its way to other Warsaw Pact countries while Czechs and Slovaks wanting to do something as modest as, say, decorate their homes, had to prowl on the black market for cheap carpets and second-rate tins of paint. A party hack, Dr. Gustáv Husák was put in charge. That didn't sit well with capable citizens proud of their independence and wit, watching the growing prosperity of the countries around them while their own children's futures were sapped.

It was, though, a real opportunity for the cautious and shrewd, the ones who had kept their mouths shut, who toed the party line, took the free trips to Moscow, and after their bosses were purged took over their desks. Charter 77 was as much a gauntlet thrown down, a demand for a reckoning with the ones who had grown fat, smug and powerful since 1968, as it was a demand for human rights.

The government briefly considered publishing the original Charter statement along with detailed rebuttals to each point raised, but hastily realised that this could prove disastrous. So they tried to suppress any mention of it. *Rudé Právo* kept smearing the Chartists, calling them "has beens and self-appointees", Dubčekites with a vengeance to regain power. Some Chartists were. Most weren't. The suggestion that they were motivated solely by their own conceits was finding little sympathy among party members expelled following 1968, and those whom Interior Minister Jaromír Obzina called the "two million former petit-bourgeosie". As for the country's remaining four million adults, many of them also nurturing memories of Prague Spring, there had hardly been spontaneous applause for the regime.

And yet most people remained silent. To keep their homes and jobs they accepted, some more easily than others, the loyalty oaths required as prerequisite to successful careers. No questions, no trouble.

But the Husák regime was going even further. Methodically, the teenage sons and daughters of expelled party members and religious couples were prohibited from higher education, forcing them into menial jobs, carrying the post-1968 purge to a second generation. In a country brought up even under the Stalinist Novotný regime of the 1950s and 1960s to hold education as a socialist right rather than a party privilege, and dependent historically on its entrepreneurial talents and skills, for this policy alone Gustáv Husák was widely hated.

The party was simply presenting every parent concerned for his or her children's welfare—and what parent isn't— with a choice: shut up and conform or your kids will sweep the streets. That was hard to refute as good jobs and chances of a comfortable life seemed fast disappearing. "I'm doing it for the kid," became in Czechoslovakia synonymous with political conformism and silence, the products of fear and "normalisation".

The Chartists were challenging all that. They were saying to the bureaucrats of the party and state, the mini-Husáks, that they should come out into public debate where they would have to string sentences together which made sense, rather than hide behind closed doors and reams of newspeak. In effect they were calling for nothing less than a miraculous rebirth of a sense of decency and openness in Czechoslovakia's national life. They weren't going to get it, of course. On no account would Mr. Husák and his minions tolerate that.

Nonetheless, to a lot of people living elsewhere in Eastern and even in Western Europe, the conditions the Chartists found intolerable were not so unfamiliar—more familiar than their own leaders or they themselves would care to admit. Measured in terms of their own lives and frustrations, the Chartists' demands made sense.

The morning of 6 January 1977, is remembered as being cold and overcast. Pavel Landovský, an actor, got up and drove to pick up his friends, Václav Havel, a playwright and Ludvík Vaculík, a novelist. They then collected piles of letters to be mailed at the post office. Suddenly at an intersection Landovský's battered Saab was surrounded by automobiles from the STB, or Státni Bezpečnost, the state security police. The letters they had intended to mail and the copy they intended personally to deliver to Prague Castle, the seat of government, were the Chartists' original decree. The last sentence read, "We believe that Charter 77 will help to enable all the citizens of Czechoslovakia to work and live as free human beings."

★ ★ ★

Six months later most people in Prague seemed to be keeping to themselves, or salving their emotional wounds with large quantities of alcohol. The pilsen beer is undeniably excellent; blond foamy steins of the stuff slopping over rough wooden benches in low-ceilinged ale houses are among the world's best draughts. The good citizens of Prague were drinking a lot of it. And they drank in a hurry, from late in the afternoon when the taps really began flowing until they slid under the tables, stumbled towards the doors and groped their way home after 10 o'clock. Alcoholism had become one of Czechoslovakia's most alarming social illnesses since 1968. It was also a way of making tolerable a card-carrying boss in the office, workmates who act as informers and a newspaper as bad as *Rudé Právo*.

The pubs, of course, had their own unspoken rules. It was too dangerous to talk openly about the Charter. It was safer to be morose. But it was more fun to tell jokes about the Russians. Not just more fun, along with drinking it was the national sport.

Prague's bars were absolutely infected with Schweik-like drunks and seditious humour. And yet I couldn't help but feel that pilsen too was fulfilling its own beguiling, yet carefully prescribed and stunting social role. It loosened the tongue but seldom strengthened the backbone. Pilsen was not only state manufactured, it was state approved.

Laté that first evening I stopped in Malostranskí Náměstí, the cobbled square in whose well-worn coffee houses lovers had met, students quarrelled and old people reminisced for over 300 years. Pale-cheeked, doe-eyed girls served cream coffee and cakes. Most of the customers were quiet, they seemed self-assured and composed. Here was the heart of Prague, unharried, patient, content with itself; nestled between the castle and the Vltava River. It was here I was to meet the film's director in three days if our little expedition went as planned.

★ ★ ★

Across the street from the Lenin Museum is a small shop. Standing in front of it, looking at items in the window, it is possible to see in the reflection pedestrians passing by the other side. From time to time the old man working in that shop looked up and winked. She was five minutes late, carrying her shopping bag in her right hand.

I didn't move until she turned the corner. By the time I had caught up she was standing in a bus queue. She got on the first one to come along. I did too. Two stops later she got off. I rode to the next stop and walked back. This time it was a bus with a different number. I took the one behind. When I saw her standing in another queue several stops along I got off and followed her into a park. It was by the river in front of a large dirty grey building with an enormous Czech flag flying from the roof, a true Stalinist megalith. I sat down next to her on a park bench.

"I thought you'd appreciate it here," she said. We were on Kyjevské Nábřeží, the Kiev embankment. She was looking straight ahead. "That's the headquarters of the Central Committee of the Communist Party of Czechoslovakia." Such was her sense of place.

"He sends his apologies." She spoke on. "He was supposed to meet you. But he's had headaches. He can't tolerate daylight. There are a lot like that. Especially among the ones who have been interrogated. We're not being thrown in jail. Instead the government seems to be trying to lock us up psychologically, trap us with fear. We've all been sacked, and there's very little money around."

Hadn't they lost, I asked.

"No," she said. "There are always the kids. when they grow up they automatically begin to think more freely. Then they want to travel, and that's not allowed. They want jobs but can't find any. And they want to read books which are banned. So, ... what can we do to help you?"

No one seemed to have noticed us. The gardener was pruning shrubs about 50 yards away. Her face was lined by worries but she had begun to cheer up. It was a sunny day and she felt brave. We decided on a little adventure, to reconnoitre the homes of some of the Chartists we hoped to interview on film.

It proved a mildly comic yet worthwhile routine. I would wait in a park, by a phone booth, near a kiosk. She would walk by the houses and flats. If there were grey-suited security men about she would walk back, her shopping bag in her left hand. I then wandered past just to check. Each time the cars and the men were there. Each time we walked past, not daring to look up for too long at the curtained windows, let alone enquire if the Chartists were at home. Contact would have to be made some other way. We would have to involve someone else.

★ ★ ★

High on the hill overlooking Prague is Hradčany, a looming fortress of buttressed battlements in grey stone. From this site in the 10th century Good King Wenceslas—he was actually a prince, one of Bohemia's first rulers—spread the gospel and subdued the neighbouring tribes. Later, Prague was to become part of the Hapsburg empire, though not entirely willingly. In 1618 the King's governors were thrown from the castle windows, signalling the beginning of a Bohemian uprising that led to the 30 Years War and the crushing defeat of the Czech nobility by imperial forces at the battle of White Mountain in 1620. A dreadful toll was then wrought on Prague's citizens. Many were killed or forced into exile. Onerous taxes were exacted from the remaining towns-people whose homes and workshops huddled against the great castle walls. Yet the Hapsburg mercenaries and nobility, grown rich on confiscated property, have proved by no means Prague's only imperial tormentors.

In the Hradčany courtyard tourists were milling about like pigeons, cameras clicking, thumbing through kiosk postcard stands, licking fast melting ice creams. Soldiers appeared by the main portal. The tourists stopped. The courtyard noticeably stiffened and hushed. Four state limousines, black Czech Tatra 663s, their windows darkned, swept past carrying Mr. Husák's cronies, today's imperial governors.

I had to make a telephone call. Someone else had to be found who would help. Two hours later they, the woman with the shopping bag and I met in an overgrown suburban park. Efforts would be made to talk with the Chartist spokesmen that evening. There was nothing to do but wait.

Three men were standing outside the hotel when I returned, one either side of the entrance and one on the other side of the street. They were still there when I went out. As I walked down the street one walked quickly ahead, another crossed behind me, the third stayed put. It was a classic triangulation technique. At the first pub one of them came inside and ordered a drink. The other two were outside when I left. At the second pub one of the others bought cigarettes. At the third he came into the washroom while I went for a pee. But by then I was drunk, the pilsen was taking effect, and I didn't really care. I stumbled back towards the hotel, taking as many crooked streets as I could until miraculously I was on a dark street alone.

The next morning the meeting took place. Times and locations for interviews had been arranged. There was little interest in my eventful evening. "Ah," they said, "you get used to that." I phoned Vienna and then went rowing on the river opposite the site where Eastern Europe's largest monument to Stalin, a towering cement colossus, had stood until 1961, when it was unceremoniously destroyed. Everything was going according to plan.

★ ★ ★

He was sitting in the coffee house, looking every bit a tourist, eyeing the waitresses, writing postcards, without his sunglasses on. Good, that meant the others had arrived, including the two women who were bringing in the camera—just ordinary tourists on a camping holiday. I sat down in the seat opposite.

"Good trip?"

"Yes," he replied.

"Any problems?"

"No."

"Shall we go for a stroll?"

"Why not."

We talked further, paid and left. Over the next half hour the film's director and I planned an interesting if mildly subversive tour of Prague. From time to time over the next several days a conscientious observer might have noticed two men speaking English at different cafes near well-known tourist sites—Hradčany, the King Charles Bridge, the clock tower in the Old Town Square. Each time they would sit at the same table, chat, write postcards, pick up their carrier bags and leave. But each time they would pick up each others' postcards, each others' carrier bags. On the first were written rendezvous for filming the interviews and for handing over the exposed film, which was in the bags. It worked a treat. There was no reason why it shouldn't have.

The logic was utterly simple. If it takes several people to make a television film, then it's more difficult to realise a film's being made if the people making it are spread out. Nonetheless it was just the sort of operation that the junior G-men of the Czech secret police would call a deeply subversive plot. And as it went undetected then, so the pinhead logic of state security dictates, no less than Western intelligence must have been involved. Needless to say, they weren't. It must be a sobering moment for the secret police sitting sipping cold coffee in their offices in Bartolomějská Street when they pause to reflect that an awful lot of their countrymen don't want them to be much good at their job. And they're not.

Jaromír Obzina, the Minister of the Interior, described his role as that of a politician only carrying out a necessary task. "I'm not a security man," he is reported to have mawkishly told an audience at the Communist Party central political school in Prague shortly after Charter 77 appeared. "I am a party official sent into the ministry by the leadership of the party to implement policy there. All the measures in this affair are implemented after consultations with, and with the consent of, the party." So he was just doing his job. What could be more rational, more matter of fact? Yet he was lying, or what he had said reflected poorly on his colleagues on the central committee. The STB's *modus operandi* was that of a bunch of thugs.

Item: Jiří Hájek liked to go jogging daily in the forest near his home. This presented problems for the less agile STB goons in the Tatra 603 squad car who kept watch on his home. So one morning while he was running they sprayed a caustic liquid into his eyes. Hájek had long suffered from bleeding retinas.

Item: Václav Havel, the playwright, had been forced to work as a labourer in a brewery even before he was arrested delivering the Chartists' first statement on 6 January. After that he was kept in isolation in Prague's Ruzyně prison for four and a half months, interrogated daily, and finally released having signed a statement saying he was no longer a Charter 77 spokesman. Later he was arrested and imprisoned for four years.

Item: Jan Patočka, a 70-year-old philosopher and Charter spokesperson met with the Dutch Foreign Minister, Max van der Stoel, then on an official visit to Prague, on 1 March. Shortly after, Patočka was arrested and interrogated for two days continuously, until he collapsed under questioning and was hospitalised. On 13 March he died following a cerebral haemorrhage.

People who wanted to discuss the Charter documents at their union meetings were sacked. Others found to have copies of Charter literature in their handbags lost their state benefits. By July 1977, dozens of Chartists were, if not in jail, lying at home in bed suffering splitting migraine headaches, shaking too much to write (if their typewriters had not already been confiscated), enduring sleepless, tormented nights after weeks of sometimes ceaseless interrogation.

And yet the Chartists continued issuing statements arguing their case and its legality. Another 500 people had had the courage to sign the original declaration. In the cement factory at Radotin, the enormous SNOP steel works in Kladno, the Avie aircraft plant in Lětnany and the Tesla electronic goods and ČKD locomotive works in Prague, workers simply refused to condemn the Charter out of hand and unseen.

Jiří Hájek and František Kriegel, both seasoned politicians, were also uncowed. Both under intense surveillance, they managed secretly to film an interview in which they calculated with obvious sarcasm how much their STB entourage was costing the state: three shifts of 15 agents each, a fleet of black Tatra 603 sedans—in all about 240,000 crowns, or $24,000, a month. "These agents," Kriegel added, "they're boys . . . What I've seen in the last forty years, they can't scare me now."

Twenty-five years earlier, during Prague's last Stalinist purge they would have been taken to the basement of the Pankrác prison on Prague's "Square of Heroes" and shot in the back of the neck. Those days thankfully had passed. We were living in what Mr. Obzinza described as "a progressive era". The fact that Chartists continued to speak openly, even after sustained police harassment, was to Mr. Obzinza's way of thinking possibly part of the price paid to keep that tolerance alive. The Chartists thought not. After all, is a society really progressive simply because it no longer murders its dissidents?

The Chartists had some sharp things to say about the West too. They were not about to make the mistake of Soviet Jews who relied so heavily on Western media and governmental support that when the Soviet government finally allowed many of them to emigrate, there was little left of a real movement in the Soviet Union to keep their demands for human rights alive. The Chartists also knew that Czechoslovakia, precious to the political hearts of European liberals as it may be, had been forgotten, even forsaken by those same Western Europeans when it had seemed convenient to do so.

"It's quite important to remind British people," Zdeněk Urbánek told us. "We really had quite a well functioning democracy during the 20 years of freedom, between 1918 and 1938."

Then Neville Chamberlain, the British Prime Minister, signed a pact with Hitler in Munich. Chamberlain, returning to London, talked of having achieved "peace in our time". It was not to be, though he had agreed that part of Czechoslovakia would be ceded to Germany.

"It was an unfortunate moment of history for us because I am afraid that all what happens here now began just at that time."

Urbánek wasn't bitter; simply resigned and tired. An historian whose book had been banned in Czechoslovakia for years, Urbánek had been arrested shortly after Pavel Landovský's Saab was intercepted by the STB. He was held for several days during which they questioned him relentlessly. His name had been found among the material in Landovský's car. The STB had taken samples of his typewriter's script, just in case he toyed with the idea of writing any more anti-state literature. Urbánek didn't sleep well. But he wanted to talk.

While I bided my time between rendezvous, Urbánek recounted to John Pilger on film where the Chartists' strength lay. "I am absolutely not afraid," he said. "I write what I wish when I start to write and this is exactly why I cannot get published." Perhaps he was just stubborn. A large whisky steadied his hands, and possibly his nerves. Who knows? He had made a decision for which he was to be even further harassed when the film was broadcast.

Others did too. Julius Tomin for one, a young Catholic pedagogue so wrought by pangs of philosophical angst that when he talked about the Charter he'd signed it proved difficult to separate his political demands from a sense of overwhelming moral torment. If the state's conformist vise was screwed tightly over the foreheads of Czechoslovakia's thinking citizens, it was visibly throbbing in Tomin's skull. And yet he, too, wanted to talk.

"I think that the Charter is the start of the experiment of combining freedom and socialism," he said. "I'm glad to meet anybody interested in this experiment, and in talking with him, this talking with him is so important for me, that if I knew that tomorrow I go into prison for it, I shall talk with you anyway."

Brave words. And Julius Tomin knew the history of repression in Czechoslovakia well. The real brain squeezers of his country had been the Jesuits, whose grip over a period of 200 years makes Mr. Husák's paltry sorties into political philosophy appear infantile. A few hundred metres up from the coffee houses in Prague's Malostranské Náměstí is the Church of St. Nicholas, designed by Christopher Diezenhofer to celebrate the reign of the Jesuits in the earthly realm of their almighty God, to say nothing of the suppression of Czech heretics.

Never in Czech life had a ruling clique been so imperious. Most of the Czech nobility was executed. Protestants fled. Never had the message been so blatantly broadcast that the rulers were omnipotent. Walk into the church. On either side of the nave, high above the worshippers, standing on tall pedestals is a gallery of courtiers to the altar of God, larger than lifesize statues of the honourable merchants, nobles and obedient citizens of Bohemia, ascending in height as they approach the transept. There, cut in white marble, as gods come down from heaven to lord over mortals, are four gigantic statues of the church's philosophers, heavily robed and adorned. Only Hitler put on pageants comparable to that, but not in stone. Czechs and Slovaks had done with that sort of pomp. In 1961, Stalin's heroic memorial had come down.

Of what remained, the most imposing was the communist party headquarters, grey, foreboding and for most citizens impenetrable. Czechoslovakia had completed a fundamental historical transmutation. Oppression could only be judged now not by what was to be seen, but by what was left unsaid. There was no longer much need for memorial stadiums and arches. Czechoslovakia's rulers had learned one of the lessons of the modern world: history has no memory for silence. The Chartists also understood that, which is why they spoke out.

But what of the country's workers? Interior Minister Obzina had characterised Charter 77 as a petty-bourgeois elitist movement, the complaint of the privileged that their children could not stand up to genuine egalitarian competition for school places. He would then deliver a tirade of dilapidated Stalinist epithets. Charter, he would say, "is anti-state, anti-people, anti-socialist demagogic slander." Lest anyone forget. Yet he was hardly dialectically perfect. There were workers among the Charter signatories and activists. But they were for the most part in gaol. It seemed that Mr. Obzina's secret police, for all their egalitarian notions, found it easier to lock up workers in a workers' state than playwrights, historians and past members of the presidium.

Two young technicians, Vladimír Lašťuvka and Aleš Macháček, both married with children, were in Litomerice prison in northern Bohemia, having been caught with "subversive material from abroad". Later they would be tried and given three-and-a-half-year sentences. Lathe operators, fitters, librarians, unskilled and un-employed workers, clerks, railwaymen, stokers, maintenance workers, priests, stonemasons and miners were among the hundreds to be tried and imprisoned over the next few years. For factory hands to have taken part openly in our film would not only have been politically objectionable, it would have been socially im-pertinent as well, the reward for which was a sure trip to Ruzyne gaol.

This was explained to me patiently and cheerfully by a garage mechanic, a young man with grease on his trousers and oil deep in the grain of his palms, who knew a thing or two about how to repair cameras, whose father had been a mechanic before him, and who was a Charter activist now. While his wife made coffee we talked. Did he feel isolated, I asked.

"No, not at all."

"Why not?"

"You see, we know we not only speak on behalf of a lot of people here. We too have friends—socialist friends—in other countries.

The Hungarians talk to us. So do the Poles . . ."

"So why don't they have Chartist movements?" I asked.

"They don't have Husák and Soviet tanks hiding behind trees in their gardens."

The answer was obvious. So was my next question.

"So why should the Poles take an interest in you?"

"Poland," he said, "we're talking a lot with them. Their time will come."

Before I left Prague I wanted once more to see the woman with the handkerchief I had met the first day. We met in U Bindrů, an ornate 19th century coffee house where the aroma seemed soaked into the cut-glass, velvet and polished wood. It was the centre of Prague from another era, when the list of coffees available in the style of Turkey, Berlin, Vienna, Greece, the Orient . . . painted on large panels over the grand salon spoke of a proud entrepôt, determinedly European and strivingly cosmopolitan, kept by the energy and foresight of its citizens from being lost to the world in the crook of the Vltava river.

"That time is gone."

"Yes, I know," she said. "It really means very little to me. You see we have always been socialists."

"But weren't you dreaming too?"

"Possibly." She paused, stirring her coffee. "We could have done it in 1968. It really was a political spring."

"And now?"

"Oh, it's different. But it's not over. He has headaches. He may have to withdraw for a while, but someone else will take his place. Someone always does. You see we are the ones who are having to teach Husák what it means to be socialist."

Perhaps, I thought; or perhaps Husák doesn't care.

Taking the film out was much the same as bringing it in. The only difference was that passengers visibly sighed, relieved once the train was in Austria. Then there was a rush to the buffet car for beer.

★ ★ ★

When the film was broadcast it finished with a pop singer, Marta Kubišová, singing the song she sang during the Prague Spring. In 1968, as the Russians were instructing the Czech government to stop the reforms, Dubček heard her sing and stood up, moved to tears. The song is very simple, a bit naive. "Oh my country, let not fear and violence establish themselves on your soil, keep yourself faithful and true . . ."

When she sang it for the film she was sitting at a picnic table at her mother's small farm in the Bohemian countryside. Her mother was ill and needed medicines the government would not provide. Marta had had her records banned, her driving licence confiscated. Today Marta is still out in the cold, harassed as are hundreds of others in Czechoslovakia, many of them charged with subversion and having paid for it in gaol.

On the other hand, in addition to the splendid work of his secret police, Mr. Husák would seem to have other more workaday reasons to feel proud. The country's per capita income has continued to fall, while prices continue to rise. Mr. Obzina has been promoted to Deputy Prime Minister. And the books of Franz Kafka, Czechoslovakia's best known author, are difficult to obtain and seldom reprinted.

By way of reply the Chartists have established a Committee for the Defence of the Unjustly Prosecuted (VONS). As one of its friends explained, "This regime is afraid of funerals and graves, anything that could be evidence to their crimes. Remember that under Stalin, after people were shot they were cremated and their ashes scattered along the roadsides outside Prague. We want to make sure we know where people are so that doesn't happen again."

Most people in Czechoslovakia, though, aren't politically active. Instead they tell jokes. Lots of jokes. The Poles are fond of them too.

5
Chad

THE BLOOD'S ALL over the hospital floor. Some of it's dried in dull brown patches. But there's much more, puddles and skid marks where the orderlies have slipped dragging the wounded, shoeless young men whose khaki uniforms are caked with dirt oozing the tell-tale red clots that mean they don't have long to live. Stomachs, thighs, necks, dangling arms; the wounds are as raw as the screams rending the stale dank air, and as utterly real as the dull, leadened glazed eyes of the ones who will soon die. It looks as if someone had run amok with a meathook in an abattoir.

African women are huddled along the walls moaning, cupping their hands over their children's ears, anxiously holding them in the folds of their faded worn saris. As the mortar rounds thump into the compound, the walls shudder and the women wail. The windows explode showering splinters of glass down the corridor.

It's "day one" of the coup in N'Djamena, the capital of Chad, a vast expanse of desert and savannah carved out of the map of central Africa by a French cartographer less than 100 years ago, as if with a straight-edge and a handful of European treaties it was possible to arrest time, the shifting Saharan dunes, nomads and Islam. The country's been bleeding from the day it was born, and more so since France decided to withdraw its colonial officers and bestow "independence" in 1960, at the end of the Algerian War. I am with Anne-Marie Grobet, a Swiss photographer. We knew there was going to be a coup. We didn't know when. So we had come early and waited. It is 12 February 1979.

A pregnant woman with a bullet near her heart lies moaning, begging on the operating table. There is no electricity. No water. The French doctors want to operate but can't. She is left panting in the dark against a blood-spattered wall. The logic is inexorable. She soon dies.

The orderlies rummage for bandages in the hospital stores, a musty medicine cupboard with a broken door. There are none. They try the emergency generator again. It refuses to work. The Russian doctors suddenly left six months before, and the minister of health had run off with the keys to the national medical dispensary.

It is at moments such as this that the term "underdevelopment" comes into its own, when the newspaper platitudes and United Nations resolutions about alleviating poverty and building the Third World lose their vague, easy indecisiveness and become wrenchingly real; when people die not from their wounds, but for the want of sutures, drugs, antibiotics and even sterile gauze. The Kalashnikovs and mortars nominate the victims. The lack of disinfectants and bandages—such as you'd find in ordinary Western homes—finishes them off.

We see men die lying face down in pools of their own blood. Yet Chad's largest hospital, a rambling two story warren of filthy wards and blocked drains, is only 500 metres down a straight dusty road from the President's grand residence. Who could sleep well knowing it was the only hospital in their town?

Outside, the rebels, dark Muslims with scarlet and yellow rags tied around their upper arms as badges, have set up a 105mm recoil-less rifle on the back of a pick-up truck under a drooping acacia tree in the hospital courtyard. They're loosing-off crates of the metre-long shells at the President's whitewashed stronghold. His men are responding in kind with heavy machine guns and 60mm and 81mm mortars, tearing walls out of the hospital, blowing away galvanised roof-sheeting like paper shredded in the wind.

Inside, a wild-eyed young rebel fighter's right leg is dangling by a few remaining ligaments from above the knee. The bones are shattered. White jagged splinters stick out of the angry red meat that was his thigh. The French doctors begin to stitch. The screaming becomes a howl, then a sobbing deep-throated moan until coma comes over him.

Another Muslim fighter is brought in, a bundle of blood soaked rags. Four of his comrades are trying to hold him together. There was no blood for transfusions. The plasma was gone. The man didn't survive. A casualty of the coup? Certainly. But a victim of underdevelopment and the arms trade as well.

Suddenly the mortars stopped. Machine guns sprayed the corridor outside. A squad of paratroopers burst in, well-dressed, well-armed, and on the prowl—the President's elite troops, Christians from Chad's southern tribes.

"Where are they?"

The commanding officer prods the huddled women with the muzzle of his sub-machine gun.

"Come on, where?"

He's impatient. His men head for the operating theatre door. The French doctor emerges, wiping his hand on his spattered apron.

"There are no combatants here, capitaine."

The doctor's not much to look at. He's short, balding and looks like a tired brasserie chef in a provincial French town. But he's got guts.

"Capitaine, this is a hospital. There no weapons here. I am in charge."

The captain has a cursory look around. Then he and his men get out. The doctor lights a cigarette, throws it away, and disappears back into the operating theatre.

More wounded arrive, but now they're heavier, darker ebony skinned full-faced blacks from the southern tribes, the President's loyal supporters. The battle had washed past, relinquishing debris like an ebbing tide.

In the courtyard young men lie dead behind trees, under burnt out cars, caught running down the hospital corridors. Shreds of corrugated metal sheeting are strewn everywhere. This was a hospital where patients shared scraps of grey rotting foam rubber for mattresses, cooked together in battered pots on the filthy concrete floors and emptied their slops into open drains. The stench, already overwhelming, would soon be laced with the sweet rancidness of death. It was a moment of calm, and incongruity.

A barefoot young girl appeared, wandering about, knitting and singing softly to herself. African women slowly emerged, collecting firewood to make dinner over crude bucket stoves. Young Muslim boys in white robes, called "boubous", climbed over the low walls and fell to their knees in the sand, praying to Allah in the setting sun. A small doe-eyed Italian nurse wearing a crucifix drifted gazing around the courtyard. "It's such a pity," was all she said, "so many broken windows and they take so long to repair."

We had had enough for day one of the coup. So we walked back to the hotel, down the 500 metres to the President's besieged palace, across the main square in front of the sandbags behind which his troops, already remote, resolute, with deep sunken eyes carefully, slowly trained machine guns on us. We smiled, chewing our lips, waving when it seemed appropriate.

They smiled back. It was their war. We were there as outsiders. And after six hours of heavy fighting they were still prepared to accept that. The walls of the President's residence were already deeply scorched and pock-marked. The sand was strewn with spent cartridge casings, the bunkered guardposts stacked high with ammunition crates.

As we passed the first trees into the European quarter, a French paratrooper crouching in a ditch with his bazooka and radio pack beside him gave us a thumbs up, lit and tossed us a cigarette. "Thanks," was all we could manage. The night barrage, with the real wreckers—the 120mm mortars, was yet to come.

★ ★ ★

Chad is often called the lost heart of Africa. By the more callous press—"a basket case." Pass two meridians through the confused continent and they intersect there, half a million landlocked square miles encompassed by that cartographer's ruler. The north of the country is Sahara. The middle, scorched Sahel crust. The south, scrub savannah. Three of Africa's great climatic belts. Over two million cattle, more than half the country's herd, are estimated to have died during the great drought of 1972 and 1973. Yet the disaster was hardly reported in the Western press.

There are officially four and a half million people in Chad, 3,850 telephones, 240 kilometres of paved roads. Everything grown is eaten and the government, when it functions, has to go cap in hand every year begging for foreign aid.

Before the coup the directory of agencies bent on saving Chad read like the guest list at a United Nations charity ball: FAO, UNICEF, UNDP, CARE, the EEC, Peace Corps, Swedes, Swiss, missionaries and pharmaceutical firms. Yet life in Chad always will be more elusive than targets set out in mimeographed development plans.

Simply put, aid agency Land Rovers may bring surplus rice today, perhaps tomorrow. But can they turn back the harmattan— the dry winds which sweep down from the Sahara wastes in autumn, blistering the fragile scrub? And can they promise the monsoon, pushing billowing white clouds as far as the Tibesti massif—the desert's rocky volcanic mountains—its life-giving rain quenching the thirsty sands? The answer is obviously no. As a wry, tired government official explained, "We welcome your experts. But let's put it this way. The weather doesn't wait for spare parts."

Even so, hours before the coup, embassy officials in N'Djamena were behind their typewriters blindly preparing the next year's grant requests. Outside their air-conditioned offices the streets were deserted. Even the goats and dogs usually browsing in the rubbish had disappeared. Bars—galvanised shacks with a few plank benches—were shuttered. No beer. No "highlife" music. No laughter and brawls. Even we knew. Anonymous tracts demanding death to the President blew aimlessly, scattered over the soft sand.

The Prime Minister, Hissène Habré, with an army of Muslim desert tribesmen secretly trained in the Sudan and calling themselves the Forces Armées du Nord (FAN) was about to attack the President, Félix Malloum. Malloum was a Christian, from the tribes in the south, enjoying French favour, French arms and advisers. Some said he was a French puppet, packing Chad's government with his own people, squeezing profits from the country's northern Muslims through taxes, road tolls and straight forward sequestrations. Like many governments, his was pocked with graft and corruption, perhaps more nakedly than some.

Hissène Habré was ambitious and shrewd. He had tasted power and wanted more, all of it. In Chad, he who is president controls the country's purse, its weapons, and what little it produces which is worth eating or selling abroad. It was a prize worth fighting for.

Four years before, on 13 April 1975, the previous President, Nagarta Tombalbaye, was machine-gunned to death when he refused to get into an army lorry. *"C'est fini,"* he said, turned and walked away. The mad logic of Chad dictates that everything, even coups, have a distinctively French flavour. The relationship is longstanding and uncompromisingly cynical.

Back at the hotel the guests were settling in for a short war. The Red Cross delegates were drafting radio bulletins for Geneva. The manager had somehow found crates of fresh eggs. French paratroopers were systematically drinking their way through the bar's cooler beer. There were over 2,000 French paratroopers and Foreign Legionnaires in town. We would be safe. So would the French ambassador next door and the French residential quarter.

Beyond that little world, well . . . who cares? It was their fight after all, or so the prevailing thinking ran. The French agency pressmen were on their way, being flown in by specially arranged military plane. Chad, needless to say, had a strategic dimension. Colonel Qaddafi's Libya was 400 miles over the sand dunes to the north. He had already claimed a huge swathe of Chad bordering on Libya, the part which probably contained uranium deposits, for his own. And he was said to be financing yet another Muslim rebel army, that of Goukouni Oueddei, a National Liberation Front called FROLINAT, whose men held captive nearly 2,000 of President Malloum's best troops in stone huts under palm frond roofs in the Saharan oasis town of Faya-Largeau. There would be plenty for the hacks to write about. There was a lot more to Chad than many of them or their readers would ever know.

★ ★ ★

For over 2,000 years the country had been plagued by remoteness, famine and war. The only news was brought out by camel caravan. In the age of the Caesars they carried gold and ivory to the Carthaginian ports on Africa's northern coast.

The Romans dreamed of the region's fabled wealth. So later did the Venetians and Philip II of Spain. In the 8th century, Arabs began travelling laterally across the Sahara, establishing Islam and sultanates from the Nile to Timbuktoo. One hundred years ago ostrich feathers and civet musk from Chad were much in demand in Paris salons.

But it was the traffic in slaves that prospered. Men, women and children captured from the animist tribes in the south were driven as pure chattel along with camels on foot up the great tracks north of Lake Chad across the rocky Tibesti massif, for those who survived to be sold and shipped across the Mediterranean to become servants in European, and the Russian, imperial courts.

In 1910, travellers reported piles of skulls around desert water-holes. Slaves were sold publicly in Adriatic market places at the outbreak of the First World War. It is rumoured that some are still in bondage in desert oases today.

It came as little surprise that there was scant record of any of this in Chad's national museum, a French-inspired repository of national wild life and ethnography. Three ramshackle skeletons: a wobbly giraffe, a hippo with broken teeth, and an elephant with its back leg propped up on a small pile of bricks, were all that stood guard over a dozen cases filled with faded tribal masks and a few stuffed birds.

It was even more difficult to imagine Chad's past when standing on Avenue Charles de Gaulle, N'Djamena's—and it goes without saying Chad's—main boulevard, a triumph of Boeing airplanes, ready-mix cement and bad taste. At one end of this dusty mile and a half would-be *grand rue,* boutique owners and hairdressers were battling to keep what passes as "Africa" at bay.

Imported satinette bedside lamps, vinyl cocktail cabinets and plywood lounge suites stood like icons behind plate glass windows under crumbling whitewashed arcades, a glut of mail order rococo dumped in the desert from a Paris warehouse.

At the other end of the avenue, barefoot men bent double tugged large wooden barrows through the market dust, disappearing into a maze of sand lanes, mud walls and open drains. There in the Muslim quarter, behind honeycombed walls, women peeled garlics, suckled babies and winnowed millet on broad straw mats under acacia trees. Most of them henna their hands with patterns as ornate as filigree. The local holy man, the marabout, sits inside a dark mud room cuddling his 18-month-old daughter while reading from a dog-eared Koran. Crates of thin Islamic tomes are piled against the wall. And in a corner are stacked the flat wooden pallets on which boys, every afternoon, drew broad Arabic script with sticks dipped into gourds of gritty black ink.

Outside, young men play cards on straw mats laid on the sand. The scene couldn't have been more composed, more traditional, possibly more timeless to the casual eye. Yet the men were wearing watches and carrying knives under their laundered white boubous. Several of them had been to Moscow, Paris and Cairo to study. They were friendly. They were also preoccupied. Some of them were soon to be carrying Kalashnikovs and hand grenades.

The French had had to grab Chad before British columns moving west from the Sudan, and German columns advancing east from the Cameroons, squeezed them out of the continent. So in 1897, Colonel Emile Gentile steamed up the Chari River from the equatorial south and arrived at Lake Chad. It was then the largest lake in Africa. Now it's shrunk to one-third its former size due to evaporation, irrigation drainage and drifting sands. Yet, today, the same tribes of fishermen still eke out a living, building their houses on matted reeds, having to chop trenches for their needle thin canoes to pass through what has become Africa's largest sponge. Gentile installed his agent with the nearby Muslim sultan of Baguirimi and left. The agent was promptly routed by the local warlord, Rabah Zubaya, with an army of black slaves. It took three years to defeat Zubaya and another twenty to subdue the nomadic desert tribes who tenaciously refused to submit. French Foreign Legionnaires threw dead cattle down wells effectively poisoning oases, and whole encampments of Muslim men are said to have been lined up and shot. Such counter-insurgency tactics are the stuff of which the heroics of Beau Geste were made.

Today the people of Chad for the most part are hardly better off. Chad's nomads and pastoralists face famine, their herds decimated by the war, foreign aid shipments having been lost and the rains having failed. The country is helplessly split between armed camps led by competing warlords. For this the French must take some responsibility.

Behind the French columns came missionaries to teach the catechism and the language of kings. They soon found ready converts among the southern tribes. But the Muslims steadfastly spurned both the faith and the tongue. When full independence was granted on 11 August 1960, the southerners were given control.

"But then it wouldn't have been any other way." An earnest priest was recounting for us the crusade to 'lift the veil' in Africa. He was remarkably frank, sitting in front of a few bookcases, the only decent library the country had.

"After all, it is only the south that the French really care about," he explained.

The reason is simple. Southern Chad is a massive rain-soaked cotton farm. Every winter, under mangoes and palms in hundreds of villages, families heap elephant-sized piles of fluffy white gold—cotton—on to the French-controlled company scales. The price is always low. There are always copious quantities of foul-tasting millet beer to put villagers in an appropriate mood. The company, CotonChad, does very well and Parisians are guaranteed the next season's fashions. The French call southern Chad '*Tchad utile*', Chad useful. The rest they dismiss with a wave of the hand. It's worthless, '*inutile*'.

The priest wasn't apologising for his countrymen's icy logic. It was too late for that. Even his pastoral mission was now in doubt. Once the cathedral had been N'Djamena's largest edifice, squatting resplendent and self-assured in the sand square opposite the Presidential residence. Now it had been eclipsed by the new mosque, a sprawling enclave of petromodern architecture set in the African market, designed in Europe and paid for by Saudi Arabia. Strengthened by the high price of oil, Chad's Muslims were demanding control of a government which had been wrenching extortionate taxes from them for years. No, the priest hadn't lost faith. He feared though, that the country had slipped dangerously close to ethnic war. On the other hand, what passed for high society in N'Djamena preferred to appear nonplussed.

The evening before the coup the French businessmen held their annual ball in the garden of the hotel between the laurel rose trees and the bank of the Chari River. The ambassador, as usual, was guest of honour. Beneath the pennants, streamers and garlands of pastel lights, under a full African moon, tall slim French women in flaming chiffon dresses and high-heeled shoes gave themselves over to sentimental tangos ground out on a veteran gramophone.

Perhaps for them the dizziness of fonder times was fleetingly revived. Perhaps the elixirs of champagne and perfume kept memories alive. It seemed so, as the sun rose and the guests drove slowly home to their cool whitewashed bungalows set deep among bougainvillaea, where houseboys waited patiently with the family dogs. Yet some of them must have known what was to come.

★ ★ ★

The afternoon of the second day of fighting there was a brief ceasefire. The sand streets were empty but for mongrels and goats scavenging in the rubbish. Where two days before fat women in

78

calico dresses, with broad smiles, hips swinging, joking, had walked with their children running behind them, there were now only a few discarded sandals scattered in the sand. Old men emerged dragging market carts on which the dead were stacked like cordwood. The wounded began to arrive, faint and motionless, awkward bundles wrapped in blood-soaked rags carried on rotten and torn makeshift stretchers to the hospital steps. War was disgorging its heroes.

I was with an International Red Cross delegate, a wealthy Swiss in his mid-thirties, impeccably dressed in fawn trousers and a neat checked sports shirt, an image of hygiene and incisiveness in the African dust. He was loading a jeep after having smashed the lock on the national pharmacy, the tin-roofed Ministry of Health stores. There was no penicillin, no other antibiotics, no plasma or alcohol. Those had been secretly sold long ago. There were some bandages and bottles of disinfectant, enough for the hospital, and enough also for Habré's troops who were loading a stolen lorry beside us.

Then the delegate began testing the tenuous sinews of the ceasefire. Some of Habré's men needed trained medical attention. By day the hospital was firmly under the President's control. By night it was lost in a no-man's-land of red tracer bullets and mortar fire. Would we take Habré's wounded there?

Slowly we drove down the main sandy thoroughfare of the African quarter, past "Market Mini-snob" where in better days customised wrought-iron bedsteads were sold. Now it was firmly closed. Next door the fruit drink stall had been ripped open by mortar fire. Nothing stirred. Rows of workshops were boarded up, shops where men sat in the dust making cheap wooden goods, repairing inner-tubes, selling second-hand motor parts.

Under an acacia tree we finally saw three men lying in the back of a pickup truck. Habré's troops were there, tense and impatient, waiting for us. Why had we taken so long? The wounded needed surgery and blood. Didn't we care?

The Swiss was unruffled. We would take two of them without weapons and return for the third. Then the trouble began. Opposite "Market Mini-snob" there was now a crowd. Men were arguing and pushing. Lying in the sand next to a pothole was what looked like a pile of rags. It hadn't been there ten minutes before. A naked little boy, his belly sticking out, was poking it with a stick. Two dogs were sniffing, not daring to go closer, snapping at each other's tails. We stopped.

The heap was a young man whose throat had been cut what couldn't have been minutes before.

"Leave him."

A man in the crowd was shouting at us. "He's an informer. He's from the south."

We picked him up. His neck swung loose all but for the bone. His oesophagus was torn open. And yet he was breathing, gurgling, rich crimson blood coming out of the gash in his throat.

"Jesus Christ," the Swiss delegate whispered. We loaded the man into the back of the car and held him together until he flopped dead on the hospital floor.

The French doctor was furious.

"Don't bring us ones like that." He spat out his cigarette. "We've got our hands full with the ones who might pull through."

Later the Red Cross delegate and I talked about our little episode. He said he was really an administrator. It wasn't his job to do medical work. He was supposed to have flown back to Geneva anyhow. We both knew that we had inadvertently challenged the French doctor's judgment and possibly betrayed our own good sense. Yet there was a difference between that man and the other wounded. He had been jumped by his neighbours who had literally torn out his throat. He hadn't been chopped down by machine gun fire, nor blown apart by mortars. These are all forms of butchery. But there is a distinction between them. It's the distinction that spans the moral gulf between warfare and massacre. The priest's vision of Chad seemed on the verge of becoming awesomely real.

★ ★ ★

That evening, the French press corps arrived. Among them were the 'taxi journalists', the hacks who write front page exclusive stories even before the cabs taking them from the airports arrive at their five-star hotels. They are 'the parachutists', the ones who jump into anything—war, famine, coup. And jump out.

The stale odour of office coffee and ashtrays was still with them as they changed from double-breasted blazers into well pressed safari suits. A French officer conveniently dropped by the hotel to give a briefing. And a few hours later copy was delivered to the French army headquarters at the airport and sent on to Paris. It was for a few of them a smooth little operation. Not one of 'the parachutists' had yet ventured on to the streets or talked to an African.

Rocking back and forth on his heels, content, standing on the hotel front steps with his hands behind his back one of the 'taxi men' was quietly gazing up at the red tracer bullets crisscrossing the deep indigo sky. He'd filed his story. Now it was time for a cigarette. I opined that Chad was turning into a messy little affair.

"No, it will be over soon." He spoke with disarming confidence for a man who had just arrived. Then he let it be known that the French ambassador and general between them would reach agreement with the two warring factions soon.

I suppose I should have been grateful, getting a tip like that from a man in the know. But then I had been sleeping under the mattress, not so much to trap stray bullets which unnervingly zipped in through the window like errant bees, as to muffle the incessant din of the 120mm mortar barrages. That wasn't to say the French weren't trying to keep matters in hand. They certainly were. Had I not run into French officers on patrol during the ceasefire, riding high in their jeeps and on both sides of the *de facto* ceasefire line? French mercenaries, flying old prop planes had bombed the radio station after Habré's men had seized it during the first hours of the coup. But wasn't it true that when they returned to refuel the French army had put oil barrels on the runway so they couldn't take off again? There were other more intriguing questions. Who was it, for instance, who had so neatly dropped a mortar round through the cockpit of the President's personal plane so he couldn't flee the country?

A squadron of Jaguar jet fighters perched like poisonous wasps along the airport runway. The French definitely held the balance in this untidy African feud. But whether they cared to admit it or not, they were hamstrung too.

To have resolved the coup would have meant committing their troops. And that was politically impossible. After all Chad was an independent country. Ostensibly French troops were there only to protect French citizens and interests—the shopkeepers and hairdressers, the ambassador and the nuns. It didn't matter that Foreign Legion fire bases had been dug-in along a line which roughly bisected Chad, keeping Goukouni Oueddei's FROLINAT army in the Sahara at bay. The diplomatic fiction of non-involvement had to be preserved.

I was becoming something of a connoisseur of how interventionist an army can be while maintaining strict neutrality. Nonetheless, I still owed the French forces some thanks. We had been at a desert waterhole outside the town of Abéché, 300 desolate miles east of the capital, when a lieutenant and three squaddies rushed up in a jeep. It was three days before the coup.

"You've got to leave now," was how he put it. I wasn't sure whether that was an offer or command. Around us herdsmen were running barefoot in the slippery mud from the well to troughs where their cattle, camels and goats prodded to drink. Arab nomad girls, their hair tightly braided into dozens of thin, long plaits ran around pulling the goats back by their tails. Anne-Marie was taking photographs having climbed a rusty water tower nearby which didn't work.

We'd been talking with the nomads and the people of the sandy mud-walled town. The previous year's millet crop had been devoured by locusts. Families had had to sell their few bags of onions to buy cooking oil and salt. When there was nothing they chewed stones and sifted the sand for grass seed, collecting enough for a meal every two days.

"Look." The lieutenant wasn't interested in anthropology. He wanted us out. "Either you come with me now or you stay here for at least the next three weeks and that's something you may well regret."

We didn't need to be told again. Abéché was on strike. The Muslim water-bearers with their sway-backed donkeys were refusing to sell to the southerners in town. The prefect, a risible, gregarious man from the President's tribe was virtually captive within his cool mansion. He had his whisky, his portable radio and his chocolates. But it was unsafe for him to venture out.

So we climbed into the jeep and sped back to the airstrip. There we drank cold beer with the French conscripts whose woeful task it was to patrol the sand-bagged, barbed wire perimeter, scanning the hills through binoculars, but mostly chewing the sand scooped into their lungs by a hot wind which never stopped.

On the way back to N'Djamena the French army DC4 touched down briefly at Ati, once a Saharan trading centre, now a Foreign Legion outpost. Elderly Chadian men proudly wearing faded European campaign ribbons pinned to their boubous dragged metal bed-frames, chickens, coat racks, coffee tables and lumpy mattresses on to the plane. Their women were dripping baskets of food. Beefy middle-aged Legionnaires who spoke German and had fought in Vietnam kept hurrying them along. It was hot. Everyone sweated profusely, trying to ignore the telltale signs. The evacuation had begun. When Habré finally attacked, Abéché was the first town to fall.

★ ★ ★

"Jesus, they took all my chickens."

Sweat was pouring off his face, beads of it pearling on to the chest of an overweight French businessman who had just returned to the hotel from his house. "I climbed through the kitchen window. They had me up against a wall, with my radio under their arm."

"Then?"

"A guy with a yellow rag around his sleeve turns up, starts yelling at them, and they put the stuff back. I've never seen that before in Africa . . ."

Inadvertently, absolutely mechanically he gulps down three bottles of beer as he talks. Then he begins frantically searching the ground.

"Jesus, now I've lost my keys . . . ."

Yet he was lucky. He had eaten. After five days the government's troops had had little sleep, and many of them no more than a cold lump of local cereal paste called 'boule'. Their sunken eyes betrayed the ceaseless rolling thunder of the 120mm mortars and heavy machine gun fire—also their flickering defiance to be alive.

One of them had run into the middle of the road, waving his Uzi sub-machine gun at us, shouting at us to lie down, staggering pathetically against exhaustion. Then a machine gun rattled behind the next building. He spasmed. His arms and legs flopped and he seemed to dissolve.

"Shit. When is it going to stop? When it is going to . . . ." He was delirious.

"Shut up soldier." His sergeant, thank god, was at hand.

"Don't tell me to shut up. Who's in charge here? I'm in charge. I'm in charge. I'm in . . ."   The soldier was burbling, pleading. His nerves had cracked, wanting to believe it was over.

When the ceasefire was signed in a deserted villa beside an empty fountain pool the French general, Louis Forest, presided. One of the rebels was wearing reflecting sunglasses which he steadfastly refused to take off. He also signed his name simply "Le Parisien", a gesture, he said, to the years he had slaved his guts out at the Renault factory outside Paris in Billancourt.

"And why not," he added. "We've won."

Europeans came out from under their beds and drove slowly and cautiously to the airport, carrying bath towels on sticks as truce flags. The goats were back on the streets like locusts, browsing for rubbish. Men began dragging carts through the market. Stalls opened selling disinfectant.

A woman pleaded with us to be driven to her home. Her sons were wounded, she said. When we got there they were lying face up in the sun covered with straw mats buzzing with flies. She knew before, they were dead. Somehow now that we had seen them she was certain.

People in the south refused to believe there had not been a

massacre in N'Djamena. A few days later in Sara, President Malloum's hometown some 300 miles closer to the Equator, life seemed timeless, idyllic and slow. Chidren swam in the river while their brothers dragged nets behind long dugout canoes. Old men sat in the evening waiting for elephants to come to the sandy bank and drink.

Yet in town, other men were walking in groups conspicuously armed with spears, knives and iron throwing sticks called *"couteau de jet d'eau"*. The market which was run mainly by Muslim traders had been closed for days. The local prefect told us there was nothing to worry about. Everything was under control. Two days later nearly 500 Muslims were massacred there in a reprisal fed on rumours, born out of frustration and revenge.

Back in N'Djamena when we saw President Malloum he had to be propped up by his aides, as ineffectual himself as the toy cannon on his desk beside his gold-plated telephone. He would soon be taking his leave. But his commander, Colonel Abdulkader Kamoungue, remained defiant, his National Guardsmen undefeated. They would fight on, ostensibly working towards a government of national reconciliation—a pious hope and stunning improbability. Goukouni Oueddei's FROLINAT troops had descended to the outskirts of town. Within six months he would be President of Chad, with Hissène Habré as Vice President. But soon Habré would quit to besiege Goukouni, defeating him three years later, in 1982. In the meantime in southern Chad Colonel Kamoungue fought to establish a formidable grip over the cotton trade. Chad was in the maw of warlords once more. Neighbouring African states tried repeatedly to sit them down to form binding coalitions, all of which failed. The French troops retreated temporarily, the cotton supplies from the south remained secure.

★ ★ ★

The plot: An insatiable black virago sucks tirelessly on the cock of a demented, megalomaniac, if sometimes enlightened, despot whose response to American intervention in his poverty-stricken country is to immolate the aid agency man on a mountain of cornflakes delivered by mistake. The backdrop: a fabled African country remarkably like Chad. The author: the American satirical novelist and critic, John Updike. The book: *The Coup*.

With only a few surfaced roads, 13 cinemas and 7,600 private cars, the temptation to portray Chad as an African freak show must be enticing. And why shouldn't its coups become grist for parody, even parody which draws as heavily on the ejaculatory fantasies of middle-aged, middle-class, white American suburbanites as on the country's chaotic present? In a way it's touching to find that American sophisticates still have what amount to wet dreams about the dark continent, where deep in its heartland, on the edge of the Sahara, naked ladies smear mysterious unguents over fat black men with prodigious pricks. One can almost hear the drum beats . . .

It's equally touching to realise that people in Chad also like a good joke. They laughed when they saw the American embassy staff carrying the ambassador's aged mother down the steps of his residence four days after the coup, followed by crate after crate of hoarded tinned food.

They laughed again when the Soviet ambassador was trying to bribe a canoe ride across the Chari River to safety in Cameroon. Imagine the sight. The plenipotentiaries of the world's two greatest powers positively whingeing with fright, caught up in a civil war in a beggared country lost on the African continent. Of course it was unkind.

Yet realistically there was little chance that either dignitary would be shot in the back. In Chad, as in much of Africa, that fate is still reserved largely for blacks.

On 22 August 1983, Chad made the cover of *Newsweek* magazine. Americans in barber shops, college boys, women in laundromats were told over five pages all about it. But why this sudden interest by one of America's leading news magazines? Was the Reagan administration about to launch a massive foreign aid plan for the half-starving nomads? Apparently not. Was it because Chad held a key United Nations vote? Possibly, but no. Was it because Americans had finally woken up to the sullen beauty of the Sahara dunes on cold, star-studded desert nights? *Newsweek*, never a magazine to labour a point, simply pointed out that Chad lies directly south of Libya where the mad Colonel Qaddafi rules.

"Kaddafi marched into the god forsaken sand trap of Chad to feed his own fantasies of a pan-Islamic empire stretching from the Atlantic Ocean to the Red Sea." So claimed *Newsweek*. "The Mischief Maker," it called him. In fact Goukouni Oueddei had simply called on his northern neighbour, Colonel Qaddafi, for some military assistance to help drive Hissène Habré's forces from the desert wastes of northern Chad. Goukouni had yet again been thrown out of the presidency and capital by Habré, and now he was fighting back. With Libyan help Goukouni soon routed Habré's troops. So there was little now lying between the Libyan and FROLINAT combined forces and N'Djamena but for a few burnt-out lorries and endless sand dunes. Suddenly American strategic interests were at stake. The republic had to be roused and American muscles flexed.

"We could have Kaddafi picking steel fragments out of his couscous for the rest of the time without much trouble," said a senior official, according to *Newsweek*. Not to be outdone, *Time* magazine drove home the point. "There is a continent-wide pattern of Libyan destabilisation, Libyan terrorist activities, Libyan aggression. We are in the middle of a small-scale, but very important conflict," *Time* quoted yet another anonymous senior official as saying. "The empire-minded Libyan despatched his Chadian client, aided by substantial Libyan forces, to overthrow President Hissène Habré." So explained the *Washington Post*.

But wait. Hadn't Goukouni drawn on Libyan support a number of times in the course of the mad see-saw desert war? And the last time, in 1982, hadn't the Libyans quit the country when Goukouni, then President of Chad, asked them to go? Hadn't also the International Red Cross delegates said that Goukouni was about the only honest and reasonable warlord in Chad they had found? And hadn't the CIA been reported to have covertly funnelled over $10 million into Hissène Habré's war chest to build up the army with which he drove Goukouni out of the Presidential stronghold in N'Djamena in 1982?

This was all patently true. And if Colonel Qaddafi was interested in anything, it was a strip of northern Chadian desert along the Libyan border, called the Azour strip, under which there were said to be uranium deposits. Western powers were interested in this uranium too. But such detail and complexity were not to clutter American readers' minds during the 'crisis'. And 'crisis' it had become.

"In an effort to check Libyan leader Muammar Gaddafi's expansionist aims, President Reagan has despatched $25 million worth of military aid, two AWACS electronic surveillance planes, eight F-15 fighter escorts and a reconnaissance plane to the area," reported *Time*. American Red-Eye missiles were being sent to N'Djamena and an American aircraft-carrier stood off Libya's Mediterranean coast. Over 2,000 Zairois paratroopers, some Zairois Mirage fighter planes, 400 tons of French weaponry and a few mercenaries were also sent to keep Habré's questionable grasp on Chad's presidency alive.

Why the fuss? The problem, of course, was that the French government was reluctant to become directly involved. Hissène Habré may have been on remarkably good terms with, and have had powerful friends in, Paris. But many Frenchmen have never forgiven him for being involved in the murder of the French major sent to negotiate the release of a young ethnologist, Mme. Françoise Claustre, whom he kidnapped in early fighting in 1974. Nor was the French socialist government eager to commit troops to defend a man who to many seemed to be becoming an American financed puppet.

Nonetheless the American press, which knew little about Chad, kept harping on Qaddafi's mania, in America a popular theme. The French government was accused of spinelessness. This proved popular in the American press too. Finally the French committed over 2,500 paratroopers and Foreign Legionnaires, as well as several squadrons of Jaguar, Mirage and Macchi fighters to the defence of Habré's dubious legitimacy.

The *International Herald Tribune* was unrepentant. In a leader page article a guest columnist wrote, "The United States should have bombed the Libyan column as it invaded Chad . . . If the Libyans had been taken out as they crossed the border into Chad, the entire civilised world would have been pleased." Muscle and money, that's what counts. But most American newspapers knew better, and having thundered so loudly were eager to move away from Chad and on to another 'crisis' somewhere else in the world where American interests were at stake and grist for their mills, or at least for a few days. After all, the much vaunted AWACS never took off. And Qaddafi and Goukouni displayed an unnervingly shrewd propensity to want to sit down with Habré and negotiate rather than push on to N'Djamena and drag him through the dust.

And so the great American public was lurched from crisis to crisis in other parts of the globe, keeping public relations for the government's foreign policy at full throttle even if there was little of substance to report. Chad disappeared into the small notices at the bottom of the inside pages, if not altogether, in newspapers from Washington to Idaho.

Since then Chad has been effectively sliced in half militarily by a line of French paratroopers more or less in the same positions they occupied in 1979. Then Hissène Habré was mounting his first coup and Goukouni Oueddei was holding much of then President Malloum's army hostage under the palms at the oasis of Faya-Largeau. The difference today is that Habré is President. N'Djamena is in ruins. Fully one quarter of Chad's population is in exile, crammed into refugee camps on the Cameroon side of the Chari River or sleeping rough in Sudan's capital, Khartoum. And Goukouni Oueddei is repeatedly thrust upon Colonel Qaddafi by Habré's refusal to form a coalition government. The country slides in and out of the news; the only continuity is the building up of arms and casualties.

When Anne-Marie and I were in Chad, women huddled against mud walls while boys went out to keep the machine guns alive. Now, few walls remain intact. It will be sometime before anyone, black or white, sips gin-and-tonics under the dripping mimosa at N'Djamena's tennis club again, some time before the hospital has anaesthetics, the farmers grain for planting and nomads water for their herds. Whatever there was of daily life for many Chadians has been long ground in a crucible of incessant and escalating war.

The day I left Chad a sandstorm came. The sun dropped like a poisoned stone into an inert grey cloud. The country was engulfed as if in the atmosphere of a dead, forbidden planet, struggling again in a battle it has known for centuries, remote, lost once more on the edge of the vast Sahara. That may have been. Now there is something else about Chad which persists. Despite the emptiness, the misfortune and the want, in the world of propaganda, the arms trade and strategic interests, even Chad has become a piece of geopolitical real estate, too important to be left alone, too insignificant to be helped, too powerless to challenge the newspeak. Such is its fate, a modern African tragedy.

6
Uganda

On THE ROOFTOP restaurant of the Kilimanjaro Hotel in Dar es Salaam they serve plates of tiny oysters and broiled lobsters washed down with local friary wine. The view stretches luxuriantly across the harbour, the green banana groves to the blue Indian Ocean beyond. On the mezzanine floor there's cold beer and whisky with peanuts and potato crisps. At poolside one can get fried steak sandwiches and soft drinks under the tropical sun. Sounds fine.

It is, if you're a tourist, or a businessman with a few days to spare. But if you're a journalist having to wait while the Tanzanian army liberates Kampala, the capital of Uganda some 700 miles away across several big game parks and Lake Victoria, where Africa's answer to Caligula, Idi Amin Dada, ran his macabre vaudeville, it can get awfully boring. You can eat only so many steak sandwiches; after a while even lobster loses its appeal, as the photographer with whom I was travelling, Bo Bojensen, and I found, even on *The Sunday Times'* ample expenses.

It was March 1979. Julius Nyerere, Tanzania's President, had finally decided to give his northern neighbour a push. After months of border provocations, 45,000 Tanzanian troops supported by some 2,000 Ugandan exiles and several hundred Mozambicans were routing Amin's undisciplined forces, pushing them daily further back into Uganda up the Kampala Road.

Nyerere knew full well that the price would be high. The deep grass verges were still well-watered and manicured around his white porticoed mansion. But most of the cattle in northern Tanzania had been slaughtered to feed his advancing army and Ugandans whose villages had been pillaged by Amin's troops. In Dar es Salaam the supermarket shelves were bare, but for odd packages of washing powder and occasional tins of cooking oil. Quite inexplicably Nyerere had suddenly obtained millions of dollars in cash to buy Soviet weapons. But part of the price paid was stiff terms for an International Monetary Fund loan. In effect the grand old man of African socialism was mortgaging his own country's 'socialist' economic experiment—one of the few, if flawed, attempts left in Africa—to get rid of an unruly neighbour. The cost was estimated at $500,000 a day. Few people doubted that it was worth it.

Yet these were not the concerns of the circus of press men assembling daily in the Kilimanjaro Hotel bar. Uppermost in their minds was the cruder, more practical question of how they were going to get to Kampala, and more to the point who was and who wasn't going to be on the first plane in. Large sums of money changed hands. Thousands of dollars worth of travellers cheques mysteriously disappeared. Seats were gambled and lost. But to little effect. Nyerere's press officer had drawn up the guest list for the tour of Amin's gruesome playground. Two favoured journalists were allowed with the troops a few days in advance. They got their world exclusive stories the day Kampala fell. A day later we, the press hoard, set off.

The plane first touched down at Mwanza, a small airstrip on the Tanzanian shore of Lake Victoria. We were told that on no account were we to take photographs or speak to the men on the ground. The plane landed to the whirr of the motor-drives of the press corps' Nikons. Along the runway were parked several MiGs, a radar configuration and a tent. Inside the tent were young blond men playing dominoes, jet pilot helmets on the wooden table beside them.

"Where are you from?" they asked.

"London," I replied.

"Ah, we are from Moscow."

Apparently so, and friendly as well I thought.

"I spend two years at the Middlesex Language School," one said. "You know Middlesex?"

Yes, I knew it well. We talked briefly about the forthcoming Moscow Olympics. Were they pilots, I asked.

"No, technicians."

"And the helmets?"

"Yes, well . . . we're technicians."

A Tanzanian stumbled into the tent and indicated with a heavy nudge that it was time to depart.

Our next stop was the Mount Maru Hotel at Arusha on the edge of Tanzania's great Ngurdoto Crater National Park. Our guide apologised profusely, something about Entebbe airport not being safe. Or was it that the new Ugandan government had not yet arrived in Kampala for us to film and interview? Or were the

Ugandans squabbling again among themselves? Or were the Tanzanians not quite sure we should be there at all? We weren't to find out. Instead, our first night was spent like a bus full of safari package holiday makers, drinking "Mount Kili" cocktails, overeating, and sleeping in air-conditioned rooms. It was not as expected, especially with that crowd.

There were the usual hacks. The thin guy from the French press smoking Gauloises. The English newscaster who knew Uganda from his Voluntary Service Overseas days. The *New York Times* reporter who had just arrived in Africa still wearing a buttondown shirt, wash-and-wear trousers and thick-last New York shoes. He'd seen an execution in Nigeria and was a bit unsettled by it.

There was the international press agency woman continually worried the Tanzanians would take offence at her company's close relationship with South Africa. And the British expatriate who had written a detailed and moving book about Amin's atrocities, and who had almost been taken off a plane when it landed unscheduled at Uganda's Entebbe airport a few years before. He seemed frightened, and disturbed that the story he had so determinedly and so long pursued was drawing to a close.

Then there were the jokers—the American hacks, the Vietnam vets who had joined the American press, who had made their way down from Nairobi in neighbouring Kenya to join us. These guys who called each other "honcho" and "dude" had been sitting in the corridor outside the American singer Linda Ronstadt's hotel room in Nairobi for over a week, trying to prove she was having an affair with California's governor Jerry Brown who was also there. Now it looked as if Amin was on his way out. "So," one of the honchos amiably explained, "we thought we might as well go over to Uganda and cover that too." Why not? The logic was faultless. All he knew was that Amin was a sick joke. I asked him to send me copies of what he wrote.

"Sure buddy," he said. We drank a few beers. We were all backslapping friends on the road.

★ ★ ★

Entebbe airport was strewn with wreckage. The terminal building was a twisted maze of partition walls and jagged struts, the linoleum floors were covered with blood and shattered glass. A huge portrait of Idi Amin hung askew, ripped in half. It was here on 4 July 1976, that Israeli commandos freed passengers from the Air France flight hijacked on its way from Tel Aviv to Paris carrying, among others, Dora Bloch. Now the Tanzanian army had had a go. Neat rows of mortar craters were stencilled across the

91

tarmac apron leading up to a Uganda Airlines Boeing 707. There the string of craters stopped. The plane's cockpit, wings and fuselage were pocked with holes, its tyres shot out.

This was the plane which along with its sister ship had been bought by Amin shortly after he seized power, with help from Israeli and CIA front companies. Nowhere in sight were the Lockheed C-130 transports which also flew Amin's "whisky run", ferrying booze, weapons, and silk handkerchiefs twice weekly from London's best department stores out of Stansted airport in Essex, keeping "Big Daddy" and his generals' appetites appeased. Behind the terminal were still unopened crates of military spare parts. On the manifests are written the names of British firms. A burly Free Ugandan sergeant swaggered up offering an open bottle of Remy Martin cognac.

"My friends, we have been waiting for you. Drink to Free Uganda."

He didn't need to insist.

"It's Amin's own." He was in an expansive mood. There were two more bottles, one each shoved into the large ammunition leg pockets of his combat trousers. Every time he took a step he clinked.

"And where did you find these?" I asked.

"In Amin's house. I'll take you there," he said. Then be began to burp.

It was the answer I wanted. If Amin's homes were being ransacked then discipline around some of his more politically sensitive offices and their filing cabinets was likely to be lax as well.

Uganda was in a holiday mood. Along the 20-mile road from Entebbe to Kampala, from out behind wooden shacks and the broad fronds of banana trees people cheered and sang, offering us fruit. Scorched patches in the dry red earth and burnt out tanks marked sites where the Tanzanians had encountered resistance. But it hadn't been from Amin's own troops. No, the airport was too important to have been entrusted to them. It was Libyan "militia men" who died there, over 300 of the thousand heroes dragooned from Tripoli's dole queues and secret Palestinian camps and shoved by His Excellency Colonel Qaddafi into Libyan C-130 transport planes to defend their Muslim brother, Idi Amin. By then Tanzanian columns were pressing ahead well inside Uganda on the road to Kampala. One of the Libyan C-130s lay gutted by the Entebbe runway, torn open by a Tanzanian rocket-propelled grenade as it tried to fly to safety. Fifty-nine Libyans were being held prisoner outside Kampala. The rest had fled earlier or were dead.

In downtown Kampala people were picking over junk outside the broken plate-glass windows of looted shops. A man was trying to balance a large refrigerator on a bicycle. Another was carting off an office desk loaded on a milk crate he was scraping along the road with a rope. Kids were scavenging in piles of paper and garbage. Someone was dragging a stuffed zebra from a travel agency a string fixed through its nose. It was a carnival of junk.

Food shortages under Amin had become more and more acute. Sugar, flour and salt had been virtually unobtainable for months. Now the Food and Beverage Depot, the Produce Marketing Board and the Sugar Depot had been broken open. Inside were discovered hoards of staples; also shoes, cooking oil, sardines, matches, soap flakes and US army surplus rations—the booty of Amin's bandit officers. Like trains of ants whole families traipsed to the warehouse, picked up as much as they could cram into plastic bags and boxes and staggered home with their loot. Along the roadside dead Amin soldiers lay bloated in the sun.

Tanzanian soldiers were enforcing a vague sort of discipline. Many of them were drunk, exhausted from two months of marching and fighting from the border to here, never getting a lift, never sleeping more than a few hours a day. They gladly handed out huge handfuls of Ugandan currency, worthless now. Someone had sacked the local banks. Someone as well had blown the safe at Barclays Bank of Uganda with an RPG, helping themselves to tens of thousands of pounds in hard foreign currency.

There wasn't much else to steal. Amin's rule had been collapsing before the Tanzanians arrived. His generals were refusing to pass on taxes to the central bank, treating their regions as personal fiefdoms, carrying on flourishing trade in contraband arabica and robusta coffee, cattle and cotton across the borders with Kenya, Zaire and Sudan. Amin's own high living was being squeezed by his henchmen's hypertrophic greed. The *nouveau riche*, the *"mufuta-mingi"*, gloating on profits made from shops taken over when Amin had kicked out Uganda's Asians, were clamouring for even more bribes and big cars. The state was almost bankrupt. Guerrillas had been active in Buganda, southern Uganda, with some notable success. A credible case could be made that Nyerere had decided to invade to pre-empt an incipient coup and uprising. But the hacks for the most part knew little and cared less about that.

On the steps of Uganda's Parliament the new President, Yusufu Lule, was sworn in. Lule was a middle-aged and modestly distinguished academic who had spent years in exile in London holding meetings upstairs in a Finchley pub. He, the judges and a student audience were all wearing academic robes. He talked of peace, justice and freedom, noble sentiments which he seemed genuinely to cherish and of which Uganda was much in need. It was a fragile and well-intentioned, if stage-managed, beginning. Most Kampalans were more interested in foraging for their next meal.

It was 14 April 1979. At the Kampala Intercontinental Hotel we tried to repair the telex by candlelight, without luck. There was plenty of vintage French claret from Amin's cellars and plates of mashed banana mush called *"matoke"*. More soldiers were drunk. There was a commotion outside the front door. A civilian man was wrestled to the ground. In his pocket was found a hand grenade. He was taken away and shot.

Later we saw another civilian bound and blindfolded by the hotel gate. He begged us to save him. The soldiers said he was one of Amin's secret police from the State Research Centre. We had our doubts and went looking for their commanding officer. Then we heard two shots. Machine gun and mortar fire punctured the night. Nonetheless Bo and I were pleased to be there. Amin had indeed been Africa's most grotesque and hideous joke. Now he'd been sent packing.

And yet there was something unsettling. Over the next several days while I talked our way past guard posts and road blocks Bo took photographs, endlessly. He worked hard, much harder than I, lugging a full pack of cameras, lenses and film over his shoulder, bent double, often having to run. As we stopped for breath he'd tell me how much he wished he'd brought his portable darkroom, another 30 pounds of equipment, with us. He was astonishing. A notebook, passport and pen were proving more than enough for me. Yet for Bo it was a much more difficult assignment, a much more taxing war. At night while we slept I could hear him grinding his teeth, occasionally crying out. There was sporadic small arms fire, occasionally an explosion. That was normal. It was what we saw during the day that was obscene.

★ ★ ★

On the face of it Amin had been living a pathetic suburban fantasy. His home at 12a Prince Charles Drive was something to which a bank manager might aspire somewhere in London's green belt: parquet floors, simple bedrooms for the kids, their school books, toys and gripe water thrown about. Daddy had a study and in the corner was his skin-diving gear and a few glossy magazines. There was even beer in the fridge. But madness crept in. The refrigerator was the one in which he was said to have hidden the dismembered body of his wife Kay. On the bookshelves beside the desk were armament sales brochures. In the top desk drawer were boxes of military decorations, Republic of Uganda medals with Amin's image on them made by one of London's foremost jewellers. Perhaps Amin was simply an egomaniac.

But no, on top of the desk were dossiers, piles of them, of state security suspects, their mug shots stapled to the corners of the files. Inside were letters from informers.

To The Director
State Research Bureau

Dear Sir:
I deam [sic] it necessary to write to you to bring to your attention the filth and lies that my wife is indulging in. She has directly and indirectly resorted to blackmailing me . . .

Sirs:
Both my parents died when I was still young . . . I married but then divorced with 2 children whom at the moment I am staying with them. My main purpose of coming here is to get employment . . .

Confidential:
Officer Nanjunda reports that in one of the shops on Ntale Road where a certain man called Kigundu came to buy himself some sugar this man got out different types of currency and . . . suspicious guerilla activity . . .

J. Edgar Hoover used to provide Lyndon Johnson with FBI files for the then President's bedside reading. Perhaps Idi Amin, VC, DSO, MC (self-awarded), since 1977 CBE, self-proclaimed Defender of the British Empire was trying to emulate, in his own modest way, no less a personage than the President of the United States.

But not everything had been going Amin's way. There were more files and correspondence. "Amin, we kindly ask you to resign as soon as possible before we take any further steps. We are tired of you . . ."

On the top of this anonymous note, written in red ink next to the State Research Centre stamp, was "For appropriate action." But there were more, always more to haunt Amin even in his own African nightmare.

Dear General Amin,
I am writing to enquire about your great stomac [sic] of state full of Amino acids. Do you get indigestion? Could it be an enemy transmitter upsetting your Great Bowels of State? . . ."

Towards the end Amin began changing vehicles in mid-journey. He seldom slept an entire night in one place, fearful himself.

Amin's lakeside home, Cape Town View, had been well wrecked by small arms fire. His official residence, Entebbe State House, high on a hill surrounded by carefully mown lawn and flowering shrubs overlooking Lake Victoria, was much as the British had left it in 1962. The ornate flock wallpaper was peeling off the wall. The chandeliers were tarnished and dull, the furniture overstuffed and uncomfortable.

Amin's town house on Nakasero Hill, a solid brick manse hidden behind shrubs, was unrevealing as well. There was film, thousands of feet of it lying in piles on the floor: Western movies and films of the president's glorious exploits—military reviews, fly-pasts and speeches. But then, even this celluloid trove was modest in comparison to what some Americans and Europeans keep for their home videos.

Sure, Amin and his generals had their white Mercedes-Benzes, all the whisky they could swallow and any woman they cared to enjoy or humiliate. But Amin, try as he did, couldn't distinguish himself as a world famous consumer. He had neither the brains nor the education to discern or choose. Repeatedly he was fobbed off with gaudy trinkets and second-rate goods at gold-plated prices. No, Amin was a man of action, or nothing at all. After all wasn't that why the British army promoted him to sergeant for shooting Mau Maus when he was in Kenya in the King's African Rifles, the bastard son of a squaddie and a tramp camp follower? Wasn't that why the Israelis helped him to overthrow Milton Obote during the 1971 coup? Amin knew how to shoot off his mouth and how to make people listen. His method was simple. Kill. And he knew how to make that exceedingly unpleasant and drawn out.

★ ★ ★

His troops weren't bad at it either. Two Free Uganda fighters, refugees who had grown up in camps in Tanzania and were now studying engineering and geology at Dar es Salaam University before going to fight against Amin had found one of his generals' abandoned Mercedes-Benz. With their Kalashnikovs beside them and grenades pinned to their lapels we set off down the Kampala Road towards Masaka, backwards along the route the Tanzanians had invaded. We talked of Dar es Salaam, of girls, and home, listening to Zairois disco rock cassette tapes in the general's Mercedes. Both we and the soldiers relaxed.

Alongside the road were the neat homesteads of Buganda farmers, rows of coffee bushes, tomatoes and onions laid out under

jackfruit trees as formal as English country gardens. In front of the
mud and palm huts women burned out the inside of water pots
with charcoal to purify them and impart a good taste. The sky was
clear and blue but for a few puffy white clouds. This was Africa at
peace, the idyllic cultivated countryside that Winston Churchill
found so attractive, the tranquillity of the English Home Counties
transposed to the Equator.

Occasionally we passed burnt out lorries stuck front-end down in
the mud beside the tarmac. Then whole swathes of trees that had
been ripped off with automatic fire at chest height.

"We footed through here," our guides said. "The Libyans, we
couldn't understand them. They drove down the road shouting
wildly with rifles sticking out the windows. We just hit them with
recoil-less rifles. Bam! Only once did we have a real battle. The
Amini (Amin's troops) dug in and we fought all night. Before, they
always fled."

The Tanzanian troops with their Free Ugandan allies had
followed simple classic tactics, marching at night and attacking
just before daybreak forcing Amin's troops to retreat. Then while
Amin's men frantically established new defensive positions the
Tanzanian's slept. Local women brought them food from nearby
villages, and water, even as they fought. The Tanzanians kept to
the countryside. Amin's men, not used to marching, stayed on the
roads. There they were open targets. It was as easy as shooting
grouse.

"And what about Amin's air force?" I asked.

"We knew exactly what to expect."

"Oh?"

"Yes, it's true. Our officers had done the same courses as his
pilots in Moscow. So when the first MiGs came over we let them
pass. It was the next ones, the ones with the rockets that we were
after. We had SAM-7s."

And they usually got them. So much so that shortly into the war
several of Amin's pilots flew to Tanzania to give themselves up
only to be sent straight back to bomb his positions as a test of their
sincerity.

Then other stories began to emerge. Of the atrocities these young
students had seen, of the men and women they had found locked in
a regional police barracks, their heads pulverised with hammers.
Of naked corpses which had been slashed to ribbons. Of little
children deliberately crushed under lorries. The two soldiers said
they had become ill, they had never imagined the smell. They said
they felt tainted just to have seen such butchery. Could we
understand, they asked. It was their country after all.

We stopped on the way back at a modest homestead. A woman was wailing on the porch of a crude brick house. There were bullet holes in the walls. Across the courtyard was a fresh grave. A man who looked older than he probably was, sturdily built, his shoulders slouched, was standing over it.

"My father," he said. "He had done nothing. He was 80 years old."

I asked if Amin's troops had shot him. The man nodded.

"Why?" I asked.

The man shook his head.

Mercenaries from northern border tribes, Amin's loyal henchmen, had little but contempt for the southern Buganda—Christian, self-confident and prosperous. But neither had Uganda's other main tribes, the Acholi and Langi, been exempt. They, too, had been slaughtered by the thousands during Big Daddy's eight-year rule. The man with sad watery eyes standing forlorn over the grave began to speak.

"My name is Thomas Kawere. I've been to Britain you know, Cardiff. In 1958 I won the Commonwealth Games welterweight boxing silver medal . . ."

He was 52. No, he didn't mind us coming by. He was glad to see us in a way, he said. We shared a soft drink, then left. "Please," he said. "Tell people in England about this."

★ ★ ★

The State Research Centre is an utterly featureless four-storey red brick office building tucked down a slope behind Amin's town house on Nakasero Hill. It could have passed as a social security office in a small English new town. It hardly looked a charnel house, yet it was the Auschwitz of Africa. From there the men in the dark glasses and bell-bottomed trousers set out in pick-up trucks and unmarked cars prowling for live meat to drag back for the basement's mutilating goons. Often, once caught, people's families were approached and offered a deal. A large sum of money could secure their loved one's release as well as his security file. It was an extortion racket in blood. But thousands of victims were never seen again. Bodies had been dug up in the nearby forests. Mass graves were found in fields and marshes.

By the roadside in front of the State Research Centre a young woman was sitting on a scrap of cardboard, crying. There was still one basement door to be prised open. The smell of rotting bodies from behind it was overwhelming. Her husband had been "arrested" only a few days before Kampala fell. His name was on one of the final "suspects" lists.

Number 25 Daniel Kakonge.
Place of Arrest: Nkrumah Road
Offence: Not Known.

His body had not yet been found. Her name was Jane Rose. They had three children: Daniel aged five; Dorothy aged three; and Festos, nearly two.

"And what have you told the children?" I asked.

"That he was in Nakasero. They will have to find out even if I try to hide it from them. Daniel keeps saying we should go to Nakasero and get him. He cries every night. The others want to know where their daddy is . . ."

She said it was her duty to wait until the door was opened. She had to identify the corpse.

The courtyard was strewn with comics written in Arabic. Inside the entrance hall were stacked crates of US army surplus rations, grenades and machine gun ammunition. On them was stencilled "Destination Benghazi". It was here that Colonel Qaddafi's heroes met their deaths, defending Amin's human sewer while his hand-picked sadists practised their dark trade with hammers and whips up to the last minutes in the basement, crushing skulls with tongs and bare fists. Once again the mad Colonel had got it wrong, badly wrong, if he thought that this was the defence of Islam.

Stepping over corpses Bo took photographs while I went looking for what I had come for, the purchasing office and its files. Amin couldn't have run a secret police without radios, vehicles, weapons and more esoteric gear. Every profession has its own technology. I wanted to know where Amin bought his.

The file cabinets had burst open like rotten sulphurous Russian Easter eggs. Suspects' dossiers had spilled over the floor. They told the same miserable story, though every one had its own bent individuality.

"Offences:

"Found on the Kampala Road with stolen chickens. Couldn't answer questions."

"Alleged politician."

"Had come back after a long stay abroad. (Terminated)"

"Having connections with a woman whose boyfriend is in Israel . . ."

There were bits of radio equipment stacked in heaps on the desk. Small arms ammunition was strewn over the floor making it slippery to walk. I kicked some of the junk off the desk, put my feet up and settled back into Major Farouk Minawa's chair. A grenade rolled off the bookcase on to the floor. I waited. Nothing happened. Minawa had been the State Research boss. I wanted to read his correspondence.

Letter dated 22 November 1977, to the State Research Centre, P.O. Box 3676, Kampala. Attention Major Faruk Minawa:

> Dear Major Faruk,
> I have now the pleasure of enclosing herewith brief details of the microwave alarm system that you requested me to find out about . . .

That one was signed by a Keith Savage in Nairobi. There were others, for police walkie talkies from Contact Radio Telephones Ltd. in Leicester, England. Security Systems International Ltd., registered in the Isle of Man and run by an American named Joe Sands was selling secret cameras, telephone tapping equipment and bomb blankets. Globe Identification System in Toronto, Canada wanted Amin to buy its finger print and photographic national identification card system.

There were others: the slippery little men, the arms merchants whose only patch is the rough underbelly of state security, the shoe-brush and hair-oil salesmen of the arms industry who were unlikely to be empowered by any corporation or government to sell Trident missiles or radar systems, the technology of megadeath. These guys sold the dirty postcards of the arms trade: the pocket dynamos with crocodile clips so that some illiterate goon could fry off some poor student's testicles; walkie-talkies so that even the dumbest thug could swagger apeing the beer-bellied state troopers of Hollywood B-movies.

Minawa's gang wasn't stupid. They knew what they wanted: telephone tapping equipment, electronic surveillance devices, short wave radios, and assassination kits. The reason was pressingly obvious. In Amin's study at 12a Prince Charles Drive I had found minutes of one of his recent meetings with defence ministers. Amin was ranting.

> Minutes of the meeting of 20 February, under the chairmanship of the Life President:
>
> You security officers the President turned and shouted at them. I have given everything that you need. You all have smart cars. You all have good houses. You all are married to very beautiful ladies. You are all rich. What else do you need! He wondered. Why do you collabrate [sic] with Guellillas [sic]? I have several times told you that all of you here have never seen what a guelillar [sic] is. His bullet has no mercy. You should know the

difference between him and a freedom-fighter. But a gullilla [sic] is a very dangerous person. 'ADUI' . . .

The answer was terror. Amin was never slow to respond. Yet such would seem to have been Amin's suspicions of corruption and graft, even within the State Research Centre, that he decided an entirely new security force was called for to stop the rot. "Major" Bob Astles, the enigmatic Yorkshireman who for years had been Amin's close adviser was put in charge of a special unit responsible only to Amin himself.

Minutes of the meeting on March 27th at Cape Town View, under the chairmanship of the Life President to security officers:

. . . Today I have opened a new special unit of highly qualified men. This group is to be headed by me directly. It will be known as "SSS Amin Operation". Everybody at this stage run wild in applause . . .

But not for long. "SSS Amin Operation", it seems, played dirty. Captain Mzee Yoswa, the assistant head of the State Research Centre, said he wanted to resign in protest. "I must tell you", the minutes read, "that Uganda has lost so many of their able sons to Major Bob Astles' boys who call themselves Ant[sic]-Water Pirate Squad. Quite a lot are now floating on Lake Victoria having been eaten by bullets. What is it to say that these young lads die like that . . ." For the rest of the meeting Amin blew his top.

Amin also needed more gear for Astles to do his job. Correspondence from State Research Centre files showed that Amin had already purchased two seven-metre "Sea Raider" patrol boats built by a firm called Specialised Mouldings in Nairobi. He had also ordered three 12-metre "Sea Rover" landing craft, each costing $70,000 from the same company, complete with radios and other electronics from Pye Telecommunications in Cambridge, England, costing another $146,555. The agent for both firms was Wilken Telecommunications Ltd, a Nairobi firm whose directors were Keith Savage, an Englishman, and Bruce MacKenzie. MacKenzie, a 58-year-old ex-RAF pilot was a most unusual Scot who had stayed in Kenya after independence to become the first and only white minister, as Minister of Agriculture, in Jomo Kenyatta's government. There had been rumours that MacKenzie had worked for MI6, British intelligence, as well as the CIA, MOSSAD and the Shah of Iran's SAVAK. His firm handled all types of security and surveillance equipment according to the files: radios, alarms and more esoteric devices worth in all millions of dollars, much of it supplied by Pye Telecommunications.

There was only one problem. Someone in Amin's entourage didn't like him. On his return with Savage to Nairobi on 24 May 1978, they had been given a stuffed animal's head as a present at Entebbe airport by Amin. Shortly after their Piper Aztec was airborne, the plane mysteriously exploded. MacKenzie, Savage and a Briton accompanying them were killed. Yet business between Wilken Telecommunications and the State Research Centre continued under the direction of Julian Savage, Keith's son. Later Julian was to explain to me that he was forced to do business with the State Research Centre largely because of what was still owed on the Uganda account.

For the moment though, I was preoccupied collecting what I could, carefully filleting key invoices from the files, rolling them into a tight package and stuffing them under my shirt. There is nothing quite so persuasive as a letter signed by himself to wave in front of a British businessman who keeps denying he knows anything about what you are talking about. By the time I finished in Minawa's office I had a large dossier of letters from British executives all of whose firms had played, in their own special ways, a small part in making Idi Amin's secret police more efficient, in ensuring that the basement of the State Research Centre was never long thirsty for blood.

The next day was Easter. Families were well-scrubbed, dressed in Sunday frocks, flowered hats and gaberdine suits. I could hear hymns from the small church near the State Research Centre. It was almost a peaceful, beautiful day. People were standing about in the roads chatting. Kampala seemed relaxed, nonchalant under a broad blue sky. Outside the church a squad of Tanzanian troops were holding two civilian men, their wrists tied behind their backs, their ankles bound, sitting on the grass at gunpoint. Later we heard the shots.

"They were Amin's men. They were trying to hide in the church," was what the sergeant said.

At the British residence the acting High Commissioner, Richard Posnett, dutifully broke the lock and dusted away the cobwebs for the television crews. The BBC man was flying in steaks and cold beer from Nairobi. The Tanzanian press officer was flapping about, the situation by then utterly beyond his control.

I wandered over to Mulago Hospital, once the best in black Africa. The wards were bare but for a few women gazing emptily at the ceiling from their dishevelled beds. There was no medicine. Many of the doctors had run for their lives, first from Amin, now for fear of reprisals. A man came up to us and said, "Come with me. There is something you have to see."

He was middle-aged, obviously educated and he seemed both anxious and relieved to have found us.

"Come, it won't take long."

What did he want to show us?

"You'll see."

We got into his dilapidated Mercedes-Benz, and while he drove out of town he told us how he had studied medicine in Edinburgh, how he had come back to Uganda because of his family, how he had found it impossible to get any other Westerner interested in accompanying him.

"None of them would come," he said. "And I told them I had the proof."

He did too. His name was Dr. Kakande. He'd studied at Harvard and Edinburgh. He was the coroner. For the previous four years he had carefully logged every cadaver which passed through the mortuary. Would we like to see the books?

"Absolutely."

"Good, but first there is something else I want to show you."

He stopped the car outside a small red-brick building a few miles out of Kampala. We got out. It looked like a chapel. And yet all I could hear was the buzzing of flies. There, caught between the windows and the screens were what must have been hundreds of thousands of them. Then he opened the door. There were the bodies: on slabs, on the floor, their eyes popping out, their bellies distended, mutilated beyond recognition.

"You see?" he asked.

Yes, we saw. I was trying to light a cigarette, trying to get the acrid smoke up my nostrils. Bo had a handkerchief tied over his nose and mouth.

"They are from the State Research Centre, the day before yesterday."

Then he showed us the books. The columns read for line after line, page after page in neat, careful handwriting, "Unknown African man brought in by unknown policeman," "Unknown African woman brought in by unidentified officer," "Unknown ... Unknown ..."

It was too dangerous to have entered the names of the State Research men who dumped the bodies at his door. And there were no papers on the corpses of course. But the coroner knew there was one way in which he could give these people identities. By doing his job. And so alongside the lists of times, dates and the "unknowns", written in the most meticulous detail was entered the exact nature of the wounds each of the bodies had endured.

This was the chronicle of Amin's pathological regime, the irrefutable documentation of his killings. Later other journalists found fields full of corpses. And yet I couldn't help wondering.

A few years ago a man named David Irving wrote a book called *Hitler's War*. Irving's argument was simple. Hitler didn't really know that all the Jews were gassed. That was Himmler's scheme. The suggestion wasn't new. Fascists and neo-Nazis have been putting it around for years, saying also that the whole story of Auschwitz and the extermination of six million had been fabricated by the Jewish-dominated press. But Irving was among the first to dress up Hitler's dubious innocence in legitimate historical clothing and to elicit correspondingly serious book reviews. How long, I thought, would it be before some other clever fellow decided to startle the world and become wealthy with the news that Amin didn't really do it, that the stories of the atrocities were also cruel propaganda, that the killings never took place?

Outrageous? I think not. Railway newsstand vendors would all too gladly carry, say, *The Truth of Idi Amin*, with a lurid cover and promises of remarkable exposés. If the Nazi holocaust was a big, and no doubt Jewish, lie, there is little reason why Amin's terror couldn't be too. The coroner's records stood as an obstacle to that. Amin should have killed him and burned the books. Instead he allowed the clerk who logged his killings to survive. That was only one of his mistakes. Some people must think it a pity he didn't set light to the State Research Centre files as well.

★ ★ ★

"Hello. Is this Mr. Q?"

"Yes."

"Are you area manager for Africa for Pye Telecommunications?"

"That's right."

"Do you sell Mascot 70 VHF radios and MF 25 FMDS transceivers?" I mentioned the catalogue numbers for several other pieces of military surveillance and communications equipment.

"Yes we do."

"Can you please tell me what they do?"

He asks who I am and I let him know. The telephone calls had begun. The Pye MF 25 FMDS is a medium wave transceiver used by Amin's State Research Centre in its Land Rovers and Range Rovers. Does Pye sell them in Africa?

"Yes."

"Well I'm glad you said that. I've just returned from Kampala where I had the unpleasant experience of stepping over a few bodies before coming across a pile of them."

"Yes, well . . . we sell to other countries in Africa beside Uganda you know."

"Your radios were in the State Research Centre. Do you know what this is?"

Then the silences begin. "No reply." . . . "I can't talk any longer." "Can you please phone back tomorrow and ask for our public relations." . . . "We make it a practice not to discuss customers' business with the press, there is an important question of commercial confidentiality involved here." He and others droned on, many of them decent businessmen who knew full well that their companies have sold nasty pieces of hardware to Amin and would rather not be reminded of it.

The man at Pye finally replied. "As far as I know they were for the electricity board, and those guys needed radios to check the sites," he said.I don't know if the police had some. I don't know if they did. It's quite logical though, isn't it." "If we didn't do it, others would," another told me. "Just because Amin's in the press a lot doesn't mean he's any worse than the others." Over the next few days an entire repertoire of tiresome clichés and limp apologies was trotted out in defence of corporate sales.

But the story, or part of it, slowly began to emerge. One of the first British salesmen to do business with Minawa's office was a seat-of-the-pants one-man-operation in Leicester: Contact Radio, run by a nervous man named Gerald Yell. He was soon arguing over payment, and Amin's goons needed a larger, more reputable source of supply. So along came Keith Savage and Bruce MacKenzie offering goodies from the French military electronics firm, Thompson CSF, and Pye Telecommunications. Mr Joe Sands, with an office on the Isle of Man, also picked up some of the action. "We've been vetted sixteen ways and backwards by the government, by everybody. We're clean," he told me. But shortly after, he disappeared, wanted by police in Britain and the United States for questioning. Lurking elsewhere were two American ex-CIA employees, Frank Terpil and Edwin P. Wilson. Terpil has since been tried *in absentia* by a New York court for gunrunning, and sentenced to 53 years in gaol. MacKenzie's widow believes Terpil killed her husband. The motive is unclear, though the arms trade, of course, is a notoriously competitive world.

Pye didn't like any of this when it was published. I wrote:

We informed Pye that their radios were in the State Research Centre, cheek-by-jowl with reports from informers, identity cards of people who had 'disappeared', and files on 'subversives'. We also described to them the scene in the basement of the State Research Centre where Tanzanian and Free Ugandan troops found rooms stuffed with the dismemebered and horribly mutilated bodies of people tortured and murdered just hours before the building was stormed. Pye's senior management have issued the following reply. It reads in full: 'Pye Telecommunications Ltd. trades in nearly 120 countries around the world including some 40 in Africa. In East Africa we are represented by Wilken Telecommunications Limited who are based in Nairobi and have responsibility for Kenya and Uganda. We trade anywhere in the world unless specifically directed otherwise by HMG (Her Majesty's Government). We are not aware of end-user application, this is particularly the case where we trade through a third party.'

Later, Pye offered to have me visit their Cambridge headquarters and read through their files, a sign of good faith on their part. I was perfectly satisfied with copies of their correspondence I had obtained in Kampala. And so the little flurry over British firms supplying Amin's killers faded away.

Bo and I parted. He was exhausted, so was I. The next week the magazine naturally carried an entirely different cover story. All that remained of Uganda for me was a pair of trousers soaking in a bucket of biological washing powder. The stains wouldn't shift. My girlfriend had refused to wash them. They were caked with Buganda mud up to the knees. The mud has a distinctly reddish hue. She wouldn't budge. So they were thrown away. After delivering the articles I slept for three days. Then I began scanning the newspapers looking for stories, looking for work again. Uganda was over for the time being. Such is journalism.

7
Rhodesia

"LOOK, IT'S A very good piece. But we think we'll just hang on to it for now. It would be better to run it when they're all sitting down at the conference table together."

Sure it would, I'm saying to myself. Then it wouldn't matter.

One of the newspaper's senior editors had just come back from the Foreign Office. It was a tricky decision, demanding a delicate judgment, at least that's how it's explained in the pub. Possibly. But seldom are stories spiked with such alacrity.

The piece was to have been the Sunday's feature story, covering the entire second leader page. It set out simply to say who was paying which Rhodesian black political group,s and how much.

It was December 1977. David Owen, Foreign Secretary in James Callaghan's defunct Labour government had spent nearly a year getting nowhere towards a Rhodesian settlement that would involve Ian Smith, white Rhodesia's Prime Minister, negotiating directly with the leaders of the guerrilla armies operating throughout Rhodesia from secret bases in Zambia and Mozambique. Owen had enjoyed American, that is to say President Carter's support. In fact seldom had both Atlantic partners seen so much eye-to-eye as on the need to get "Smithy" and the guerrillas at one table together. Yet each of their attempts—the most recent called the Anglo-American proposals—had been neatly sabotaged, either at the conference tables themselves, more usually long beforehand.

Now something was in the wind. Lord Carrington, Conservative Shadow Foreign Secretary, was known to be formulating privately an entirely new British approach to the war in its errant colony. There would have to be a general election in Britain within little over a year and the Tories stood a good chance of winning. The rate of inflation was over 10%, unemployment was rising by over 100,000 a month touching one and one half million at Christmas, a figure then thought to be stratospheric. The public service unions, fed up with wage restraint, were to embark on widespread industrial action leading to a "winter of discontent". Whatever David Owen wanted to do in Rhodesia would be hostage to these domestic problems.

On the other hand the alignment of political forces, as the guerrilla groups called them, had seldom been so propitious for Ian Smith to launch an initiative of his own. The Zimbabwe African National Union (ZANU), led by the Marxist Christian Robert Mugabe, and Joshua Nkomo's Zimbabwe African People's Union (ZAPU) knew that. While their men fought in the bush the two leaders held together an uneasy alliance called the Patriotic Front. The black Rhodesian leaders who had never or no longer effectively commanded guerrilla forces knew it also: Bishop Abel Muzorewa, the 52-year-old head of Rhodesia's United Methodist Church and the political United African National Council (UANC); Reverend Ndabaningi Sithole, one time leader of ZANU, now after years in prison and no longer in touch with the guerrillas, almost alone in the political wilderness; and Chief Jeremiah Chirau, for years Ian Smith's acceptable black, never short of funds to preach against the nationalist cause, wholeheartedly seeming to back the country's white minority's policy.

Ian Smith announced his move on 3 March 1978. Sitting beside him at the Governor's Lodge in Salisbury were Bishop Muzorewa, Reverend Sithole and Chief Chirau, three black faces co-opted for the first time into the previously all-white government. As a sign of good faith the hanging of political prisoners in Salisbury Central Gaol was to stop. Elections were promised by the end of the year. It was called the "Internal Settlement". The guerrillas and their political organisations were excluded. The war would inevitably carry on.

It had seemed a good time to find out what shrewd Western businessmen thought a likely Rhodesian outcome; more crudely put, to find out where the smart money was. It had been known for some time that virtually all the black political groups had been soliciting funds throughout Europe and the United States. I wanted to know which corporations had stumped up, how much and for whom. After all if I was a guerrilla fighting in the bush I'd like to know with whom my leader had supped at the corporate table. Conversely, if I had shares in any of the companies involved, then I'd like to know who they were backing, particularly if I as a shareholder took a different view of the likely outcome of the war. So I wrote:

The financial dealings behind the Rhodesian nationalist groups are as complicated and clouded as the political manoeuvres which led up to the current talks in Salisbury and the collapse of the Anglo-American peace proposals.

They could hardly be otherwise. All the nationalist groups need funds to provide for their supporters—whether in refugee camps in Mozambique and Zambia, or canvassing in Salisbury's suburbs. They also need someone to pick up hotel bills, airfares, and expenses tabs for their jet-setting diplomatic forays.

The black leaders themselves, Joshua Nkomo, Bishop Muzorewa and Reverend Sithole prefer not to discuss money, and admonish their supporters to do likewise. 'We are struggling for a free and independent Zimbabwe now. We will write the history of that struggle later,' one aide told us.

The truth is that without substantial financial backing from the mining moguls of Southern Africa—Lonrho, Anglo-American Corporation, Union Carbide, a host of others and Ian Smith's government itself—the nationalists would be hard pressed to send diplomatic missions to New York and London, and to campaign for elections inside Rhodesia.

In return the nationalists have gone out of their way to give reassurances that Zimbabwe (as it will be called) will welcome private enterprise.

A senior American diplomat who has been watching these affairs says, 'I promise you the CIA is no longer "blackbagging" the nationalists. You know, covertly financing them. The truth is, we no longer have to...'

The piece went on to describe in some detail who and how much money was involved. The *Sunday Times* withdrew the story late on a Friday evening. It was an editorial judgment which I felt could best be described as sublime.

Today, under new management, one can only wonder what the *Sunday Times'* attitude would be.

★ ★ ★

On 19 September 1978 the *Report on the Supply of Petroleum and Petroleum Products to Rhodesia* was published on behalf of the Foreign and Commonwealth Office: 296 pages, price £4.75. The report set out the findings of Thomas Bingham QC, and Mr. S.M. Grey FCA, a chartered accountant, charged by David Owen's Foreign Office to investigate sanctions-busting by British oil firms to Ian Smith's illegal government since 11 November 1965, the date Ian Smith issued his Unilateral Declaration of Independence (UDI). There were few surprises, especially as much of the evidence had already appeared in the press. Executives of British Petroleum

109

and Royal Dutch Shell, Britain's largest corporations, had stood by as their South African subsidiaries had been party to schemes which circumvented the United Nations and British government sanctions against trade with the technically illegal regime. British Petroleum had two government-appointed directors on the board. Further, the British government was proved to have known, but did nothing to prevent the vital supply. Indeed, this trade had continued systematically through a complicated series of interlocking companies since shortly after UDI. And the oil flow had enabled Smith's regime and the Rhodesian economy to survive.

The days surrounding the press leaks and eventual publication of the Bingham Report could only be tiresome for anyone well acquainted with the British establishment's ritual of bewailing its own hypocrisies. Hair shirts and sackcloth and ashes were the order of the day in Westminster and at Shell Centre on London's South Bank. Fleet Street leader writers vied with each other in sonorous tones of moral outrage. Even so, Mr. Bingham's report told less than the full story. The names of the Shell and BP executives who caballed to provide all the oil that was then used to keep Ian Smith's armoured cars on the roads and put petrol in white residents' estate cars whisking from Salisbury's shopping centres to the golf clubs, were leaked to the press only months later. A more fundamental question wasn't even asked. If Smith's regime had been able to buy all that oil and petrol over a period of 13 years, worth in all more than £500 million, how did it pay? Rhodesia was barred from receiving World Bank loans. South Africa was generous with its support. But this did not extend to a several hundred million pound hand-out.

The answer, of course, is that Rhodesia had quite a lot to sell, in particular tobacco and metallurgical grade chrome ore. Anti-apartheid groups and United Nations committees had tried from time to time to find out where the tobacco went, but with little success. There were rumours that Thailand had become an intermediary through which boycotted Rhodesian leaf—among the best in the world—was illicitly channelled to cigarette rolling mills in Europe and the United States. Mulching machines were used to shred the Rhodesian weed, making it difficult if not impossible to identify. There was no clearer evidence of brisk trade than the droves of overseas buyers who began gathering every April in Salisbury for the auction of the Rhodesian crop. "Will the boycott work? Opinion in Rhodesia is cynical: they quote the old adage 'Commerce will always find a way,'" wrote Michael Barford, the well-informed editor of the trade journal, *World Tobacco* at the outset of UDI. Thirteen years later over beer and

110

brisket in a pub not half a mile from the British Parliament he confided that his prognosis had been borne out. Barford should know, being Rhodesian himself. If successive British governments had been remiss in uncovering sanctions busting by their own oil firms, where tobacco was concerned—tax revenue on tobacco sales brings well over one billion pounds into the British Exchequer each year—they didn't even try.

Yet in business terms tobacco's only a money spinner. It's not a strategic mineral, short in supply, high in demand, not just for car bumpers and cooking pots, but as a basic ingredient in the manufacture of all the world's stainless steel alloys. That's chrome. And Rhodesia (now Zimbabwe) is thought to have greater reserves of high quality chrome oxide ore than any other country world-wide, as well as being a leading exporter of ferrochrome.

The argument is simple. Since the famous OPEC meeting in 1974, not just the price of oil, but that of many other raw materials had shot sky high. Southern Africa, including Rhodesia, is a major source of several of those minerals without which modern economies, and more specifically their armouries, cannot be maintained. Leaving aside gemstones, gold and other precious metals, others such as chromium, nickel and lithium are essential for the manufacture of sophisticated weapons systems including fighter planes, missiles and bombs. Southern Africa must remain open to the West at all costs. Rhodesia must not be allowed to fall into Marxist hands.

This little piece of geopolitical logic was made great play of by pro-South African British Conservative MPs. Their *locus classicus* was a bluntly stated, thinly disguised anti-Soviet tract entitled *The Southern Oceans and the Security of the Free World*, edited by Major Sir Patrick Wall MP, and published in 1977. Wall wrote,

> The USSR, has, of course, little need for South Africa's minerals for it's own use as it is largely self-sufficient . . . [but] . . . Should the USSR ever be in a position to control their cost or to deny their production to the West they would have succeeded in striking a blow that could well cripple Europe's industrial economy as well as gravely damaging that of the USA. In the short term such a blow could well prove fatal in undermining Europe's will to resist Soviet domination.

Similar dire warnings began appearing regularly in the press.

As leader of the opposition in the House of Lords, Lord Carrington quietly tolerated this sort of flummery from the back benches. Privately he took a different, considerably more sophisticated view. If supplies of Southern African strategic minerals were in fact being interdicted on the high seas, he argued, then Britain and the United States would already be at war. So why all the fuss? The best way to keep more of Southern Africa from falling into anti-Western hands was to do business with the newly independent regimes whether they called themselves Marxist or not, and to encourage agricultural production so their people could feed themselves. As far as minerals were concerned, he was interested in fostering stable regimes that could guarantee delivery to contract.

Carrington held other somewhat heretical, almost radical views, to the minds of many Tories. He firmly believed that Britain had not one, but two antagonists in the Southern African region. One, for sure, was Dr. Vassily Solodovnikov, the Soviet ambassador in Lusaka, Zambia, spinning his web to a grand Soviet strategic design. The other was American multinational corporations eager to snap up business that had been largely a British prerogative since the imperial heyday. Sitting on the boards of Rio Tinto Zinc, Britain's largest mining firm, and Barclay's Bank International, he knew at first hand how Americans, allies to the end in the face of the ever-touted Soviet threat, had been remorselessly squeezing British firms out of business throughout the Commonwealth and what had been the Sterling Area. Southern Africa had become not only the most recent theatre of anti-colonial guerrilla warfare, but a corporate battleground of this particularly Anglo-American feud. Rhodesia looked like one of the last British bastions about to fall. When it comes to business matters, as the world now knows, Americans don't just stand around. Later, Carrington was to become the butt of their anger. For the time being it was David Owen and his friends in Jimmy Carter's administration.

As often as Andrew Young, President Carter's Assistant Secretary of State for African Affairs, talked of the Anglo-American peace proposals, North Carolina's Senator Jesse Helms pilloried them on Capital Hill. Full-page advertisements were placed in major American and British newspapers promoting a book called *Rhodesia*, written, the cover blurb said, "out of first hand experience with literary skill and with a passionate concern to make plain the truth." The book "reveals how Andrew Young and his British cohort, Foreign Secretary David Owen unwittingly are working to install a marxist dictatorship in Rhodesia . . ." The author was Robert Moore, writer of half a dozen right-wing thrillers and anti-communist warnings to the Free World.

For the Rhodesian venture Moore installed himself as "American ambassador" (self-appointed) in Salisbury, a defiant plenipotentiary sitting under his own "crippled eagles" embassy shield, an emblem of America's supposed post-Vietnam flaccidness. The American political crackerjack, the kind that delivered votes at hustings in the days when men who ran for governor also sold snake oil.

Preferences for particular black leaders in a post-Ian Smith Zimbabwe were beginning to emerge. Robert Moore couldn't have been more explicit. He described Robert Mugabe as demented, Hitlerish, possibly syphilitic; Joshua Nkomo as like Idi Amin and a two-bottle-a-day drunk. Bishop Muzorewa he saw as a moderate. But for a man in whom good, civilised Free World Christians could put their trust, well, . . . Chief Chirau was the man Moore preferred. The chief, according to Moore, "says most tribesmen can't understand ballots and, as in the past, are apt to vote for the opposite of what they want."

The coarseness of Moore's judgments is offensive to all the black nationalist leaders, to say nothing of the Rhodesian people. Many of them had suffered and campaigned indefatigably for 20 years trying to right what they and much of the rest of the world saw as an intolerable wrong. It seems curious that papers such as the *New York Times* carried full-page advertisements for such junk. Rhodesia, for sure, was not South Africa. Ian Smith's government had no formal system of apartheid. Nevertheless, Rhodesia's over six million blacks had to register to move, were barred from designated "white areas" at night, needed special permission to buy property, to go to certain schools and to use many of the government's facilities, all of which was nakedly discriminatory solely on the basis of race. The country's vast majority had no vote or other say in a government entirely in the hands of a quarter of a million whites.

Change was inevitable. The question was into whose hands the government of independent Zimbabwe would fall. In the circumstances, the interest of corporations in cultivating political leaders for the new country is obvious and explicable. But is it surprising that black leaders also showed themselves as accommodating towards, and in fact went much further to solicit private Western sources for support? They after all had no public exchequer to draw upon, nor a tradition of well-heeled public hypocrisy such as in Britain, for example, where MPs are under no obligation publicly to declare the full extent of their private business interests. It was widely reported that Joshua Nkomo's armies received training and arms from Eastern Europe; that Mugabe's army based in Mozambique had primarily Chinese help. Bishop Muzorewa was said to have benefited from substantial subventions from American Methodists for years. But these apparently were not enough, as I soon found by talking with Rhodesian nationalista and British and US businessmen who had dealings with them.

★ ★ ★

In January 1977, Bishop Muzorewa, on his return from a Geneva Conference—only one of a succession of attempted Rhodesian settlements which failed, met with a senior executive of the Anglo-American Corporation. Muzorewa was desperately short of cash, his aides told me, even to pay his delegation's hotel bills. Anglo-American is the largest minerals house in the world. The mining magnate listened to the good Bishop but at the end of the meeting, according to Muzorewa's followers, stumped up a lousy $4,000.

Muzorewa's aides thought this an insult. More than 400,000 blacks work in Southern African mines, many of them on contract living in closed compounds, not seeing their families for a year at a time. In that year alone the millionaire's constellation of corporate giants declared over £150 million profits after tax. For a corporation that publicly talked of the need for gradual yet real change in Southern Africa, it was exceedingly tight-fisted. As much out of embarrassment as shrewd calculation Muzorewa's associates decided to cover the matter up.

They had not been idle elsewhere, they explained, lobbying for funds from conservative Arab states such as Kuwait and Morocco, though these too were said to have turned him down. Yet there were indications that British businessmen were sympathetic, as was the Union Carbide Corporation, one of the largest industrial consumers of chrome ore in the United States.

Muzorewa's assistant, George Nyandoro, had had a private meeting in London with leading figures in the Conservative Party. Nyandoro, a man both jovial and cunning, also met with a few senior members of the business lobby, the Confederation of British Industry (CBI). Yes, both bodies were interested in offering help, he was told. The Tories realised full well that supporting Muzorewa, a peaceful church leader without troops, and especially in light of the Labour government and President Carter's apparent openness towards the guerrilla armies of Robert Mugabe and Joshua Nkomo's Patriotic Front, could only strengthen their hands domestically. British businessmen for their part had had to stand by gnashing their teeth ever since UDI, watching good British business go to German, Japanese and French firms better placed to break sanctions with impunity. Now they were looking for a political vehicle to get back into the Rhodesian market. At least some CBI executives were enthusiastic. "Yes, we'll have an aeroplane on the runway full of British executives ready to fly out

114

as soon as sanctions are lifted," one told me. Frankly I couldn't imagine the sight.

Nonetheless, in early Summer 1977, Muzorewa was in London to meet with John Methven, the director, and others at the CBI. At the same time he visited banks and firms in the City of London, lunching with, among others, executives at Booker McConnell, Britain's largest international agribusiness consultants. "He's more bourgeois than Benjamin Franklin," a director from one firm said. "He's a good chap, but we'll just wait and see," another explained, adding that his firm had made available a few scholarships for Muzorewa to dispose of among his supporters. It was also decided that he would attend the forthcoming Conservative Party conference.

On 10 October, at a pre-conference meeting in Blackpool, held under the auspices of the Young Conservatives though arranged by Tory senior foreign affairs spokesmen, Muzorewa duly criticised David Owen's Anglo-American peace proposals. The Conservative leadership was there. Yet curiously the *Sunday Times* decided that none of these developments were to be widely aired.

In fact, Bishop Muzorewa was consistently finding himself with the short end of the corporate stick. Diehard American anti-communists knew that power doesn't come so much from the pulpit as from the barrel of a gun. They, among others, wanted a man in Rhodesia who could get the guerrillas to lay down their arms. Muzorewa was a good man, but Ndabaningi Sithole was for them.

Sithole's aides told me and Sithole himself later confirmed that in November 1977, the 57-year-old ex-guerrilla leader flew to the US to begin one of the most curious tours of the whole Rhodesian war. After meeting with UN Secretary-General Kurt Waldheim, he flew on to Washington for brief meetings with Secretary of State Cyrus Vance, and Andrew Young. Then a consultant, who had worked for various government agencies including the United States Information Service in South East Asia at the height of the Vietnam war, began helping to arrange Sithole's itinerary.

Sithole was paraded through the congressional offices of America's hard right. "I told the boys to go into the bush. Now I'm telling them to come out," he repeated *ad nauseam*. Then he flew to Southern California to address businessmen uncomfortably close to the John Birch Society. Accompanying him for part of his tour was another ultra-right American who admitted he had worked in intelligence as well as, oddly, a Rhodesian department store. These were hardly the sort of people one would expect to find espousing the cause of Zimbabwe's black majority. But who cared?

Among the American strategic minerals lobby the word was that "Sithole definitely has his head screwed on right."

The man speaking was E.F. Andrews, vice president of Allegheny Ludlum Industries, one of America's largest clients for Rhodesian chrome ore. Andrews made no secret of his views. Testifying in front of the Senate Foreign Relations Committee's Sub-Committee on African Affairs he explained Rhodesia's place in the world. During the period since UDI, he explained, South Africa had brought massive new deposits of low-level chrome oxide ore into production which could be refined owing to a new process patented by the British firm, British Oxygen Ltd. Consequently there wouldn't be a strategic shortage of chrome in the US if Rhodesia was lost. But, he told the committee, "If our access to Rhodesian chrome is cut off, our dependence on South Africa as a source of supply will increase. Should we lose access to both Rhodesian and South African chrome and ferrochrome we would become substantially reliant on the Soviet Union." In the United States that sort of argument tends to carry the day.

Over the telephone Andrews was equally straightforward about his support for Reverend Sithole. The ageing ex-guerrilla commander was the only man, Andrews said, who could stop the communist rot. And yet there was more involved. For if Bishop Muzorewa and Ndabaningi Sithole were having to cast their nets so widely in search of friends and funds it was largely because they no longer enjoyed the favour of one man, Roland W. "Tiny" Rowland, managing director and chief executive of Lonrho Ltd. Edward Heath once rather grandly declared that Rowland epitomised "the unacceptable face of capitalism." This may have been an apt description, though with so many other candidates it seems unfair to have singled Rowland out. Nonetheless regarding Rhodesian matters "Tiny" Rowland was in a class of his own.

★ ★ ★

Rowland's executive offices on the sixth floor of Lonrho's Cheapside headquarters near St. Pauls was the one place in London where Rhodesia's black nationalists all claimed to be welcome. Nkomo knew it well. Sithole claimed that he used it as an office. Some of Mugabe's men told me they were once frequent visitors. And Bishop Muzorewa's close assistants earnestly described how he too had paid a visit enquiring about funds. Rowland was, after all, deeply involved in various attempts at a Rhodesian settlement.

At the Salisbury Conference in early 1976, when Ian Smith and Joshua Nkomo sat down opposite each other and talked for several days, Rowland saw to it that Nkomo's bills were paid, his advisers flown out, and telex and other facilities made available through Lonrho's Rhodesian offices. When James Callaghan wanted to send a new set of proposals at one point in the proceedings, they were transmitted via Lonrho's and not the Foreign Office telex machine. Nkomo's aides and his British advisers spoke openly about this.

There apparently seemed nothing unusual in this. Rowland's own legal counsel had acted on Nkomo's behalf at the Victoria Falls Conference with Ian Smith the year before. Rowland had also been instrumental in arranging secret meetings between Ian Smith and his advisers and Kenneth Kaunda, President of Zambia, at least one of which Nkomo attended.

The relationship between Nkomo, Kaunda and Rowland had been close for years. And it was by no means an entirely one-sided affair. When the British Department of Trade criticised Rowland in its report on Lonrho's business methods, Kaunda informed the British government that all Lonrho's Zambian assets, which were considerable would be nationalised should Rowland be dropped from the board. He wasn't, of course.

At the much vaunted but ill-fated Geneva Conference in autumn 1976, again Rowland was reported to have picked up Nkomo's tab, reputedly for about £35,000, which was said to cover not only meals and drinks, but the Presidential Suite and an entire floor at the Intercontinental Hotel. At the time Rowland was thought of very much as a Nkomo man. The tycoon was arranging to have printing presses shipped from the newspaper Lonrho owned in next door Zambia—*The Times of Zambia*—to Salisbury. A young African journalist was put in charge of the new black newspaper—*The Zimbabwe Times*—with financial backing. But such largesse was not without complications. It was darkly rumoured within the nationalist community that some of the money advanced to Nkomo's aides for their political cause had been used instead to buy land and fast cars.

Clearly, while Joshua Nkomo is a charming man, there was much more at stake in the relationship than just friendship. Rhodesia for Rowland was a very special place. Not only had he gone there as a young man, the son of German immigrant parents, to become one of the colony's largest ranchers, and then owner of some of its most profitable gold and copper mines, but Lonrho, which is a contraction of the name London and Rhodesia Company, also owned the pipeline which ran from Umtali in Rhodesia to Beira on Mozambique's Indian Ocean coast. Through it most of Rhodesia's oil was to have flowed. Sanctions scuppered that. So it was not surprising to find Rowland profoundly interested in the search for evidence of sanctions-busting by BP and Shell, and later attempting to sue them for colossal lost pipeline revenues.

Rowland's friend Kenneth Kaunda was then providing safe haven for Nkomo's troops. In effect Lonrho was deeply involved in the corporate war for the reapportionment of southern Africa's mineral wealth. The company was said to have challenged the Anglo-American Corporation in Angola but with little apparent success. In the black South African puppet state of Bophuthatswana, Lonrho owned considerable interest in large platinum mines. A Rhodesian settlement would be an important move on the corporate southern African chequer board.

Shortly after the Geneva Conference it was suggested to Nkomo that some funds might be forthcoming from the Shah of Iran. Nkomo's aides say that Rowland lent a hand in helping to arrange a meeting with the latter-day emperor of the Peacock Throne. Nkomo flew to Teheran and, according to his aides, presto! Some $500,000 was said to have been made available.

This sort of touting for jet-set cheque-book support may not have gone down well with the fighters, "the boys", slogging it out in the Rhodesian bush, but it looked attractive to their leaders—short of cash, trying to maintain credible international presences and attend the many diplomatic conferences. It also had a definite and predictable effect on morale. As a member of a delegation at the Geneva Conference told me "After a point you don't care whether you're right or wrong. They're sitting down every night to platters of steak Diane while you're sneaking out the back door for hot dogs and sauerkraut. That begins to wear on you after a while." And yet those who giveth do so at a price, as a chagrined Ndabaningi Sithole found out.

The reverend had gone into business the year before with two black Rhodesians living in London, one of whom bragged ostentatiously about having some sort of working relationship with Rowland. I used to contact this man, who wore fine suits and carried a beautiful, expensive leather briefcase, through Lonrho's Cheapside offices. The two black Rhodesians had been entrusted to run "Primrose", a trust into which they said some £50,000 had been deposited, ostensibly to help ZANU, of which Sithole had once been leader. The problem was that several thousand pounds apparently never arrived in Rhodesia for the purposes intended. Over steak and Burgundy in one of London's finer pubs, the man with the briefcase confirmed this, and several other matters regarding confidential corporate

118

funding for the nationalist groups, to myself and a *Sunday Times* colleague. In the meantime Reverend Sithole was in exile.

In April 1977, while sitting dejected in the lobby of London's Waldorf Hotel, Sithole decided he had to get back inside Rhodesia to have any hope of surviving as a political force. He told me that he went to see Rowland, among others in London. Secret negotiations with Ian Smith followed which made possible Sithole's return to Rhodesia that July. And so he became the first "terrorist" leader to be allowed home. He soon had offices and vehicles at his disposal in Salisbury.

Sithole was less fortunate elsewhere. At the Geneva Conference he had met Miles White, a no-nonsense American living in Monte Carlo, who told me that in return for the possibility of commissions on agricultural contracts once Zimbabwe became free, he would try to help arrange some $5 million for Sithole's campaign fund. That seemed fine.

Sithole also took advice from Group Captain Richard Dupont, a relative of Ian Smith's ex-Minister of Justice then living in the English home counties. Dupont, who was entirely above reproach, unfortunately helped Sithole get in touch with some gentlemen running an office called the International Banking Corporation, in London's Hanover Square. Shortly afterwards, and having nothing to do with either Dupont or Sithole, the IBC's files were seized by the fraud squad and three of the company's directors were arrested on charges of conspiracy to defraud. From then on Sithole's cause was lost, floundering among international white-collar crooks, stacked like lumber rotting somewhere in the right-wing American political wilderness.

Spirited on by his rivals' audacity and his own pressing need for funds, Bishop Muzorewa was only slightly more discreet when he, too, approached Cheapside in spring 1977. Muzorewa's aides told me that at the interview the Bishop explained to Rowland that though he had not come before, he could now see few differences between them. He had heard about Nkomo's successful audience with the Shah and wondered if a similar trip could help himself.

Whether it was Rowland or someone else who eventually helped is unknown; Muzorewa talked with several corporate executives. Later in the year Muzorewa's men were back in London, and excited. The Bishop was about to set off for Teheran. There was only one problem. For all their astuteness, Muzorewa's aides had ineptly failed to realise that the Bishop had scheduled to arrive in Iran during Ramadan. The trip had to be postponed. When Muzorewa finally got there a few months later, I was told, he was whisked from the airport by limousine, and ushered into his audience with the Shah, who listened politely. The Shah, apparently, said he had no doubts about the Bishop's commitment to capitalism – that had been forcefully put. But his highness would have to consider the matter. No funds were immediately forthcoming, though some eventually arrived. A few months later, in March 1978, the Bishop accepted Ian Smith's embrace, becoming, along with Reverend Sithole and Chief Chirau, the first black ministers in the previously all-white minority government. The pact sealed their political death.

✱ ✱ ✱

The unpleasant truth was that in the absence of representative government in Rhodesia, power did come from resistance and out of gun barrels. No amount of jet-setting would change that. Unless Ian Smith could be brought to settle with the guerrilla movements, any election would be hopelessly at risk, at best a cruel and probably bloody historical farce. Tiny Rowland knew that, which would have figured in his reasons for promoting Joshua Nkomo, leader of the ZAPU branch of the shaky Patriotic Front. He also appreciated the value of making gracious overtures to Robert Mugabe. They weren't well received.

When Mugabe came to London in 1976, he was informed that Rowland would welcome him paying a visit to Cheapside. One of Mugabe's aides, present throughout the subsequent meeting, described to me how, in the course of their conversation, Rowland reminded the guerrilla leader of Lonrho's previous assistance to ZANU. Instead of showing gratitude, Mugabe apparently exploded, storming out of Lonrho's offices swearing to his aides and supporters that ZANU would never take money from Rowland's organisation again. The problem, of course, which was possibly as embarrassing for Rowland as it was shocking to Mugabe, was that much of the money had gone astray. Mugabe had never known, until that meeting, that any financial arrangement had been made, or that any men claiming to represent ZANU had accepted such corporate funding.

Back at his wife's home in London's Notting Hill Gate, Mugabe began a reassessment of ZANU's representatives abroad. No evidence came to light that Mugabe authorised or took part in any other efforts to elicit corporate support. In this among Rhodesia's black leaders he seems to have stood alone, suggesting that his confidence lay elsewhere, in the ZANU armies and overwhelming popular support. I asked Paul Spicer, Tiny Rowland's public affairs assistant at Lonrho, about support for black nationalists. He declined to comment.

This was the gist of the story the editors saw fit not to print. In all probability, there were other payments and favours promised by or asked for from other corporations that remained private. Yet here was enough to begin a serious discussion. In the pub with the editors after a few pints had loosened a few tongues there were mutterings about "rocking the boat" and "we've got to be patient, the right time will come".

I couldn't deny that there were some tawdry elements in the whole goings on; that several of the black Rhodesian leaders, as much as their corporate counterparts, had shown serious lapses of judgement, not to say political acumen. And yet to me, therein lay a whole world of anxiety, as well as crass calculation—the more visceral reality of a world which goes by the name of diplomacy. At the time, Rhodesia was foremost in the British overseas news. There were daily reports of innocent people shot, "caught in the crossfire", "suspected of being guerrillas", of "new initiatives just around the corner". It was a very dirty colonial war and not an easy one to follow. Knowing who was paying whom would have offered some clues to Sunday readers as to what was to come.

★ ★ ★

So my story was spiked. But there was something more at stake. Rhodesia was to be a war fought by honourable men, by responsible men striving earnestly for a solution to a complex and difficult situation. That at least was the way it was portrayed by much of the British press and, I believe, sincerely thought of by many of the participants—that is the white ones. What can be called for want of a better term "the British establishment" too much at stake in Rhodesia to think of their involvement in terms other than that. It was a war after all, being fought by "kith and kin", ever close to the British emotional bone. Those "kith and kin" may have been morally and legally wrong to have declared UDI in 1965. But, by God, you had to admire their pluck, was a common refrain—the Battle of Britain spirit of "Good Old Smithy", the ex-Spitfire pilot who, if anything, could be said to be an idealistic rebel living just a bit beyond and behind his time.

Several British newspapers openly admired the way Ian Smith's illegal regime was "standing up to the blacks." The most compelling stories were those of white farms which had been raided by the guerrillas, the residents hideously murdered, their machinery smashed, their bedrooms and sitting rooms sacked and defiled. These were horrible tales of unspeakable atrocities. But there was another horror which by and large was going untold. The horror of daily police beatings in Salisbury's destitute black shantytowns, the burned villages, the bayonetted women who refused to stop giving their sons—called "terrorists"—clothing and food, the babies who fried when their parents' village huts were burned. According to official figures nearly 1,000 white people died, many of them horribly, in ten years of the Rhodesia war. According to those same figures more than 14,000 black Africans were killed. Most of their bodies lie in unmarked graves. Most of their stories were never told.

At around the time my piece was pulled I spent a night in a cheap Bristol hotel. With me were two young prison guards then working in Bristol Gaol. In the bedroom on the vinyl-topped table around which we sat was a bottle of whisky and a tape recorder.

"We used to pull their legs, honest we did. You know for the ones that wouldn't die when the rope jerked their necks. We used to have to tug on their legs after they had been hung, to make sure they were dead." One of the men, in his early thirties and now safely back in England with his wife and kids, was speaking. "It was disgusting," he said.

"Well, why did you do it?" I asked. Why had they volunteered to be on duty for hanging the "terrorists" in Salisbury Central Gaol? The answer was simple. Money.

"We used to get a few dollars extra for everyone we hung. At the end we were doing five at a time. Then we'd cut them down, stack them in the lorry, and take them out to be buried near the flower garden at Chikurubi prison outside town."

The men had documents which substantiated everything they said. Yet soon they began complaining, almost whining about what had happened to them. They had been working in Belfast prison, having volunteered because the money was good, better than in gaols on the British mainland. Then one of their wives had seen an advertisement in a popular Sunday newspaper offering jobs in security positions to men looking for adventure with experience. They had applied, gone for interviews at an office near Trafalgar Square and off to Rhodesia they went to become prison guards in Salisbury Central Gaol.

"They didn't tell us before we went out", one of them said, "that there was not really enough overtime. The basic money wasn't any good. I was really sour. So what the hell, I said. Somebody had to do the hangings, and well, why not us? . . . Mind you," he said, "it was disgusting. I feel awful every time I think of it now."

The two men went on to explain how they also supplemented

their salaries by volunteering for weekend police pillaging raids into Mozambique, bringing back handfuls of Portuguese escudos to change on Salisbury's thriving currency black market, how they beat the prisoners with sticks, how they spat on them, how the prisoners were locked away when Red Cross delegations came to visit the gaol.

Here was the documented personal testimony of two men, both British citizens wearing Her Majesty's Government prison uniforms serving in the prison service, employees of the Home Office, recounting the naked sadistic turnings of the worm right at the core of the blighted Rhodesian state. For months the International Red Cross in Geneva had tried unsuccessfully to gain access properly to inspect Salisbury Central Gaol. Church leaders the world over had spoken out on behalf of relatives whose men had disappeared there. The two prison guards' testimony, simply as evidence, should have been told. Yet again the newspaper didn't want to know.

As with the covert funding of black nationalist leaders on their international tours, so the tugging of hanged men's bare feet until they were dead was not the sort of behaviour that honourable men, whether they be Ian Smith, British journalists or Foreign Office mandarins, cared to face up to.

And so a lie was propagated and sustained, especially in the closing stages of the war: the lie of the "Honourable Men", written by honourable men, for the most part about men remarkably like themselves on both the British and white Rhodesian side. Nowhere are men expected to behave more honourably than in the army, and nowhere was there a greater lie.

For the rot had set in. Ian Smith's regime was doomed, as Lord Carrington and others who shrewdly observed the Rhodesian security forces knew. Smith's army was no longer made up of men who could draw on the RAF and Battle of Britain as sources of their spirit and heroism. On the contrary, despite many of its highly trained officers and loyal black squaddies, the Rhodesian army had grown heavy with the leaden sadism and grasping ambition of hired thugs, ex-convicts and ill-adjusted Vietnam veterans— mercenaries recruited through the small advertisements of the Western press to swell its fast depleting ranks. The Bristol prison. guards were only two of an entire band of carpet-bagging killers eager to be given a Rhodesian uniform so they could carry a gun.

The prison guards had quit when their chances for earning special pay, the hangings, were stopped as part of the Internal Settlement. The others stayed on to forage and kill in one of the world's few remaining and fully authorised high technology "nigger hunts". Rhodesia's army, under the command of Lieutenant General Peter Walls, used these special units to telling and ruthless effect. Terrorising blacks helped drive the guerrilla leaders towards concessions at the negotiating tables. But the price paid in Rhodesia was high—men, women and children "caught in the crossfire", some "zapped" indiscriminately by 20th century bounty hunters.

On 20 April 1978, Lord Richard Cecil was killed in Rhodesia. The 30-year-old son of the Marquis of Salisbury, great-grandson of Lord Salisbury who gave Rhodesia's capital its name, ex-Grenadier Guard and Special Air Service (SAS), had turned journalist to report on and make a film about the Rhodesian war. He was shot by guerrillas while filming a Rhodesian army raid on a village where guerrilla suspects had been spotted.

Cecil's colleague, Nick Downie, who was also a trained soldier turned journalist/filmmaker, completed the film, called "Frontline Rhodesia", which was later shown on British television. It showed Cecil in action in an army uniform he often wore; among others a young white Rhodesian paratroop officer who was later killed, and a dead black man. "This time an innocent civilian," the film's commentary coolly observed about the black man. "But in this war the man who shoots first survives." There were also scenes of captured black Africans being dragged, bleeding, by a rope to a waiting helicopter.

Throughout, the film's commentary stressed the professionalism of the Rhodesian units compared to the rag-tag ill-disciplined behaviour of "Mugabe's terrorists". The implication was clearly spelt out in the film's closing moments. "For Rhodesia the future holds despair," the commentary solemnly intoned. "The scene is set for a black civil war. If white morale collapses or the army is dismantled, there will be total chaos. And while the whites may escape, the African civilians will die in countless thousands. At least 16,000 Rhodesians on both sides have died so far. That figure could fade into insignificance."

But that hasn't happened. And a lot of people thought it wasn't going to. For many blacks the future of Rhodesia held not "despair" but a chance to go to decent schools, to earn a living, to be genuinely equal citizens in their own country. And then there was the question of General Walls' army's mercenary killers . . . None of this was even alluded to in Downie's film. I asked him why not. We had a row, and haven't spoken to each other since.

Richard Cecil had been a close friend of P.K. van der Byl, Ian Smith's Minister of Information and Foreign Affairs. On Thursday 27 April, Cecil was buried after a service at St. Mary and St.

Bartholomew's parish church in Cranborne, his family's county home. Lord Carrington, William Whitelaw and Harold Macmillan were among the mourners. A fortnight later a memorial service was held in his memory at the Guards' Wellington Barracks. Cecil was no doubt a courageous and probably genuinely honourable man. There were other honourable men fighting in Rhodesia, on both sides. But the men who'd come into the frontline of "Smithy's" war, his racist propagandists and gutter soldiers, were not among them.

★ ★ ★

Most weekday mornings John Carbaugh, Senator Jesse Helms' political adviser, takes breakfast in the dining room of Hay-Adams Hotel. The hotel was originally the Washington residence of Henry Adams, 19th-century American essayist, philosopher and conservative pundit. The panelled walls and leather armchairs breathe comfortable respectability and wealth. Political breakfasts are a Washington speciality.

Carbaugh's late. His red Jaguar sports car is in the garage again. He's rich, he's from Helms' state of North Carolina, and he's just been profiled in *New Yorker* magazine. He's also a Vietnam war veteran with a tongue out of a Saigon bar. He's not in the habit of wasting words.

"That bastard Carrington bugged our hotel rooms. There's no question about it. He rigged that whole Lancaster House thing from the start, he and that black commie Mugabe."

With Carbaugh you know where you stand. But why had he traipsed to London for the Rhodesian settlement in autumn 1979 in the first place? Salisbury, it seems, is not such a long way from Dixie Land. And if Bishop Muzorewa could possibly be helped to throw a large spanner into any chances of a British arranged settlement which would have led to free and open elections, well, so much the better.

Carbaugh is intelligent. Like most people who bothered to forget the rhetoric and actually count, it was obvious that Mugabe would win such an election. Mugabe is a Shona, as are approximately 80% of Rhodesia's blacks. Nkomo is from an Ndebele tribe. Ndebele make up about 15% of the black population. Muzorewa, from one of the minor Shona tribes, could hope to win only if the guerrilla leaders were not candidates.

On the other hand, in May 1979, the Tories won the British election and Peter Carrington became Foreign Secretary. Only a Tory ever really stood a chance of bringing Ian Smith to a conference table with the likes of Nkomo *and* Mugabe. Carbaugh and his friends sputtered and fumed in London during the first stages of the Lancaster House Conference. But to no avail. Carrington got the parties to agree to a ceasefire followed shortly afterwards by British supervised elections.

Robert Mugabe's party won, of course, and he became Zimbabwe's first Prime Minister. He was then 56, and had spent over 10 years in Rhodesian gaols. The Lancaster House Conference was seen by many as the British Conservative government's first, and some argue most notable, success. Lord Carrington was widely congratulated. As *Time* magazine said, "The prospect of peace, international recognition and an end to economic sanctions has turned all but a handful of Rhodesia's diehards into fans of Carrington's and Prime Minister Margaret Thatcher's."

Possibly there was an easy irony here in that Lord Carrington, the very epitome of a Tory patrician, should have engineered the first peaceful transition of power to an espousedly Marxist leader in Africa. Yet for those who knew him this was not inconsistent with the policy he had pursued all along. And it was clear that he had accomplished what a Labour leader probably could never have done, holding the confidence of Tory backbenchers—and therefore an automatic parliamentary majority—as well as Ian Smith, in reaching agreement with the guerrillas.

In turn Robert Mugabe has been remarkably pro-business. The oil can now flow through Tiny Rowland's pipeline. Ferrochrome, nickel, gold, asbestos and copper is all being exported openly, much of it to the US from mines still owned by Lonrho, Rio Tinto Zinc, Union Carbide and Anglo-American Corporation. This year's tobacco auction was, as usual, well attended. And South Africa, as ever, is the country's main trading partner.

And what about the other black leaders, who at times frantically and possibly misguidedly cast about so widely for banker and board room sponsors? Bishop Muzorewa sits as MP for Mashonaland in the Zimbabwe Parliament, that is when he's not in prison. Reverend Sithole is almost forgotten, working out of a downtown Salisbury office. Joshua Nkomo, who had been Minister Without Portfolio, fulminates with good cause at the steady encroachment of one party rule on any genuine power sharing among the two dominant tribal groupings, the Shona and Ndebele.

In the meantime Mugabe's uniformed henchmen were terrorising Nkomo's supporters in the Ndebele homeland, Matabeleland. There had been several small press reports. Then on 15 April 1984, the *Observer*, owned by Tiny Rowland, carried a full page expose by its editor, Donald Trelford. "Agony of a lost people", the headline screamed. Trelford went on to describe eyewitness accounts of "widespread killings and beatings by the notorious Fifth Brigade of the Zimbabwe National Army."

Rowland immediately apologised to Robert Mugabe. Trelford threatened to resign. The row was patched up quickly, but it was curious behaviour on Rowland's part, given his longstanding friendship with Joshua Nkomo. By then some 2,000 people were said to have been killed by the Fifth Brigade. Today the Fifth Brigade still has a lot to learn to match the indiscriminate sadism of Smith's troops in the last years of the war. Yet Mugabe knows that with every killing his vision, and that of his countrymen and women who endured so long for independence, turns sour.

★ ★ ★

Shortly before the Zimbabwe elections, on 13 December 1979, the *Sunday Times* ran a front page lead story about the Shah of Iran's covert political gifts. Labelled "Exclusive", the newspaper revealed that Bishop Muzorewa had received three separate gifts of $200,000 from the emperor of the Peacock Throne. The story went on to say "that Muzorewa's rival, Joshua Nkomo received $500,000 from the Shah in 1977 and this prompted Muzorewa to appeal—successfully—for the Shah's financial help. Both gifts are well known in Salisbury."

Fancy that, I thought, now that the battle was over. Better to publish part of a story sometime than no story at all. I also thought back to the night one of the newspaper's editors spiked a larger truth, having just returned from the Foreign Office. How many times, I wondered, had this distinguished newspaper done that before? How many times had it claimed to lead with the news, when in fact it seems to have chosen the different road, and dutifully followed.

8
Guatemala

THE AIRPORT AT Guatemala City is among the busiest in Central America. The runway takes jumbo jets. Pan American has its regional headquarters there. And more private airplanes are said to be parked on the tarmac than anywhere else between the Mexican Border and the Panama Canal.

So there was nothing unusual, on a clear morning in September 1979, when our small plane took off, banked over the city's slums clinging precipitously to the thin, steep-gullied ravines that become torrential cascades of mud and refuse every time it rains, and headed north towards the jungle.

There was the pilot, myself and Don Campbell. There was nothing much unusual about Don Campbell either. He was a typical eager Canadian geologist in early middle-age, fit, even chirpy, a man who believes in his own hard work and enterprise in the hope of some day making considerably more than a few bucks. Campbell, like so many geologists, dreamed of striking it rich. And he earnestly believed he was within a hair's breadth of doing so.

We were flying over jungle, dense green foliage suffocating small hills between which were nestled soft cushions of fluffy white cloud. Two hundred miles away, just inside the Guatemalan border with Mexico, was our destination, his particular El Dorado, the Rubelsanto oil field. Campbell's company, registered in the tax haven of Luxembourg, was called Basic Resources International SA. He was executive vice president. That day he was showing me around.

There was one thing unusual though, if not about Don Campbell, at least about his company. Earlier in the year it had been taken over by one of Britain's more enigmatic entrepreneurs, Sir James Goldsmith. Until recently Goldsmith had owned one of the largest food conglomerates in both Britain and France. He had also taken over the bankrupt Slater Walker group of companies at the behest of no less than the Bank of England.

Indeed, Sir James was a very wealthy man. He was only 46 when his Paris-based holding company, Generale Occidentale and its affiliate, Banque Occidentale, obtained controlling interest in Basic Resources for some $6 million, plus another $13 million in convertable debentures and a welter of fine print. But the path hadn't been without twists and complexities, few of which he was at pains to explain to a zealously enquiring press, especially business journalists on the *Daily Telegraph*, *Sunday Times*, and more especially the satirical rag *Private Eye*.

In private, like most of us Sir James had his ups and downs. These were his own affair. Basic Resources wasn't. The company was expected soon to be pumping oil out of the Guatemalan jungle, the only firm to do so. It also held an extraordinary 1,500 square mile concession, the largest in Guatemala and comparable only to the exceptional privileges once enjoyed in its heyday by the American corporate banana giant, United Fruit. If there was as much oil in the Rubelsanto fields as the French Petroleum Institute said there could be, Basic Resources could have been a tapline to fabulous wealth. More ominously, though hardly reported in either the local or international press, throughout Basic's concession was raging one of the bitterest and most ugly guerrilla wars in Latin America. Basic Resources had become unwittingly heir to that too. It deserved finding out about.

★ ★ ★

Don Campbell liked to talk. There was little else to do besides stare at the jungle out the plane window. So he told me how an "old timer" geologist, Bill Bradey, an American with a pick and a mule, had wandered down from Cuernavaca in Mexico towards Rubelsanto prospecting for sulphur. He'd found some, and with a bit of money to a Guatemalan businessman to satisfy the nationality clauses in Guatemalan law, easily staked out the giant concession. "Who'd ever heard about sulphur?" Campbell rhetorically asked. He and his partner, John Park, another Canadian mining executive, certainly had. They had also heard that along with the sulphur there might also be oil. So they quit their Montreal jobs and for ten years drilled small test wells, often not knowing where their men's wages would come from, often having to fly at little notice to New York to sort something out. It was all good pioneering stuff, the sort that self-made men like to talk about in aeroplanes and hotel bars.

But there was a problem. The oil had to be pumped from the well 233 kilometres across jungle and flatlands, across what in Guatemala is called the Transversal del Norte to the Caribbean

129

coast. The pipeline was estimated to cost about $30 million, which they didn't have.

First they had turned to Serge Semenenko, one of the West's more enigmatic and flamboyant financiers, once director of a finance house called the First Boston Corporation, which he miraculously steered several times through some remarkably deep financial rough water. Semenenko told Campbell he could effect introductions and joined Basic's board.

Then came Louis D'Olivet, an urbane and somewhat mysterious entrepreneur, resident in Paris, said to be Hungarian by birth, a man whose financial hand lay behind, among other things, the first James Bond films. Middle-of-the-night telephone calls from New York and London hotel rooms followed. Campbell thought D'Olivet knew Goldsmith's wife, or lived next door to him in Paris, or something like that. He wasn't sure. But that is how, he said, he and John Park met Sir James.

At the time, they were talking to other possible investors in Belgium. Campbell said Goldsmith insisted on complete control of Basic or nothing at all. He got it. On 22 February 1979, Goldsmith's London public relations firm, John Addey Associates announced:

> Basic Resources International SA (BRISA) announces that Sir James Goldsmith and Mme. Gilbert Beaux have been elected to the Board of Directors and Executive Committee of the company. Sir James Goldsmith has also been elected Chairman of the Executive Committee.

It was an investment which Sir James' hagiographer, Geoffrey Wansell, a journalist from *Now!* magazine, was to call "ecologically sound". Sir James described it to me as "a speculative company, a pioneering company operating on a shoestring... It was desperately short of money, had a lot of hope, a lot of optimism, a lot of pioneering spirit which I personally share." There was no doubt either, in Don Campbell's mind, that Sir James had been his redeemer.

In effect Goldsmith was bailing out Basic Resources. The company's July 1979 prospectus prepared by its London stock broker, Mead and Company, explained the relationship: "... the company has raised significant finance from Banque Occidentale and related companies, the consequence of which is that the new group could be in a position to influence or control some 40% of the shares of Basic Resources." In City of London parlance this meant that Goldsmith now held "a commanding presence". As an exercise in freebooting initiative and daring there was nothing to offer but congratulations and admiration to the fledgling oil firm. "But," I asked Campbell, "what's it like doing business in Guatemala?"

"No problem," he said. "The Quetzal is pegged with the dollar. There are no restrictions on repatriation of profits."

Campbell was thinking as a businessman should. The Quetzal is Guatemala's currency, named after a rare jungle bird worshipped by many of the country's Indians—who make up nearly half its six million population.

"So it's an investors' paradise?" I offered.

"Absolutely."

"What about the government?"

"No problem," he said, "but you got to know who you're dealing with."

I was becoming impatient, and I suspected that had begun to show. "I mean what about the stories about killing the Indians? Isn't President Lucas a tinpot dictator, and a pretty nasty one at that?"

"Well . . ." Don Campbell wasn't going to be hurried. No. Not this time. He paused and thought, then said, "He's fighting a war against communist insurgents."

"On Basic's concession?"

"Yes, within the concession area as well."

"And?"

"We do what we can to help."

Campbell then explained how when the American administration under Jimmy Carter stopped further arms shipments to Guatemala because of its dreadful human rights record, Basic was among those companies which put the Guatemalan generals in touch with other arms dealers, primarily French and Israeli, so they wouldn't go short of spare parts. He also explained how Basic's Guatemala City management dutifully attended security briefings given by the army through the local Chamber of Commerce, how they had actively lobbied for the automatic death penalty for kidnapping business executives or their families, and how they depended on the army to protect the oil wells. Yes, Basic was in the front line in the fight against communism. Campbell had no qualms about that. In a nutshell he felt that if you wanted to do business in Guatemala you would be too if you're smart.

"Here the army are in politics," he explained. "Keeping the balance, stepping in if things become too extreme one way or the other. In the United States most politicians are lawyers. Here they're soldiers. You don't call the United States a dictatorship of lawyers, now do you?"

The high jungle mountains had given way to curious small, steep green hillocks, bumps surrounded by what looked like dense swamp. Campbell explained that the bumps were called "domes", often a telltale sign that oil was to be found. A few miles away I could see a rough runway hacked out of the foliage, then a handful of drillheads came into view and pipelines leading to storage tanks. This was Rubelsanto, Basic's oil field.

Outside the small office that passed for a control tower, half a dozen Guatemalan troops loitered aimlessly, kicking the dirt, waiting for a plane to take them out.

"They guard the stores, the dynamite," Campbell said.

We then took a jeep along a narrow levy through the swamp, jungle dripping on either side, to a small clearing—the pumping station, a maze of carefully laid parallel and crisscrossed pipes. The workers were local Indians. As it was lunchtime they were dishing up tortillas and black bean mush. Some of them were throwing rocks at alligators swimming in the green water not 25 yards away. The sun was blistering the metal sheeting on the rough dining shack. The heat was suffocatingly intense.

"In a few months this will be pumping oil to the coast." Campbell was proud of his achievement. I could understand that. There were vipers and boas in the jungle. When the Indians found them they smashed their heads and stuck them on the fences. It was Campbell's blithe confidence that oil would be flowing "in a few months" that caused me to reflect.

In London, John Addey Associates had issued a series of statements saying progress was being made. Yet there were sceptics. The Montreal Stock Exchange, for one, on 6 April had ordered that trading in Basic's shares be stopped unless and until some explanation of recent heavy buying was forthcoming. The Canadian officials also insisted that Basic register with the American Securities Exchange Commission.

But Goldsmith and his fellow directors instead moved sideways, applying to sell shares on the Toronto Stock Exchange and to get a listing on the Hong Kong market where, to the astonishment of people who know that part of the financial world, they failed. There was something perplexing about Basic Resources. Could it have had to do with the eminently practical questions of how much oil there actually was in the jungle wells, and how it was going to be got out of the swamps?

★ ★ ★

Back in the plane Don Campbell found himself answering questions about investors' confidence.

We were flying low along the path of the pipeline from the wells to the sea. Below us it snaked, a thin shining tube only 12 inches in diameter lying on its freshly turned track around hillocks, across streams, along miles-long red gashes carved straight through the jungle. The forest was peppered with handkerchief-sized patches in each of which stood a tiny shack surrounded by stubble corn. These were homesteads. Corn takes but three months to mature, fast enough so that uprooted families don't quite starve. Once harvested, the soil bled of nutrients, the Indian and Ladino farmers, called "campesinos", move remorselessly on, slashing and burning fresh jungle, clearing it for the ranchers and plantation owners who at a more leisurely pace inevitably follow.

I'd asked Campbell about problems with the Indians when we'd first met at his office in Guatemala City. "Yes," he said. "They keep moving nearer to the wells and we have to get the army to keep moving them out." But for the most part the Indians were hard workers, eager for jobs at Rubelsanto. The company had few complaints about them. There was, though, the question of the guerrillas. "They keep descending on the villages and promising the peasants freedom and justice, that sort of thing," he explained. "They call themselves the Poor Peoples' Army, the EGP." But then again, the army was after them, with officers who, Campbell confided, had been specially trained in counter-insurgency at the United States' School of the Americas in the Panama Canal Zone. "Those military marching bands you see in the city during holidays, that's all for show," he said. "The real troops are special forces. They're out in the countryside, doing a first-class job."

Nevertheless, there had been a few problems at the wells. "You see, the army helps us by bringing in supplies and new pipe by military helicopter. And I suppose the guerrillas thought it was the army once when our own employees were actually aboard. So they shot it down." Then there was the incident a few years before when the guerrillas burned the stores and unsuccessfully tried to make away with the company barge.

"The army went after them, and took reprisals in a nearby village. About 20 people were killed. I think they got the wrong ones." But these were mere pinpricks. Campbell assured me that the guerrillas didn't seem bent on destroying the wells, or the pipeline for that matter. They just wanted to make their presence felt. No, there was no reason from that quarter why the opening of the pipeline should be delayed.

Below us the land was now more open, large tracts grazed bare by longhorn cattle. There were flocks of sea birds. We were nearing the coast. Campbell was pointing out spur roads, small bridges and minor earthworks. All of them had been built by Basic's engineers from the Paris-based firm Entrepose. That's where the trouble had been. Landowners were claiming "right of way" fees for allowing the pipeline to cross their property. Some had asked for more, a bridge here, a small access road there, not just in lieu but in addition. And most of the landowners were military officers.

In fact President Fernando Romeo Lucas García's career had close parallels to the oil company's own. When Campbell and his partner first went into the jungle, El Presidente was a lowly colonel in charge of the nearby garrison. They built the first local airstrip together. Then Lucas was made commander of the region, the Transversal del Norte, responsible for the economic development of the land the pipeline crossed. Now, after a typically chaotic Guatemalan election he was El Presidente with near absolute powers to dispose and deny. Among the largest estates, producing timber, cattle and cardamom, were his own that stood in the pipeline's path. But Basic's miseries only began there. Lesser holdings had been hastily purchased and legally registered by majors, colonels and generals shortly before the pipeline was laid. Each one was entitled to a fee. "The amount was more or less set by a senior air force officer," Campbell told me. The greedy ones asked for small engineering works to be carried out on their estates as well. It would have been impolitic, in many instances, to have refused.

The scheme seemed an elegant way to dispense largesse to Guatemala's military, and other, landowners; a bit extortionate perhaps for the hapless oil company which had to pay over $60 million for a pipeline that was supposed to cost only half that amount. But business can be tricky in banana republics as even a man of Sir James Goldsmith's stature was beginning to learn. Several times he and his Parisian business partner, Mme Beaux, had flown to Guatemala City to discuss their "pioneering" venture with El Presidente's government.

According to press releases issued from Basic Resources' office on Fifth Avenue, New York in May, the pipeline "should be completed in July 1979". But it wasn't. In July the company announced "construction of the pipeline is proceeding at a satisfactory rate." Basic Resources had forgotten the interest of the Guatemalan navy.

Fifteen shore patrol boats and one landing craft hardly constitute what most people think of as a navy today. Nonetheless, it was a proud force, fiercely independent and aware of its historic role in Guatemala's defence. Admirals don't expect to be ignored, especially when it comes to being asked about an oil pipeline which had to cross under the Rio Dulce. In Guatemala that's the navy's domain. There were, after all, possibilities of pollution, environmental factors to be considered.

Far fetched perhaps. But true. Before we touched down, back in Guatemala City, Campbell assured me that with a little sorting out the oil would soon be on stream. I had begun to suspect that either he knew something I didn't or one of us was a bit of a fool.

★ ★ ★

It had been raining all morning,—heavy, black, rolling clouds bucketing torrents on to the capital. The drains were mud filled courses; what had been intersections were swirling pools of garbage and water; water steamed off the streets. Throughout much of the day El Presidente had stood stiffly erect, resplendent in his dress uniform, gold braided and beribboned on the balcony of Casa Presidencial. With him, milling under the 19th-century balcony portico, were Guatemala's cabinet and chiefs of staff, their matronly wives and stunningly beautiful daughters talking among themselves, waving occasionally with white handkerchiefs to the crowd below. The rain had only made them seem more remote. Through the balcony's double glass doors could be seen shimmering the mansion's grand pendant chandelier.

September 15 is Independence Day, celebrated throughout Central America to commemorate the day in 1821 when Spain withdrew its governors and allowed the resident Spanish colonialists to account for their own affairs. The traffic police were carrying carbines. President Lucas was taking the salute.

From behind the parapets shock troops trained machine guns on the crowd. In the square Indian families stood on benches, bewildered. A few were straining for a better view. The rest stood glum and bemused, soaked through. The Indians were colourfully dressed. Yet many were in rags. Their children had dirty faces and runny noses. Special buses had collected them from the countryside for the annual carnival: and they had little choice but to stand in the square until evening to be taken home.

As the clouds lifted, the street vendors appeared. There was candyfloss, coconuts and ice cream. The damp air rattled with brassy trumpets and snare drums. From around the corner of the square marched troop after troop of high school students dressed in comic opera uniforms carrying wooden rifles. As they paraded past the President each class performed its own bizarre and utterly complicated manual of arms. Lucas acknowledged each in turn with a stiff salute.

Here was the spectacle of a president saluting school children carrying toy guns with all the pomp of Wellington after Waterloo. Wasn't it a bit ridiculous? Then a mother explained to me. "If your son doesn't march on Independence Day, he doesn't stand much of a chance to graduate. That's the way things are in Guatemala," she said.

The newspapers colluded, carrying full-page advertisements from foreign firms congratulating the country on its fine president. The local television commentators were hysterical in their effusiveness. Lucas García, as perhaps other general-presidents before him, had twisted Independence Day into a celebration of national obeisance.

But not entirely. Taped to the windows of one of the larger banks in the modern district of the capital, where the roads are paved, where pedestrians walk on sidewalks and traffic lights work, were photographs of an ordinary-looking young man, his hair combed, wearing a shirt and tie. Underneath was an appeal by the bank's clerks. "Kidnapped", it read. "We protest strongly against the kidnapping of our companion Benvenito Antonio Serrano. What has become of him?"

There was a war going on in Guatemala, a secret and dirty war, grown dirtier since Anastasio Somoza had been overthrown in nearby Nicaragua, when only two months before, on July 17, the pot-bellied dictator had fled to Miami, his air force bombing Managua, the capital he left behind. To Guatemala's solid right-wingers' the US had betrayed and abandoned Somoza and was likely to do so to them. They were now alone in the battle against communism.

"A warning to the Guatemalan people", a full-page newspaper advertisement sponsored by the Movimiento de Liberaicón Nacional read: "The war in Nicaragua, sponsored by the United States, Cuba and other satellites culminated in a government which constitutes a threat to the order, peace, liberty, justice, property and lives of Guatemalans. To fold our arms and rely on the government is suicidal. We must defend our institutions. No political sermons in church. No red teachers. Do not give your children to communists, even if they are wearing religious habits. Don't feed ravens. They will only pluck out your eyes."

Was it not President Jorge Ubico, the man who signed the original contracts with the United Fruit Company in 1931, who built a miniature Eiffel Tower straddling Guatemala's main street, who said when he was finally deposed in 1944, "Beware of communists and clerics?" And was not the Nicaraguan Foreign Minister a priest, and hadn't members of the Nicaraguan junta been trained in Cuba?

"Guatemala is in danger," another newspaper warning read. "In its blue skies there are black clouds . . ."

That evening I had a rendezvous in an ill-lit room lost somewhere in the older part of town. The streets were awash with refuse, pocked with gaping holes and puddles. In places were soft pools of light under the few street lamps. The rest was dark. The district was known to be safe only for dogs and police on the prowl.

Along most of Guatemala's highways a blond effervescent girl and a swarthy handsome man smile from billboards, beckoning motorists and Indians pushing barrows to join the good life, "Drink Coca-Cola". But life at the bottling plant, Embotelladora de Guatemalteca, is different. The personnel manager comes from the army and carries an automatic pistol, I was told. His bodyguards have submachine guns and shoot up crates of bottles for fun, it was explained to me. Three years earlier the workers had organised a union but the American franchise holder from Houston, Texas, never really accepted it. My contact that night was with lawyers from the banned union. The story they told was gruesome.

The management, they said, had first tried to bribe the union leaders, offering them mortgages and loans. But it got nowhere. Then the gunmen stepped in. In November 1978, the union's general secretary, Israel Marques, was ambushed as he drove home. He survived that and two subsequent attempts on his life, one by escaping from the factory hidden in the bottom of a bottle truck. The next month two men on motorcycles shot dead the union's financial secretary in broad daylight as he was delivering Coca-Cola in his truck. In January 1979, a young couple living in Israel Marques' home were machine-gunned. The man died, the woman survived. So Marques fled to Costa Rica and a new general secretary took his place. Within a month, as he was delivering 7-Up to a store two men jumped him and stabbed him to death. The lawyers talking to me were named in a recently published death list. We drank bitter coffee and I finally left, walking the last mile back to my hotel.

★ ★ ★

In the Camino Real Hotel lounge, heavy-set men in dark glasses regularly slouched in the settees. By the back entrance Indian children scavenged in the alley for cold tortillas and leftover black bean mush. In the restaurant tourists talked about how beautiful the volcanos around Lake Atitlán had seemed. Like most visitors they had taken a boat across the deep purple lake, climbed the steep stone road to the village of Santiago Atitlán where Indian women sell ornate brocades patterned with magical birds and beasts. Few if any of the tourists knew that only weeks before, Anastasio Somoza, Nicaragua's ex-president on the run, had briefly decamped near Lake Atitlán waiting for a special plane to fly him to exile in Paraguay. Nor were they aware that just above the village was a radio station run by the local Indians broadcasting in their own dialect. The man in charge lived in a two-roomed shack with his wife and children and a pile of black corn in the back—the family larder. He had jaundice. He also lived in fear for his life. A year later he was shot dead by the military in the back of the neck.

No, the men who knew Guatemala, and they let it be known they knew Guatemala if one could talk about a country almost in a biblical sense, were the hard men, the guys who'd fled Nicaragua and El Salvador, their businesses bombed or confiscated. Eyeball to eyeball over some of the world's dryest martinis in the dimmed hotel bar they droned on about free enterprise and the communist threat, about how they lost "a hell of a lot" of money when Somoza was overthrown. It took a calloused sense of justice and a strong stomach to do business in Guatemala. But, by God, it would soon be the only place left where a man with guts and the drive to get rich could hope for a break.

I'd heard it all before in bars throughout the Caribbean, in Africa, even Hong Kong. The same emphatic thrust, the tightly clenched fists, the several too many drinks. Intellectual lockjaws who kept banging their heads against a world that for them was hopelessly complex. A lot of them were Vietnam vets, guys who popped peanuts into their mouths while telling you how they squirted the Cong. Fuck the villagers. They deserved what they got.

But there were others too, shrewder, cooler, more experienced by far, Frenchmen and Germans and a few Americans who knew the backdoors to construction contracts, skimmed a percentage off whisky imports, who knew when to offer a fat bribe or a girl. They kept more to themselves. And when they spoke it was with a deadly sense that someone would be called to account if their schemes went awry.

Nonetheless, they too were small beer. The ones who mattered calmly asked for any messages at the reception desk, walked straight to the lifts and disappeared. They had better places to talk than the bar. What they said blessed more discreet ears.

I had had enough of what passes in Guatemala City as business life. I had also obtained the results of a secret Jesuit study into life for Indians along Basic Resources' pipeline. Whereas President Lucas' generals and colonels had more or less been given whatever they had asked for by way of compensation for "right of way", the

Indians living in the pipeline's path were either thrown off the land or legally roughed up by a tough local lawyer drafted especially for the job. The Indians were paid a pittance, and usually on condition that they left within a few days. According to the Jesuit report, many of those who didn't were effectively coerced. Fences were built against their shacks. Livestock disappeared over night. There was no work. Water became scarce.

With a car driving north it is possible to get within a few miles of the pipeline's route. Along the road women with brightly coloured bundles on their heads carried chickens to markets in the towns along the way. Children ran beside them. The jungle skirted the road dripping heavy-scented vines and huge branches over the lanes.

I stopped at a village just inside Basic's concession area, a few miles south of the pipeline. Children were bouncing balls against the rough whitewashed wall of the church under the broad-leaved trees of a dirt square. Inside more Indian women were kneeling, praying while organ music scratched out from an old tape recording. Pictures clipped from magazines of Pope John Paul II were taped to the pillars. A basket of fruit lay by the door.

Priests were having a difficult time nearby. The year previously in the town of Ixcan about 50 miles away on the other side of the concession, the priest had been blown up in a plane. Yet there was little mention of this in Guatemala's heavily censored press. Then the priest who replaced him was deported. Again little mention was made of this incident. I wanted to see the priest in this town but I'd had no way of contacting him beforehand.

It takes a confident man to speak to a total stranger in the circumstances. Nonetheless he did, about a particulary bloody incident in the village of Panzos. A year before, on 28 May 1978, several Indians had been shot when protesting after having been informed they were to be prohibited from farming land they believed was theirs. The government promised to investigate the shooting, but despite widespread protests said little other than that 43 people had been killed. The press was banned from the area.

Yes, the priest could help. Somewhere hidden in the diocese were tape recordings he and others had made with eye witnesses to the massacre shortly afterwards. They were the only direct evidence which he knew existed. If the tapes were found by the authorities he believed several more people were bound to be killed.

And what did they say? That it appeared to have been a premeditated affair. The landowners were in town that day riding lorries, carrying rifles and had soldiers with them. When the protesting campesinos refused to disperse they opened fire.

Women and children were among those shot as they fled. Some 138 people died, many more were seriously wounded. "And did it have anything to do with the pipeline?" I asked.

"Frankly, I don't believe so myself," the priest said. "But you won't be able to convince my parishioners of that. You know, even now some of them go out at night and try to chop through the pipeline with hatchets."

We talked on. I could hear children playing outside and the strange song of jungle parrots. He had another concern. The evangelists. American Protestant missionaries who were flooding into the Transversal. In every village the priests spoke of freedom and justice, and Protestant sects spoke of property ownership and order. They seemed to have the army's support. There were now more American missionaries in Guatemala, he said, than foreign Catholic priests. One church was fighting another. The priest was sure that the time would soon arrive when the Jesuits and those such as himself would be pressured to quit, or face unpleasant consequences.

I drove back to Guatemala City through the rain and mud. I had asked Don Campbell about the Panzos incident as we had flown somewhat north of the town. He said he didn't know much about disappearances in Guatemala in which the army and landowners were said to be involved. Amnesty International was at that time saying that there had been over 2,000 political murders in Guatemala in the past year. What did he make of that?

"There are none," he said.

I was dumbfounded.

"No. You see, there may be a few. But there are none, nothing like on the scale Amnesty International talks about."

"But certainly their figures, if not precise, indicate a scale of violence that's quite exceptional even for Central America," I replied.

"No." Campbell was steadfast. "This is a small community. If ten people disappear then you're bound to hear about it. And I've heard nothing like that."

We said nothing more for a bit. It was getting late in the day. We were both ratty after several hours flying in a small plane. Yet I couldn't believe that businessmen could be as blithely uninformed as Campbell apparently preferred to appear in Guatemala. Neither did Guatemala's Vice-President, Dr Francisco Villagrán Kramer, when I told him.

Villagrán Kramer, by profession a professor of law and corporation lawyer, had a nice way of putting it.

"Anyone who says there are no disappearances here is trying to blot out the sun with his thumb."

With that he stuck out his thumb—splat!—as if to squash a fly, and took another drink of whisky. We were sitting in leather armchairs in the book-lined study in his home in Guatemala City's most fashionable and security conscious residential district. Both his assistant and one of his sons were there. Our conversation was matter of fact and nonchalant. And yet they were on their guard. Outside standing by the porch were four soldiers.

"When I became Vice-President I said, 'you have to protect me,' I said, 'Gentlemen, I do not hire gunmen. I have never hired or paid a gunman in my life. As a public official I am to be protected by the authorities. So I want a military protection.' They're out there now . . ."

Manuel Colom Argueta and Alberto Fuentes Mohr, leaders of Guatemala's liberals and social democrats, had been assassinated earlier in the year. A month before he was shot Colom Argueta was reported to have said, "We do not have political prisoners here. We have dead politicians."

"You know," Villagrán said, "Manuel Colom was shot the day he was to come here. He was the head of the social democrats and he was to come over here so we could make a coalition, his party and my liberal conservatives. Then bang. I waited and waited. Dinner was ready. He didn't arrive. Then there was a telephone call. That was in March."

He took another swig of whisky.

"Now you tell me, with criminality like that, what do you call this government?"

I knew what I called it. What I wanted to know was how he could remain part of it.

"I made a mistake. I actually thought we'd be able to influence them. In the last election the army put up the money and we delivered the votes. Now it won't be long before I either leave the country, I get killed or they kick me out."

Villagrán was being remarkably frank. He was also the only notable civilian left in Lucas' government. Did he mind if I wrote about our interview?

"No, just send me a copy."

I would. And yet I knew too that Villagrán wouldn't be long in Guatemala. He was being excluded from cabinet meetings, forced to rely on his purely formal powers as head of the Council of State to have matters raised. At the same time El Presidente Lucas García was becoming more paranoid, sleeping on a camp bed in his office instead of going home at night, anxiously grasping for more absolute power. And what about Amnesty International's allegations of the thousands missing and killed?

Villagrán got up and went to his desk. "Wait a minute," he said. He returned with a file. It was full of newspaper clippings. "For the past two years", he explained, "I too have been doing my own research. Cutting out all the notices, no matter how small, of these incidents. Then I compare them with the police reports. And I try to find out what happens to the men they arrest."

"And?"

"And," he said, "you learn some remarkable things. Sure, there are a lot of criminals in this country. There would be anywhere there is as much poverty as there is here. But if you compare the number of convicts the police put in prison and the number of people they arrest who are never seen again then you can only conclude that the convicts must be continually escaping and being rearrested five or six times."

I was confused. I admitted it. What did he mean?

"Look, there are so many fewer convicts than arrested criminals here, they're unaccounted for. Do you know what I think happens to the rest? They're the ones who are taken out and shot and found dumped by the roadside."

So much for Guatemala's criminal justice system. It was tedious and time-consuming arithmetic, but Villagrán was a lawyer after all. And what about his researches into the reports from the war zone, the oil concession land?

"My God, the killings there are terrible." He seemed surprised that I had even asked. "I estimate that at least half of the killings Amnesty reports are done by the security forces and the police. Anyone who says less is a fool."

We had another whisky, and I drove back to the hotel, back to the bar where two American engineers, hard men, were speculating on Fidel Castro's sexual habits over peanuts and cold beer.

In March 1951, Jacobo Arbenz Guzmán was sworn in as Guatemala's first socialist president. In March 1953, his government announced the expropriation of some 200,000 acres of uncultivated land belonging to United Fruit. On 27 June 1954, 15 months later, Arbenz was overthrown in a bogus civil war, the CIA's first successful piece of social engineering in Latin America. Allan Dulles was then director of the CIA. His brother, John Foster, was President Eisenhower's Secretary of State. Both brothers had at some time previously worked as lawyers on behalf of United Fruit. Several other senior members of the American administration had either worked for or had close relatives who worked for United Fruit. The night before CIA-backed mercenaries invaded Guatemala to unseat President Arbenz the American ambassador, John E. Peurifoy, apparently told his staff, "Well, boys, tomorrow at this time we'll have ourselves a party." Shortly after, they did. The CIA had proved itself as the covert arm of corporate policy in the White House.

In the subsequent 25 years Guatemala had ten presidents and over 30,000 people were either killed or "disappeared". The cash economy has flourished: bananas, cardamom, nickel and small engineering exports have boomed. Multinational corporations—Coca-Cola, Union Carbide, Dow Chemical, ITT, Colgate Palmolive, and especially pharmaceutical firms: Merck and Company, Squibb, Bristol-Myers, Eli Lilly and several others—built comfortable offices and air-conditioned depots, surrounded them with well-watered lawns landscaped with trees along the country's main highways. Sheraton and Westin Hotels build high-rise hotels in the capital with direct dialling international telephones.

And yet, somehow something had gone wrong. The vast majority of the population, the campesinos, were still living on tortillas and black bean mush. Indian toddlers had developed new forms of malnutrition as their mothers began feeding them Coca-Cola instead of milk. And then of course there were the killings. Private death squads with bizarre ritualistic names such as "The White Hand" and "The Secret Anti-communist Army" claimed responsibility for hundreds of assassinations in the name of God, the state and Western civilisation. The army killed many more. And they weren't nice about it. Amnesty International's dossier on Guatemala read like a diary of a charnel house. It spoke of secret cemeteries, mass graves, of old people and children "shot, hacked and bashed to death."

The day I left Guatemala I had two calls to make. The first was to President Lucas' offices where his private secretary, an urbane officer, immaculately dressed and manicured, explained to me in an ornate ante-room that like Ireland, or England or anywhere, Guatemala too had its own level of violence and criminality. "You shouldn't over-exaggerate these things," he said. "And what about the Yorkshire Ripper? Doesn't every country have its own level of violence?" There seemed little point in drawing finer distinctions with him.

"You are here," he set forth. "You can see there is freedom in every sense, freedom of expression, to work, to travel . . ."

And Amnesty? As far as he was concerned it was part of an international communist conspiracy. "They're trying to destroy Guatemala's tourist industry." So that was it, the killings and the disappearances were make believe. He was paid to lie with a smile.

The other visit was to a chicken shack in a refugee camp on the outskirts of the city. There it was possible to taste Guatemala's "freedom in every sense". Inside, a campesino waited, shivering. He had just run away from a village near Basic's oil wells. He was afraid. "They came for me twice," he said. "The first time I was out in the fields and I saw them, about 20 of them, so I hid. The second time I was hiding under the corn. My wife knew. She said, 'They have come to kill you'."

"They" was an army patrol. His crime was to have talked of setting up a cooperative among the Indian homesteaders in the jungle.

"I have six children. My wife said, 'You can't let them take you. What do we do if something happens to you?' So we left early in the morning and walked all day and night to the town where we could get a bus."

The man was relatively safe in that chicken shack on the outskirts of the capital. But in his mind he was back in the jungle near the oil wells. And he was still shaking, afraid.

★ ★ ★

Villagrán Kramer soon after fled Guatemala to Washington where he found work with the World Bank. President Lucas was re-elected in March 1982. Within a fortnight he was overthrown by young officers who installed a three-man junta led by General Efraín Ríos Montt. They suspended the constitution, closed the legislature and announced rule by decree. General Ríos Montt was said to be a member of a born-again American Gospel Outreach of Eureka, California. He soon dropped his two colleagues and declared himself president. Immediately reports increased of Catholic priests and union leaders murdered, campesino home-steaders tortured and killed, their shacks burned, their children mutilated—all part of a born-again crusade keeping communism and the anti-christ at bay. Ríos Montt was then overthrown by yet another general, Mejía Victores. The killing continues.

In the 16th century Spanish conquistadors were required by Spanish law to read out official decrees, called "Requerimientos", to the Indians informing them of their obligations to the Spanish crown and the true church before savaging them as infidels and laying waste to their villages. The "Requerimientos" were written and read in Spanish, which meant nothing to the Indians of course. But at least the Spanish horesemen observed some, albeit rudimen-tary, proprieties. Generals Lucas, Ríos Montt and their col-leagues have dispensed with such niceties. They also kill priests.

According to Amnesty International, political murder in Guatemala reached a staggering 850 people a month, most of them summarily executed by the army. President Jimmy Carter knew enough about the Guatemalan regime to ban arms sales to it. Ronald Reagan knows enough about Guatemala to have seen those shipments resumed.

★ ★ ★

Yet Basic Resources were not an enormous success. The EGP guerrillas have had the infuriating habit of raiding the wellheads, ambushing troops on patrol and trying to cut the pipeline. They also successfully kidnapped and then held for a considerable ransom the son of one of Basic Resources' Guatemalan associates.

Basic Resources had larger problems still, of a different sort. As Sir James' biographer Geoffrey Wansell deftly put it, "Guatemala has not been quite the success he had hoped . . . but it had taught him a lesson." It certainly did.

Shortly after I left, Basic's directors were supposed to have met in Guatemala City, in early December 1979, for a gala pipeline opening. Instead they found themselves deep in renewed negotiations with the government over just how much commission it was going to be paid as well as how much oil was going to be pumped. The government had suddenly become keen to ensure that Basic didn't intend rapidly to suck the existing wells dry, run off with the money and scupper plans to explore the concession further.

John Addey put a brave face on this last minute fit of national resource husbandry from Guatemala's president. But the chances for quick and continued profits for Basic's shareholders had suffered a setback. The Guatemalan government would from then on have considerable control over the oil flow, which when compared with Basic's originally published expectations was more of a trickle. On the other hand, Basic had on its hands a pipeline costing twice the original estimate. Several of Basic's major shareholders abandoned the company, now tied and bound by the Guatemalan government. The "pioneering spirit" was a thing of the past. By early 1982 Basic's shares were on the floor, at one-third the price they had been just over a year before.

Basic Resources had run into problems. The company is still operating in Guatemala, though it has been plagued by more government demands, guerrilla attacks and legal action. Sir James had staunchly defended the Guatemalan regime. And yet Lucas García and his cronies seemed strongly unappreciative. They ambushed Basic Resources, once the important initial investment had been made and the oil was on stream. The people fighting against Lucas García and Guatemala's bloodthirsty little military gang could have told the company to expect that. Instead, Basic Resources built the generals their very own pipeline.

9
Hong Kong:
The Boat People

ON THE TENTH floor above a multistorey car park overlooking Hong Kong harbour is an office which for a few months in 1979 was extremely busy. And secret. The only entrance was through double-locked doors beyond the elevator. The only people allowed in were those showing special passes. On the walls of the room were the photographs of 20 ships. Below them were dossiers of the ships' histories, their last sightings and their probable destinations. There was only one problem. Many of those ships were said to have been previously sunk, abandoned, stove in, disappeared without a trace in the South China Sea.

Hundreds of thousands of pounds in compensation had been demanded of Lloyds underwriters by the supposed owners, trying to collect massive indemnities for "lost cargoes" in a rash of insurance frauds. Yet now some of the same ships, miraculously afloat again, their names painted out or re-registered through the Panamanian Consulate in Hong Kong, were suspected of being used to carry refugees from Vietnam. These were the "boat people", collected from anchorages off Vung Tau, Ho Chi Minh City's, and what had been Saigon's, main port, and ferried to the supposed safety of Hong Kong, Singapore and Indonesia. It was a racket in human cargoes run by well-heeled Hong Kong businessmen and Kuomintang officers from Taiwan. At least four criminal syndicates were thought to be involved. It was a racket the British government was at pains to stop.

The man running the car park headquarters was Captain Tim Frawley, officially of the Hong Kong Marine Criminal Investigation Department. It was widely believed that his operation was steered by MI6, the British secret service. Through radio telephones, secret "hot lines" and telex he was in constant contact with Royal Navy spotter planes, the Hong Kong police, the Governor's office and the Foreign Office in London. It was, in effect, a covert side to Lord Carrington's approach to the refugees.

The Foreign Secretary had flown to Hong Kong on 29 June. Refugees were then landing in the colony at a rate of over 1,000 a day. "I don't think that anybody who saw what I saw today could fail to have it brought home very dramatically to them the human misery involved in what is happening to the Vietnam refugees," he said. Then came the punch. "Over the years we have taken a very large number of migrants," Carrington explained. "There does come a moment when a country must have some regard for the social conditions and how much it can do. Given that, we obviously have to consider how much we can do . . ." The answer, of course, was very little in the face of a crisis perpetrated by a country, Vietnam, for which the Foreign Office had very little sympathy, and organised by Asian gangsters who had already been trying to defraud one of the City of London's most venerable institutions and now seemed bent on dumping boatloads of human flotsam on Hong Kong's already overcrowded shores.

Already three large ships had slipped into Hong Kong harbour or run aground on the outlying islands, having steamed past the naval patrols, on some their tillers and throttles tied down on collision course, their crews having abandoned them, leaving the terrified refugees on board to the mercies of the rocks and Hong Kong authorities. The rusting hull of the "Sen On" lay beached on an outlying island. She arrived on 26 May, carrying some 1,433 hungry and emaciated refugees, mostly Vietnamese Chinese. After 23 days at sea they were incarcerated in a makeshift refugee camp at the previously abandoned Kai Tak North airbase.

The "Huey Fong" lay, another dilapidated shell, in Hong Kong harbour, permission having finally been given to disembark 3,318 refugees after having waited three weeks at anchor. On 29 June, Hong Kong citizens were able to watch on television police unloading human cargo from the "Skyluck", ferrying them in small launches, then lifting them ashore to climb the steep rocky path on Lamma Island to waiting buses to be driven to huts behind barbed wire fences in Chi Ma Wan prison camp. For 142 days the 3,500-ton, Panamanian-registered "Skyluck" had sat at anchor in Hong Kong waters, the authorities unwilling and unprepared to allow the 2,651 passengers to disembark. Sanitation on board had become unspeakably inadequate. The refugees had had to sleep in their own slops. The ship had become a stinking, floating sewer—a supposed deterrent to other refugee boats heading for Hong Kong. Rations had been ferried out daily by the Hong Kong police. There had been several riots on board. Why hadn't the refugees been allowed ashore sooner? "We don't want too many people to think they can come here too easily," a British superintendent in the Hong Kong police told the press. It was a considered if callous reply. Only a few people beyond the police and Frawley's group knew what potentially lay in store.

Over half a dozen other ships had been spotted or were believed to be waiting off Vung Tau to collect refugees. In all likelihood they would head for Hong Kong. The reason was simple. Off Thailand, boat people were often attacked by pirates, the women raped, the men thrown overboard, their boats looted and sunk. In Malaysia they were being dragged back out to sea or quarantined on Pulau Bidong, a hopelessly overcrowded, fetid 30 acre island. Malaysia's Deputy Prime Minister told newsmen that boat people in his country's territorial waters would "be shot on sight". He then claimed to have been misquoted. "If they try sinking their boats they will not be rescued," he also said; "they will drown." The Indonesian authorities interdicted boats attempting to land, turned them around and sent them back to open sea with enough food and water for three days. In Singapore there were reports of harbour police ramming the refugee boats then failing to fish out those who were flung overboard.

In Malaysia also lay the "Southern Cross", a small 850-ton Honduran-registered freighter which had brought out 1,200 refugees who now sat, dumped, in Indonesian detention camps. The entrepreneur behind the voyage, Mr. Tay Kheng Hong, was have alleged to have made over half a million dollars. He was now firmly behind bars in a Malaysian gaol. His second in command was also under arrest, languishing in solitary confinement in Singapore's Queenstown Prison. For both the ferrymen and their cargoes it seemed most sensible to steer a course for Hong Kong. It was Frawley's unit's task to dissuade them from doing so.

★ ★ ★

Frawley gave a brief interview on BBC's *Panorama* programme. "We receive intelligence reports from various sources—and action is taken on receipt of information to pre-empt vessels putting to sea," he said. "We are inviting people to come and see us, pointing out to them the error of their ways, advising them of the penalties . . ." There was little more. The rest of the Western press, almost to the man, was caught up in the media bean feast.

"Cast adrift," read the *Sun*. "Fury as Malaysia tows 2500 boat people out to sea . . ." "The plight of these tragic refugees, driven from their country by racist warlords is stirring the conscience of the world." "The Death Voyage Begins," screamed the *Daily Mail*. "Children left to perish at sea," read the *Daily Express*.

Suddenly there were victims in South-East Asia who could

immediately be felt for, free of the ideological complications of having been napalmed by American jets, unfettered by intellectual complexities such as coming from a country whose capital readers couldn't pronounce, let alone spell. Untrammelled by political doubts, Western journalists began churning out heart-rending, desperately tragic stories. No one doubted that they were true. Yet as anyone who has ever been in real need knows, the bestower always decides upon whom their beneficence is to fall. More crudely put, nobody seems to like a good victim more than some editors if the victims confirm their views.

"The new [Vietnamese] regime's programme of revolution is so evil, so inhumanely cruel, that it is inconceivable for the younger generations of the Western world," wrote the *Daily Mail's* all-knowing pundit. "Older people who can recall the fear-ridden days of Nazi Germany when the S.S. called in the night to take a father away from his family may begin to understand the creeping terror that has gripped the lives of the Vietnamese."

"Jimmy Carter . . . should say to the Soviet Boss: Vietnam is YOUR ally. YOU supply them with weapons," argued the *Sun's* editorial picking up on the theme. "PUBLICLY tell them to end their atrocities."

It was almost as if the Vietnam War had never been fought, as if all the wrenching self-doubt that war had engendered had been misplaced, as if the United States, General Westmoreland, Lyndon Johnson, Henry Kissinger and their friends and allies had been vindicated. "Decency cries out for every country to do what it can. But humanitarianism is not enough. The time has come for the opinion of mankind to focus on the principal source of the misery: the government of Vietnam." So wrote Anthony Lewis, a bell-wether of American liberalism, in the *New York Times*.

Yet to anyone reporting on the boat people tragedy, two quite different aspects of the affair should have been glaringly apparent. Whatever the boat people's true predicament may have been, and it was awful, they were mere pawns, even if dramatic pawns, in a megalithic ideological brawl in which journalists themselves, wittingly or unwittingly, were also unmistakably involved. Inevitably the boat people were to be bruised. It was also obvious that whatever good intentions so-called sympathetic governments professed, there was to be little forthcoming for the refugees in terms of such simple necessities as clothing, a place to rest and food.

British policy was twofold: keep as many refugees as possible away from the Crown Colony, and give Margaret Thatcher and Lord Carrington their first major foreign policy victory—a boycott of Vietnam in the name of humanitarian anti-communism. The publicity could prove as considerable as that which Jimmy Carter had attracted with his human rights campaign. We were told that Hong Kong press statements about the refugees were first cleared in Whitehall.

It wasn't difficult to find the refugees in Hong Kong. "Just go to the government godowns on Canton Road across the harbour in the Kowloon docks," we were told. "They'll be there." And they were. Ramshackle junks and fishing smacks crowded, bumping against each other, scraping against the cement of the quay. For their human ballast the voyage was over. They had arrived during the night. And they were tired. On average it was three weeks of days and nights on the open sea from Vietnam to Hong Kong for those who set out in open boats, most of them never having put to sea before in their lives.

Children were lying under crude awnings on the decks; a few scrambled among cooking pots, sacks of rice and bundles of worn clothes. Old women squatted over tin can stoves. The boats were stacked with cane baskets and crude mattresses held on with chicken wire. Men huddled beside the masts or dozed. Many of them just gazed, exhausted almost beyond endurance, looking like people driven over the edge of every world they had ever known.

Behind the skein of ripped sails, bleached masts and frayed riggings lay the harbour with its workaday ferries, oil tankers and merchant ships, some of them stoking up in the morning sun. Beyond them the shimmering white skyscrapers, the pure milky opalescence of Hong Kong's f sweatshop profits and the property boom.

Back on the quay some of the young refugees, several of them in tattered green Vietnamese army uniforms, strained to get ashore. Infants squatted naked while their mothers doused them with buckets of water. As the morning wore on families began to find their bearings between the water taps and the boats, scavenging for bits of food and shreds of news about neighbours and relatives who might have made it to Hong Kong. Soon that was stopped.

The Hong Kong police, in stiff khaki shorts and with regulation swagger sticks, were to be the refugees' first instructors into the Crown Colony's mores. First the refugees had to stand in a line. Then they were told to squat. Which they did, patiently, quietly, waiting like a row of waddling ducks for the next command. The policemen paraded along the line, towering above the day's batch of new charges, occasionally prodding them, shooing away stray children, throwing away pans, cooking utensils and bed clothing the refugees hugged dearly having brought them with them,

151

keeping everyone and everything under tight control. Heads were counted from the front of the queue, and then again in reverse. Off they were marched to be registered and to be told that under no circumstances should they take it upon themselves to try and get out.

Fifty yards away beyond a high wall and a string of barbed wire were the Kowloon streets, full of traffic, pedestrians, people jumping out of the way of buses, shopping, hurrying home—that tantalising world of which the refugees had begun to dream, of which they had even caught glimpses, yet which for them was out of bounds.

Once registered, the refugees were decamped into a cavernous customs shed to lie on the floor or in roughly rigged hammocks and wait patiently for communal meals. The doctors were French volunteers and young interns from Hong Kong hospitals.

"How's it going?" we asked.

"Sort of okay," came the reply.

"What does that mean?"

"We can treat the cuts and open wounds. But nearly all the children have dysentery. The old ones are suffering from exposure and malnutrition. We have some penicillin, but it's not enough . . ."

They catalogued the empty medicine chests. I wasn't really listening. One expects as much in places like Chad, Bangladesh or El Salvador. To find the same neglect in Hong Kong seemed frankly obscene. The colony's government could certainly afford a few crates of medicines. Where were they?

★ ★ ★

23 March, 1978. The People's Committee of Ho Chi Minh City decreed: "Bourgeois tradesmen who engage in speculation, deal in the black market and hoard goods and cash have monopolised the economy and the market, increased commodity prices and disrupted the collective purchasing operations of the state, causing confusion in the market and illegally enriching themselves . . ." Such had been the official beginning of the boat people's exodus. In all there were said to be well over a million ethnic Chinese living in Vietnam, many of them merchants. Private trade was abolished in Ho Chi Minh City, shortly afterwards throughout Vietnam. All old South Vietnamese bank notes were recalled and exchanged. Chinese families were shifted from their shops to farms in the countryside. Some committed suicide. Others fled across the border to China. Others took to boats on the open sea.

On 17 February 1979, some 200,000 Chinese troops invaded Vietnam, driving columns up to 15 miles into Vietnam along

152

much of the 450-mile-long border, destroying ricefields and power stations before withdrawing two months later as suddenly as they came. "We must teach the Vietnamese another lesson," Mr Deng Xiaoping, China's Deputy Premier, told Dr Kurt Waldheim, Secretary General of the United Nations. But why a lesson? Because in neighbouring Kampuchea "the Vietnamese aggressors, aided and abetted by Soviet social-imperialists" had put in power "a handful of shameless traitors and national scum," the Chinese government announced. The Chinese people would "do their utmost to support and aid the Kampuchean people in every way." Such were the views of the great patrician mandarins of Beijing.

Such also is the newspeak of South-East Asia, where national chauvinism is dressed up as revolutionary progress, naked ethnocentrism as ideological purity and moderation as implacable renegadism. Not surprisingly it sounded strangely foreign to differently attuned Western ears used more to phrases such as "the defence of enterprise", "the right to prosperity", "the security of democracy"—those altogether softer cadences, the mellowed self-assurances and finer hypocrisies of a more cushioned world.

Nonetheless the newspeak made crude sense. If the Chinese had given the Vietnamese a bloody nose, then what seemed more logical than for the Vietnamese to retaliate? The Vietnamese economy was in near ruins. The Chinese government had unilaterally and suddenly cut off all aid the year before as Vietnam joined Comecon and signed a security pact with the Soviet Union. The Chinese merchants, particularly those in the Cholon district of Ho Chi Minh City, whose businesses had blossomed with the GI-fed consumer boom of the Vietnam War, were now refusing to relinquish their wealth despite orders to do so. And certainly at least some of the ethnic Chinese living in the invaded border areas had acted as spies.

If China was to persist in sniping at Vietnam from all quarters, then what could be more just, appropriate and easier in the South-East Asia imbroglio than to let the Chinese and their new-found allies look after their own? So what if it meant throwing whole communities into the sea? A policy which had originally been introduced to cope with Vietnam's harsh economic problems soon became irredeemably cynical. It was also nakedly extortionist. Many of the boat people had to pay 12 taels of gold, worth approximately £2,000, to obtain what was ironically called an exit permit.

Yet the question lingered on as to whether the whole tragedy could have been avoided. How much, in effect, had the Vietnamese government acted under duress? To businessmen and governments

in Thailand, Malaysia, the Philippines, Singapore and Indonesia—
members of the ASEAN security pact—the Vietnamese posed an
awesome threat. "Each junkload of men, women and children sent
to our shores is a bomb to destabilise, disrupt and cause turmoil
and dissension in ASEAN states," ranted Mr. Sinnathamby
Rajarathnam, Singapore's Foreign Minister.

The ASEAN countries were deeply in hock to Western banks,
dependent on corrupt puppet armies, and awash with peasants
driven into the cities looking for work and a modicum of justice.
By comparison Vietnam, even if economically weak, appeared
politically united, disciplined and strong. It was also the proud
possessor of some $5,000 million worth of American arms
including over a million and a half rifles, as well as jet fighters,
helicopters and tanks left in working order, well oiled and greased
from the morning of 30 April 1975, when the Viet Cong boldly
marched into Saigon. Then too, there were over 100,000
Vietnamese troops in Kampuchea, having just deposed the
butchering cadres of Pol Pot's regime in an Asian blitzkrieg which
drove the Khmer Rouge into exile, allowed ordinary Kampucheans
to return to their homes and some semblance of normality, and
installed a friendly Kampuchean government under Heng Samrin.

On the other hand, from Hanoi it looked as if the "Free World"
was ganging up on them, as if there had never really been a peace
following the war. Shortly before the Chinese invaded Vietnam,
the United States and China established full diplomatic relations.
Zbigniew Brzezinski, President Carter's National Security Adviser,
had flown to Beijing, setting the tone of the new accord in his
banquet speech. "Only those aspiring to dominate others have any
reason to fear further development of US-Chinese relations," he
said. Off the record he called the Soviets "barbarians" and spoke
ominously of the Vietnamese to an even incredulous American
press. Visits by other high ranking US officials followed. The
American Congress passed laws compelling American delegates to
vote against international agency loans to Vietnam, including
those from the World Bank and the United Nations. There was also
no sign that the US would pay war reparations, once promised by
Richard Nixon. The combination spelled the end of the tenuous
Vietnamese-American rapprochement. It was also said to have
proved the personal undoing of Vietnam's more liberal-minded
ministers who had been counselling their more hardline colleagues
that the country's salvation lay in securing such loans and
pursuing a conciliatory policy towards neighbouring states.

The sticking point though was Kampuchea. From American
supported refugee camps just over the Thai border, Pol Pot's

Khmer Rouge mounted raids against Heng Samrin's troops. It was in ostensible support of them that China levelled the crops and blew up irrigation dams, schools and hospitals and systematically razed entire towns in northern Vietnam. The British and Americans had a number of options. They could have kept out of what was in many respects a timeless regional feud. They could have offered to mediate. Instead they refused to recognise Heng Samrin's government as Kampuchea's legitimate representative in the United Nations.

The policy was remarkably simplistic and crude. Most people who read newspapers knew that it was Pol Pot who, upon liberating Kampuchea's capital, Phnom Penh, on 17 April 1975, drove the city's entire population into the countryside. Those who couldn't or didn't work were summarily murdered, their heads staved in with hammers and shovels; many had their arms ripped off, their testicles crushed. Evidence that Kampucheans were being butchered in staggering numbers by their Khmer Rouge brothers and sisters was first reported in horrific detail by a French priest, François Ponchaud. "The smile of the leper-kings has frozen into a grimace of death," he wrote in his book, *Cambodia Year Zero*. The United Nations Human Rights Commission put the figure at between 500,000 and a million dead. The Vietnamese government, having surveyed the evidence after driving Pol Pot out, say that up to two million people may have died or been murdered.

Yet now both Atlantic allies were effectively sustaining the claim of Asia's number one mass murderer, the man who boasted of his "politics of blood", as the legitimate heir to Kampuchea's United Nations chair, even though he was hiding in exile in a refugee camp. Within the EEC, Britain argued to have much needed food aid for Vietnam and Kampuchea stalled, and then stopped. Was it surprising that the Vietnamese decided to loose half a million anxious, hungry, stateless persons on to the glib complacencies and strident self-assurances of its neighbouring pro-Western states?

★ ★ ★

Sir Murray MacLehose, Hong Kong's Governor, was all too familiar with the endless tangles of South-East Asian politics. He also had a fine sense of what was required of him and what his colony's residents would tolerate. He had been governor for almost eight years, during which he had kept the colony among the biggest money spinners in the world. Whatever may have been his idiosyncrasies, he was not a man content to be wise after the event.

As the boat people arrived in Hong Kong, MacLehose jumped a

plane to London and Washington to argue for a concerted resettlement and relief programme. "The cause of the furore is the Vietnamese Government," he wrote in the *Daily Telegraph*. "It is clear that a decision has been taken to remove ethnic Chinese from the normal life of Vietnam." He then turned to his main theme.

> Hong Kong has so many other problems to deal with that it is becoming increasingly frustrated by the flood of Vietnamese arriving daily in small boats. As in other East Asian communities anxiety and tension are mounting. As we see the numbers piling up and potential host countries offering no hope of adequate relief, it is not surprising that humanity is inclined to snap, that the prospect of this invasion going on is causing countries to drive the refugees even to their death.

The argument found favour among even some of the colony's more liberal, socially-conscious residents. "There are families living on boats in the harbour who have been waiting for flats for years," an experienced social worker renowned for her unstinting work among the slum dwellers lectured us indignantly. "Why should the refugees be given preference? We have enough problems here. We have our hands full."

No doubt that was true. Yet to argue that the refugees were little more than scroungers poaching the colony's welfare benefits, one had to take a profoundly magnanimous view of what in Hong Kong passed for social justice. Was there really a possibility of refugees depriving Chinese families living in the city's squalid catacomb of high-rise slums, working all day in poor light for legendary low pay, of government-furnished flats and play schools? I think not. Such amenities hardly existed. It seemed much more likely that the refugees' need for homes, hospital treatment and decent diets served dramatically to highlight just how inadequate Hong Kong's existing services were.

Sir Murray was putting the government's view. Also disturbing to him, besides the boatloads of exhausted Vietnamese straggling into Hong Kong harbour where they could easily be rounded up and detained, was the prospect of hordes of disenchanted Chinese taking advantage of the crisis to slip into Hong Kong undetected.

It was a tricky business. There were estimated to be up to a quarter of a million illegal or unregistered Chinese already living in the colony, and over 15,000 more arriving every month. The British lease to the colony had nearly 20 years to run before it would be handed back to the Chinese in 1997. In the meantime not only did civil peace have to be maintained, the Chinese government had to be placated.

Mao was dead and China's new leaders were making little pretence any longer of ruling a purely communist state. Ostensibly there was little reason why anyone should want to run away from the Oriental paradise. Yet almost every morning Royal Navy patrol boats fished several Chinese would-be escapees out of Mirs and Deep Bays, either exhausted from swimming through the night or already drowned. Army and police patrols also collected the dead bodies off the coral and oyster beds where they had fallen, cut to ribbons and bled to death.

The survivors were rounded up, their hands tied, and handed back to the Chinese at the border. More than 40,000 had been returned since the beginning of 1979. Even so, over 100,000 illegal immigrants were going to make it safely to downtown Kowloon that year to disappear into the slums, near slave-labour for the cheap goods workshops. By mid June, in addition to the 2,500 British troops previously stationed in Hong Kong, two companies of the 10th Gurkha Regiment were dispatched to man the border along with 600 Argyll and Sutherland Highlanders, "Mad Mitch's" men, the troops who had distinguished themselves for ferocity in the Crater in Aden in 1967.

★ ★ ★

Kai Tek North is an old Royal Air Force base a few miles from Hong Kong's international airport, beyond the Hidden City, the ancient Chinese settlement buried deep in the chaotic heart of Kowloon. It's surrounded by high barbed wire fences. Outside small groups of people anxiously looked in, occasionally throwing packages, cigarettes and messages over the fence. Within the perimeter some 13,000 refugees were allowed to walk about. But not to talk to strangers. And not to receive gifts. Some squatted in the shade of the huts, watching, waiting. Others shuffled in the dust. Others were being instructed in how to fold blankets.

"Just one word of caution. If they get nasty, you know, a riot, don't stick around. Just head for the gate. They don't know you're not one of us. And, well, journalists held hostage by refugees . . . it wouldn't do us any good."

A sandy-haired English ex-policeman had just taken my colleague Michael Beckman and I through the police cordon. As a Hong Kong Government Information Service official, it was his job to show journalists around the refugee camps. Soon we were inside the small office used by the camp guards. We were sat on some wooden chairs square in the middle of the room. We were given Coca-Cola. The guards, most of them ex-British policemen, hung about. It wasn't that they didn't trust us, their commander explained. It was just that it was highly unusual to allow refugees to talk to journalists. We might get the wrong impression of camp life. "They don't understand some of the things we are doing for them," he said. Having gone so far as to allow us access, the commander and the ex-policeman now needed some reassurance that we agreed with them.

It wasn't forthcoming on our part. The man with whom we wanted to talk, Mr. Le Van Trang, had been tossed a packet of cigarettes over the fence. Then a guard took the pack, ripped off Mr. Trang's glasses and crushed them with his boot, or so Mr. Trang had told us previously. Mr. Trang had been an English teacher at Saigon's Phu Tho University. He was an educated man who liked and needed to read. Now he couldn't.

But Mr. Trang was patient. He was shuffled into the office wearing crude wooden sandals. "The guards took my shoes," he said. Perhaps we could bring him some magazines. Friends could read them. "You see," he said, "we really have little idea of what's going on outside, of what people are saying is going to happen to us." Mr. Trang then told us about his voyage from Ho Chi Minh City. He was to explain a good deal of the boat people racket that Captain Frawley and his colleagues were at pains to stop.

Le Van Trang's family lived in what had been South Vietnam, were Christian, and while they didn't support the Deng regime, weren't Viet Cong sympathisers either. He was the bright son and went to college. Until three months ago he, his wife and five children lived in Ho Chi Minh City where he taught. They were glad the war was over. Mr. Trang was now 41 years old.

The trouble had begun the year before. He was earning $15 a month from his teaching and as an educated man had no privileges to obtain rice at the government's cheap rate. The family were near starving and his brother, previously a lieutenant in the South Vietnamese army, couldn't get a job. When the local commissar announced that ethnic Chinese were to be allowed to leave, Mr. Trang decided to change his name, pose as an ethnic Chinese, and try to emigrate. His wife and three of his children escaped successfully with his brother to Indonesia. Now he and his two remaining children plotted their departure. But there were fees to be paid, formalities, no matter how ad hoc and dubious, which had to be observed.

What had happened? We knew that Le Van Trang had arrived with some 1,400 other refugees in Hong Kong on 26 May aboard a racketeer ship, the *Seng Cheong*, now known as the *Sen On*, a 160-foot, 387-ton Panamanian-registered freighter which steamed up and on to the beach of one of Hong Kong's outlying islands to avoid being quarantined. We also knew that in the same detention camp were nine "organisers", once wealthy Chinese businessmen from Saigon who had each agreed to recruit 200 people for the *Sen On* at a price of 15 taels of gold (approximately £2,500) for each adult, half that for each child.

Mr. Trang sat quietly. Then he handed us several small sheets of "Coca-Cola" headed notepaper covered with cramped writing in pencil. It began: "A premeditated attempt to murder 1,400 Vietnamese refugees."

On 20 April, Le Van Trang left the school near Ho Chi Minh City where he taught and went to the home of Madam Su in Bien Hoa, 30 kilometres away. Mme Su had been married to the regional chief of the South Vietnamese police. As he was put in a re-education camp after the war, Mme Su had remarried the new Deputy Chief of Public Security in the same province. "Mme Su, she is a very influential woman," Mr. Trang said. To his surprise, the night he went to see her several other families were there also. and they were told the same story.

Deposit the tax with Mme Su and she would see that it was paid to the appropriate authorities and that transport to Hong Kong was arranged. It was the beginning of an extortion scheme which was to milk the refugees for everything they were worth, down to the gold fillings in their teeth. "She told us that 13 taels would get us exit visas from the Vietnamese government, and two taels would get us passage on a ship that would wait off the harbour at Vung Tau." Mr. Trang paid, as did 1,400 others, netting Mme Su and others like her, the Vietnamese government and the boat racketeers, over £3 million in gold.

On the night of 23 April, Mr. Trang and his two children assembled in their town to be picked up by a bus which took them to a small wharf. "But it was dark," Mr. Trang explained. "I don't understand why we were treated that way. There were Vietnamese troops there, pushing us along. We couldn't all get into one boat, we had to leave things behind. They told us there would be plenty of food on board." They were then ferried out to the *Sen On*, a rusting cargo ship bought a month earlier by a Macao-based syndicate for a mere £12,500.

"When we got on board the crew took our bundles from us. They said we wouldn't need them. Then I knew something was wrong. There was not enough room for us to lie down." So the refugees would have to sit in their own vomit and excrement, even the children. The ship departed. And arguments began.

"Mr. Lee, the ship's boss, he was very nice, a decent dresser, always calm," Mr. Trang told us. "The first day we had food. The second day he gave us water and rice soup. But after that . . . He summoned the passengers and said the communists had cheated him, they didn't pay all the gold, only 2,000 taels, not the 2,600 he had been promised. So he said we would have to pay from now on. He stopped the ship's engines."

Mr. Trang was dumbfounded and shocked. The crew had turned pirate on their own ship. "They came and took everything, bracelets, earrings, they went through our clothes. We had to pay, 200 taels in all for some bags of ready-to-eat noodles and water mixed with oil. I paid one tael and two rings. I had to feed the children around me. I just drank some water, and a few noodles. I was so exhausted . . ."

After five days the ship had almost no water. The hygiene was appalling. There were slops all over the deck. Fortunately the ship ran aground on the Chinese island of Hai-Nan. Mr. Trang believes that Mr. Lee wanted to abandon them there.

"Mr. Lee, he and the crew tried to escape. But the Chinese detained them. The people were very kind. They brought us sweet potatoes, food and water." After nearly a month, the ship repaired, and Mr. Lee some 100 taels poorer having had to pay for the job, the *Sen On* set off again for Hong Kong.

On 25 May the *Sen On* was off Macao, Portugal's vestigial peninsular colony 20 miles from Hong Kong. The engines were stopped. A small fishing boat came alongside and Mr. Lee got into it. He was carrying a heavy briefcase and a gun. "It must have been our jewellery and gold. The boat headed towards Macao. We never saw him again." That night the crew set the tiller and the engines on a crash course for Hong Kong. Several miles out they too left the ship in a small boat. At noon the next day the *Sen On* with its abandoned cargo beached on one of the colony's islands. For the first time in over a month Mr. Trang says he felt relieved. From there he and his family and most of the other refugees were taken to Kai Tak North detention camp.

As he talked Mr. Trang became noticeably anxious. He began talking very quietly and insistently. "Please, now come to my hut and see. Three hundred people in there. You see my beard. I had a razor. They confiscated it. They broke my glasses . . ." The English ex-policeman, our man from the Hong Kong government press office, intervened.

"Look everything is being done for you Mr. Trang," the government press officer said. "You know that."

Mr. Trang looked him in the eye. "Sir, the air isn't free here," he said. "This is a prison."

This time the press officer answered very slowly and deliberately.

"Be thankful for your freedom," he said. "Be thankful for your freedom from communism."

Mike and I were escorted out. Mr. Trang and other refugees had tried to contact relatives in the United States and elsewhere, but largely to no avail. They didn't know where they were going next. They had volunteered to get jobs and work in Hong Kong but these had been refused. Would we buy some magazines for Mr. Trang? We'd see what we could do. Some of the other refugees gave us letters which we smuggled out. Some were to addresses in France from where they would be posted back into Vietnam, to let relatives and neighbours know they were safe. Others were to the United States. To post them was easy. It proved much more difficult to discover where the gold from the *Sen On* had gone.

★ ★ ★

Macao is six square miles, a quarter of a million inhabitants, an old fort, several banks and one casino. The syndicate which owns the casino more or less controls Macao. The syndicate's managing director is Stanley Ho. His sister, brother and brother-in-law are also on the board. The family was said to be the wealthiest in the colony. A visitor to Macao, on stepping off Stanley Ho's hydrofoil from Hong Kong across the bay, passes first some jerry-built tin shacks where soft drinks and tea are sold. Beyond them are more shacks where most of the colony's families live. It's a tropical slum. The city centre is built of crumbling Portuguese colonial stucco. Portuguese troops stationed there enjoy the climate, the rest and their leave in Hong Kong. Promotion prospects are minimal. On weekends the island is flooded with Hong Kong residents bent on throwing their money away on Mr. Ho's roulette and blackjack tables, betting wildly on exotic Chinese games. Gambling is illegal in the Crown Colony. Macao, as Nassau is to Miami, is Hong Kong's offshore and very makeshift Monte Carlo.

Could the Portuguese commander help us in our search for the man with the sack of gold? He wanted to. He was a young officer, educated, intelligent, a man who seemed to have played a respectably progressive role in the 1974 Portuguese revolution. But alas, the commander had few men at his disposal, and there were too many suspicious boats skipping in and out of the harbour. The one we mentioned, yes, he had heard some talk about it. But, again, these sorts of things are so difficult to prove.

We drank tea as he showed us a topographical map of the colony. So many inlets, so many places to hide. Perhaps, we asked, he had heard that William Ho had been involved, that he owned the *Sen On*? Yes, he had heard. And Stanley Ho? Yes, some people said

Stanley was his father. But it wasn't true. Well, where could William Ho be found? At the Banco Oriental, where the ubiquitous Ho family, it seemed, had an interest as well. We thanked the commander for his help. He apologised with considerable charm, saying something to the effect that given the circumstances in Macao there was little he could do.

The Hong Kong police wanted William Ho. They wanted to talk to him about that briefcase of gold, and about the "financing" of a number of the other boat people ships. They were sure he was one of the key men in the refugee extortion racket. But their jurisdiction didn't extend to Macao, and William Ho was avoiding Hong Kong. The young man was safe in his family's colony. Nonetheless he was a bit taken aback when we walked into his office unannounced.

"Please sit down," he finally said. We did. He picked up a very large paper tissue from a box on his desk and with a little flourish began pampering his nose.

"I feel so ill," he said.

We were sorry to hear that. He sniffled.

"Allergy," he said.

So we asked why he didn't go to Hong Kong and have it seen to.

Another handkerchief came out of the box and was waved in the air before landing gently under his nose. He was young and fat and very well dressed. On a shelf behind him was arranged an impressive display of tonics, aspirin, concoctions and inhalers. We told him we knew that the Hong Kong police wanted to have a chat.

"I'm not worried about that," he said and began to relax.

But it meant he was stuck in Macao.

"No. If I want to go to Europe or the United States all I have to do is take a boat up the river to Canton and fly out from there."

Nothing could be simpler, we had to agree. But what about the briefcase? It was our understanding that it contained in the region of £300,000 worth of gold, that the boat used to pick up the "agent" belonged to our young banker, and that it was well out of the tiny Portuguese colony now.

"That man, Mr. Lee, you know he causes me so much trouble. He is such a crook." William Ho repeated himself. Then he fell silent.

Alas, our interviewee was not about to admit to any wrongdoing. He would tell us, however, that it was said there was actually much less in the briefcase than the police suggested, or at least that's what he had heard. And yes, we were probably correct, it would be foolish to suppose it was still lying about Macao. And perhaps we would like to leave?

162

Another paper handkerchief was waved in the air. There was little we could do but tell him we hoped he felt better. It was all tantalising gossamer stuff, about as difficult to prove as the reality of his allergy. But then disingenuousness typified much of the boat people's experience too. Theoretically they were accorded the utmost sympathy, in keeping with Hong Kong and the West's highest ideals, whereas in fact they were getting screwed.

★ ★ ★

The Hong Kong police were nobody's fools. Working in tandem with Tim Frawley's unit they too were trying to crack the refugee gold racket. The previous 23 December, Hong Kong residents and refugees first learned what that was to involve. The *Huey Fong* had arrived just outside Hong Kong waters with 3,318 refugees on board, claiming they had been picked up drifting at sea. Conditions on board were, as usual, atrocious. Families were squatting on deck. Most of the children had developed heat rash and diarrhoea. Old people repeatedly fainted. Not surprisingly the captain asked permission to enter Hong Kong harbour. The police refused. For the next five days the refugees were left without food. Only then did helicopters begin dropping biscuits and tinned meat, a dry diet carefully calculated by Hong Kong government nutritionists to keep the refugees barely alive.

It was a ruthless approach. Ostensibly the reason behind it was that the Hong Kong police had yet to identify the man who had organised the voyage and who they believed was on board. For the next three weeks while Hong Kong police commanded by Senior Superintendent John Clemence, an ex-Scotland Yard detective, searched Kowloon rooming houses, one-room empty offices and piles of coded telexes, the refugees were confined in their own squalor.

The man Clemence was looking for was Kwok Wah-leung, a 26-year-old ethnic Chinese Hong Kong resident who used to live in Saigon. He had been contacted by a Mr. Lo Wing, a Chinese businessman who arrived in the colony on one of Hong Kong's regular but little known "mercy flights" from Ho Chi Minh City the previous 23 October. Lo Wing, who had had a profitable preserved-duck business in Vietnam while the Americans were there, had been allowed out by the Vietnamese authorities to obtain a ship for refugees. Kwok Wah-leung found him the *Huey Fong*. Shortly after, Lo Wing was sending coded cables to a colleague in Ho Chi Minh City to arrange the deal. The refugees were referred to as "ducks", the rendezvous with the *Huey Fong* as "the wedding", and the date as "the party". The price for each refugee was to be ten taels of gold plus two taels for passage.

The refugees were ferried to the *Huey Fong* anchored off Vung Tau. So too were over 4,500 taels of gold (£700,000) for the hire of the ship, about one-fifth of what the refugees had paid altogether to the Chinese organisers in Vietnam. Those who could not raise the gold arranged for relatives overseas to deposit money in designated accounts in Hong Kong banks in return for "loans" from the organisers, thereby indenturing themselves and their families in return for the voyage.

Clemence found and arrested Lo Wing. During the night of 19 January, under intense interrogation the preserved-duck merchant broke down. Kwok Wah-leung was on board the ship. The next day the *Huey Fong* was allowed to enter Hong Kong territorial waters and the refugees were given their first cooked meal. Clemence then had himself seconded as an immigration officer and as Kwok disembarked carrying £10,000 worth of gold, separated him from the other refugees to go to a different compound. After ten days Clemence called for Kwok, confronted him and obtained a confession which took four days to record.

By June the *Huey Fong*'s captain and crew were on trial in the Victoria District Court high above the older part of Hong Kong's vegetable market, listening as Kwok gave evidence in return for immunity from prosecution. The *Huey Fong* lay, a hulk, at anchor in Hong Kong's Discovery Bay. The bridge and captain's cabin had been gutted, the engine pistons lay on the engine room floor, casualties of Clemence's determination to find the gold he knew to be on the ship—and to cripple it permanently. The gold, 3,273 taels worth (about £500,000) was finally found by police divers in four sacks submerged in oil and water under the propeller shaft. But this was all the police would discover.

In Victoria Crown Court the *Huey Fong*'s crew, diminutive, worldly Chinese, sat impassively throughout the hearing. They knew they would receive heavy fines and prison sentences. They also knew it was worth their lives to stay silent.

London's insurance underwriters could look after themselves. They could cover losses and bogus claims worth many times what had been paid to owners of boats fraudulently said to have sunk in the South China Sea. There were other ships whose names had been changed several times to disguise the fact that they had been reported scrapped. Whole consignments of Japanese television sets and other electrical goods reported lost were probably now being sold in Western high street shops. Other ships were immobilised, writs nailed to their masts. These were questions of lost property. Lives were not involved.

The traffic in boat people was another matter. Not only did it presage waves of unwanted refugees. The whole scheme was nakedly exploitative, to the extent that whoever was behind it was in all likelihood skimming, in many cases, as much from the refugees as the Vietnamese government with its emigration "tax". Both the police and Frawley's group knew with whom they wanted to talk, the owners of rusting hulks with names such as the *Tung An, Tak Ou, Wing Fu, Lucky Dragon, God Pioneer,* and *Toni Maru* and others. But in many cases they couldn't. The suspects were believed to be in league with wealthy Hong Kong entrepreneurs and Kuomintang businessmen in Taiwan. But the Taiwanese government was unlikely to agree to allow such eminent personages to be interrogated, let alone charged and extradited, nor would the Hong Kong government welcome policing so intrepid as to cause scandal and diplomatic embarrassment.

And so every week the Hong Kong police had to stand by and watch as hundreds of thousands of pounds' worth of gold was transferred out of the colony by men owing allegiance to Taiwan, usually after it had been melted down and recast into anonymous bars in the laboratories of the colony's larger jewellery shops. The racket worked with such efficiency largely because it was the same network which had profited so much during the Vietnam War. Overseas Chinese merchants in Saigon then sold to GIs goods bought on credit from other overseas Chinese in Hong Kong, who in turn remitted profits back to bank accounts of Kuomintang associates in Taiwan. Such had been the business of many Chinese who fled the mainland following the communist victory under Mao.

Now they were working the syndicate in reverse, ostensibly rescuing their Vietnamese-based business partners, and in the process squeezing them for every ounce of gold they possessed. The Macao connection was possibly only a small part of a large operation. We even found refugees who had had to promise that their relatives in the United States would make donations to specified political funds; others who had pledged their own and their children's labour in Hong Kong sweat shops for the next several years in order to secure passage on one of the suspect ships.

The *Far Eastern Economic Review* carried a detailed account of a part of the boat people racket. But little was mentioned elsewhere then. Such revelations were hardly in tune with the prevailing accusatory and self-righteous anti-Vietnamese mood. There were also much more immediately heart-rending and available stories about the boat people to be written, especially about the 40,000 refugees marooned under Malaysian police guard on the island of

Pulau Bidong. Elsewhere along the Malaysian coast refugee boats were towed back to sea. So too were they in Singapore. And yet at an ASEAN meeting. Singapore's Foreign Minister Sinnathamby Rajarathnam was reported to have said, "A poor man's alternative to the gas chamber is the open sea . . . Today it is the Chinese Vietnamese . . . Why not Thailand tomorrow, and Malaysia, Singapore and others who stand in the way of Vietnam's dreams?"

Ordinary people around the world gave generously once they heard of the boat people's plight. Yet it was never made clear how much of what they gave was spent on barbed wire, instead of medicines and rice.

★ ★ ★

Occasionally, while travelling in the United States, I see the boat people and other Vietnamese refugees. Some of them are doing fine, as students on America's broad, leafy university campuses, their parents in business or working for multinational firms. Others aren't. Squatting on a rock beside the Charles River in Boston with two children sitting earnest and intent beside him, I saw a Vietnamese man, he must have been about 50, fishing with a simple line and worms for his family's dinner. He was barefoot. He was wearing rags. I had seen his picture thousands of times before during the Vietnam war. Behind him then had been helicopter gunships and GIs in armoured personnel carriers. Now it was the freeway and commuters speeding home to barbecues and TV.

The fisherman and his children squatted quietly. Across the river a huge American flag flew above the buildings of the Massachusetts Institute of Technology. From its laboratories came much of the pure and applied science of the weapons and space races, the commercial electronics boom and the Vietnam War. On each of these Hong Kong had thrived. The Free World and its technology are said to hold out so much promise. Perhaps they do. But for whom? That evening that Vietnamese refugee and his children squatting beside the Charles River were putting their trust in worms.

10
Argentina

THE RESIDENTS OF Denbigh Gardens in Richmond are a bit better off than average. Quite a bit in fact. Some are solicitors, others businessmen; a well-known international journalist lives on the street. There are plenty of trees, the homes are spacious, two-storey suburban houses well-gardened both in front and back. They are what estate agents call desirable residences in a professional neighbourhood, five minutes' walk from Richmond tube station, a few minutes' more to the nearest golf club.

One of the finer homes was owned by a man in the Foreign Office. But he had been posted overseas, so the house had been let in mid 1979. The man who now lived there was in his early thirties, with thick black hair and a moustache. He dressed well, with a marked preference for Chemise Lacoste sports shirts, Burberry raincoats and Yves St. Laurent accessories. He and his attractive wife had a young daughter who played with the neighbouring children. And they had two cars, a white Renault and a large maroon Peugeot. The Peugeot had been imported directly from the factory near Paris. It was bulletproof. The neighbours didn't know that. They knew though that the family spoke Spanish.

Most mornings Alberto Gonzalez Menotti took the tube to Victoria Station in central London. From there it was five minutes' walk to his office, 128 Vauxhall Bridge Road. There was a guard on the door. The office was that of the Argentine Naval Commission for Europe, the main purchasing agency for the Argentine Navy and Naval Air Force throughout Europe, Israel and the United Kingdom. Gonzalez was a lieutenant. He worked in the aeronautical section, buying equipment for the navy's secret intelligence service and the coast guard as well. He had an office on the second floor. Elsewhere in the building other officers purchased munitions, electronics, ships—everything needed to outfit and keep supplied with spares the country's substantial, if varied, fleet.

It was a good posting, allowing opportunities for the officers' wives to travel and shop in London, for their children to learn English, and for the men themselves to engage in a little import/export business for their own personal enrichment on the side. High quality European televisions and cars are scarce and expensive in Buenos Aires. A man who could import one for himself, tax free, and arrange similar deals for others could go far.

Purchasing on behalf of the navy was good experience as well. Ever since the coup on 24 March 1976, the navy had played a leading role in Argentina's national affairs. True, the president of the junta was then General Videla, the army's man. But then, in the last analysis the army always dominates. As they say in Argentina, the navy can steam up the River Plata and shell Buenos Aires, the air force can bomb the Presidential Palace, but the army will always control the streets.

Admiral Eduardo Emilio Massera, Gonzalez's supreme commander at the time of the coup, was believed to have tried several times to upend Videla. If so he failed. Nonetheless he managed to become extremely rich in the meantime, acting as middleman on World Cup contracts, promising to deliver substantial naval contracts to European shipyards, hobnobbing with bankers. Of one thing he made certain: that the Argentine navy would have the money to buy an entirely new generation of modern communications, radar assisted delivery systems and weaponry. A man with that sort of money to spend could walk through many important doors. And Gonzalez did too. He was known at Rolls Royce, Westland Helicopters, Hawker Siddeley, BAC, Lucas Aerospace and Short Brothers in Belfast—the blue chip companies of the British armaments industry. In France Gonzalez dealt with Dassault; in Italy, with the aircraft manufacturers Machi. Some of the work was routine. According to the firms it involved simply checking orders and filling in forms. Nonetheless, for a young officer on the way up in Argentina's gentleman service it was a significant step forward.

The commander of the Naval Commission in London was Admiral Luchetta, a tall, dignified man from one of Argentina's better families. In spring 1980, he was replaced by Admiral Walter Allara, a similarly well-heeled officer who'd been transferred from Argentina's delegation at the United Nations. Both were relatively well-known and well-liked in London's wining and dining diplomatic circuit.

Less well-known, but the man who did much of the work when the admirals were away or indisposed was Captain Jorge Raúl Vildoza. He, too, had arrived in spring 1979. And he too lived in

168

suitably urbane circumstances, first in the leafy suburbs of south London, later in a comfortable home in Kensington. Vildoza was a bit older, about 45. He, too, had a moustache, but his hair was greying around the temples. He had what used to be called a Clark Gable manner, preferring impeccably-cut, blue wool or cashmere coats and English-style woven suits to the flashier continental cuts. Most mornings he drove to work, parking his grey Peugeot estate car in the diplomatic parking space especially reserved for him just off Vauxhall Bridge Road. He would park, lock up, and trudge, his shoulders slightly stooped, around the corner to his office hardly looking at passing women, the traffic or anything else London had to offer.

In his office Petty Officer Victor Cardó would usually be waiting for him. Cardó had been Vildoza's assistant back in Buenos Aires. In London, as there, he sat in an anteroom outside Vildoza's door, fetching and dispatching whatever the captain required. Cardó looked the part. He was young, in his thirties but gaunt, with a weasel-like moustache made more assertive by his reddish brown hair. He had a square angular forehead, and he walked briskly, like a man who moved through crowds with his elbows, the social antithesis of Gonzalez with his debonaire airs.

Why dwell on three officers buying weapons for the Argentine navy from its main European office on Vauxhall Bridge Road? It was still a year before the Falklands War. Cecil Parkinson, chairman of the Conservative Party, had toured not just Argentina, but Chile and Uruguay as well shortly after Mrs. Thatcher came to office, looking for firm orders for Britain's recession-struck arms firms. Indeed, Neville Trotter, the Tory shipbuilders' MP from Newcastle-on-Tyne, had just returned from a two-week all expenses paid tour of Argentina laid on by the navy. Captain Vildoza accompanied him as personal host and guide. In England life seemed pleasant enough. Vildoza had a passion for motorcycles. He and Gonzalez occasionally would fly private planes. They seemed personable chaps.

The trouble was that Vildoza had been named as a torturer in a document published in Paris by Argentine emigrés. It claimed that he had been in charge of a secret extermination camp run by the Argentine navy in Buenos Aires during and since the 1976 coup. His unit was called GT3.3/2, which meant target group for terrorists number 3.3/2. Housed in a building of the navy's technical training college, the Escuela Mecánica de la Armada, the alleged death camp was just visible to motorists driving out of Buenos Aires along the highway beside the River Plata.

Inside the building, according to the document, prisoners lay in cramped narrow cubicles under the eaves, their ankles and wrists manacled, with coarse woven sacks—called "capuchas"—over their heads, forbidden to talk. The basement housed the torture cells. For over two years Vildoza was said to have been the boss, during which time over 4,000 men and women were secretly kidnapped and incarcerated there. Less than 100 were known to have survived. The rest simply "disappeared".

The document said that Vildoza was known as "Gaston". Gonzalez was named as one of his most enthusiastic torturers. He was called "El Gatto", the cat. Cardó, we discovered later, had been head of the guards. Guards were called "pedros", dogs. Cardó was "Pedro Morrón". With pasts like that, living in London must have been somewhat of a change of scene, not to say a relief. After all, while in England they were not only protected by diplomatic privilege and immunity, they were well fêted and dined, prevailed upon to "Buy British" when ordering arms. We decided to investigate these special guests. As the police are fond of saying, the innocent have little to fear.

★ ★ ★

Students of what has come euphemistically to be called "counter-insurgency techniques" might well find much to mull over were they to make a careful study of Captain Vildoza's sordid little operation. Torture, of course, proved to be crucial to his extermination scheme. But then, it so often does. And Vildoza and his buddies wanted to do the job well. So they read the appropriate books.

Jean Lartéguy is a French thriller writer who for nearly 30 years has been pumping out "anti-subversive adventures" while at the same time seeming to advocate strong measures. The books which originally made his reputation, *The Pretorians* and *The Centurians*, read like accounts of the exploits of Colonel Jacques Massu and his French paratroopers in cleaning the FLN out of the casbah in what has become known as the Battle of Algiers. For tips on breaking underground movements, and all that involves, Larténguy's books on some points are hard to beat. Whether he liked it or not, his books were also required reading for Vildoza and his boys.

So, too, was Leopold Trepper's autobiography, *The Great Game*. Trepper had run much of the communist underground in Western Europe during the Second World War before he was finally captured by the Gestapo. Tortured and interrogated, he nonetheless through guile and duplicity managed to beat the Gestapo at their own game, and escape. Trepper was, to people in Vildoza's particular line of employment, the grand historic ad-versary. To defeat him, to defeat the Montoneros in Argentina, to defeat communism—that was an ambition, a calling, an achievement to which only certain formidable men could aspire. As President Videla had said, speaking to the nation shortly after the coup, "It is a serious crime to assault our Western and Christian style of life and to try to change it into something we do not like. If the army has to take the responsibility of guiding the country, we are going to end the venality, the chaos and disorder once and for all." The sentiments may have been noble, but the experience was hardly edifying in Vildoza's torture cells.

Aside from reading "the classics", the naval officers at the Escuela benefited from guidance and training provided by Americans and ex-Nazis, augmented by their own sense of what was fair and foul. We met a woman, the wife of a guerrilla leader who "disappeared" shortly after the coup, who herself had been kidnapped by one of Vildoza's snatch squads. Bundled into the back of an unmarked Ford Falcon sedan by men in civilian clothing, she was blindfolded and tied, to see light again only once she was in the Escuela's basement.

Cardó was there with shears to cut off her clothes. Then he and some of the other guards tied her face upwards and naked, splayed spreadeagle to a low metal bedframe. One of the electrodes was attached to the bed which was bolted to the floor. The other they prodded and jabbed into different parts of her body. They poured cold water over her to improve the electrical contact.

Did she scream? Yes. Did she shout? Yes. What did it feel like?

Like an animal. Like your whole body is being ripped apart. I can't tell you . . . you gasp for breath but there is no air. You feel your heart is going to burst its way through your chest. I had no clothes on. They kept shoving the picana, it's called a picana, a short stick with two points on the end, they kept shoving it in my lips, my nipples, my vagina, and shouting at me. They would hit me and shout some more. They were covered in sweat. The room was small, with only one door. Outside in the corridor they kept playing popular music, very loud, Julio Iglesias and Joan Manuel Serrat, I remember that. A few songs especially, "La Saeta", "Fiesta", "Las Moscas" . . . Do you know them? No. It doesn't matter. They kept playing the music so that no one could hear. But I could hear. I could hear other people screaming, being tortured in other cells.

And what about Captain Vildoza? Did she know him? We showed her a selection of photographs of a dozen or so men we had taken in London. She identified Vildoza instantly. "This is the man who watched me being tortured. He would come into the room from time to time and stand back and watch. He kept asking how they were getting on. He made some dumb joke, I don't remember what it was. He was supervising what was going on."

The woman's name is Sara Solarz. She never saw her husband again. Today she is living in hiding somewhere in Europe, one of only a few score prisoners from the Escuela known to have survived and lived to flee Argentina.

Painstakingly we made contact with half-a-dozen other ex-prisoners from Vildoza's correctional institution, all of them hiding as refugees on the continent. They told a similar story, yet each recalled some detail, some incidents, flesh to the skeleton of daily existence in Vildoza's little seraglio. After people had been tortured they usually desperately wanted to drink. But to drink even water after such electric convulsions tends to make people retch uncontrollably. And many died. In the corridor a guard sat playing the music during the torture sessions. And where did the records come from? "They had an enormous collection, Vildoza and his men," one of the ex-inmates explained. "They stole from the people they kidnapped, their records, their books, television sets, washing machines. Sometimes when they kidnapped men and boys from their homes, they stayed behind to fuck their wives."

And Gonzalez? "Gonzalez was one of the torturers. I saw him coming into the rooms where people were tied down and I heard the screaming," one man told us. "They used to shut the door when they tortured and put on loud music. But the screaming of the people was louder than the music and came through the door. It was the screaming of people who are broken, a scream that passed through walls. I heard that scream many times, and I saw Gonzalez going into the room and then coming out with his shirt wet and his face angry . . . You know how Gonzalez broke one man? For ten minutes he jammed the picana into his balls." He thought for a moment. Then he said, "You know, I think Gonzalez is one of those guys who tortures to suck up to his boss."

Londoners obviously knew nothing of the background of the Argentine Naval Commission staff. Most knew pardonably little about the March 1976 coup in Argentina. *The Times* had given it a rather muted reception, as had the *Daily Telegraph*. Soon it was relegated to the slumberland of small items buried deep inside newspapers.

The American press took a more muscular view of what needed doing in Argentina and what was being done. It didn't question the uncomfortable fact that coups in Latin America tend to be messy affairs. *Newsweek* magazine quoted an unnamed diplomat as saying about the new junta, "They are very image-conscious. They wince at any mention of Chile." Within a few months the International Monetary Fund had announced a $300 million loan. In London the Anglo-Argentine Society chaired by Viscount Montgomery welcomed the turn of events at its offices in Belgrave Square.

Slowly, different news from Argentina began to emerge. Wives and mothers were reported to be weeping after enquiring unsuccessfully at police stations as to the whereabouts of their missing fathers, husbands and sons. Citizens stood by, agape as plain-clothes men in unmarked cars tackled, kicked and then bundled away pedestrians walking along the streets. Bodies were found on the Buenos Aires municipal rubbish dump, their hands cut off, their faces mutilated beyond recognition. Within six months of the coup, human rights organisations were claiming that at least 3,000 men and women in Argentina had simply "disappeared". As well as people undeniably active in the underground, trade unionists, teachers, journalists and Jews were among them. Alas, many of Argentina's leading military figures were outspokenly anti-semitic. Citizens who had originally welcomed the military as a respite from the incessant street fighting in Buenos Aires between left- and right-wing political gangs began to feel even more uncomfortable and disturbed.

Someone had certainly been kidnapping and killing people in Argentina under the junta. But who? When asked, General Videla tended to assume a stargazed histrionic tone. "This is really war. In a war there are survivors, wounded, dead and sometimes people who disappear," he told the nation. "When the social body of a country has been contaminated by a disease that corrodes its entrails, it forms antibodies. As the government controls and destroys the guerrilla, the action of the antibodies will disappear, as is already happening." Few dared press him to elaborate on exactly what he meant. The documents we had and the survivors with whom we had spoken left us in little doubt. A number of special hit squads had been set up by the military immediately following the coup. It was their task to wipe out the left-wing opposition, physically. That meant extermination. And as extermination is currently unpopular in the Western world, let alone the United Nations, it had to be done secretly. Vildoza's little operation and his macabre clinicians were the Argentine navy's contribution to this civic task. It was their job to liquidate the Montoneros and anyone else who aroused suspicions in the Buenos Aires region.

That is what we believe to have happened. In fact we were sure.

So too were several other journalists. But was the testimony of a few survivors from Vildoza's butchery and photographs of bodies without hands on rubbish tips enough to convince, say, a court of law or a television audience, or the hardbitten sceptics who culled opinions from the daily press? We enquired whether anyone else in Europe had begun taking an interest in the Escuela Mecánica de la Armada and the strange goings on there. They had.

★ ★ ★

The Swedish Foreign Ministry was particularly helpful. Yes, they knew about the Escuela. And yes, they were familiar with the names of our London guests. But they were more interested in getting hold of Captain Alfredo Astiz. He, they believed, had been in command of a plain-clothes snatch squad from the Escuela when a teenage girl with Swedish citizenship, Dagmar Hagelin, had been shot and kidnapped. She hadn't been seen again. Dagmar was seventeen. Her father was a minister working in Buenos Aires. Astiz was now in South Africa along with an Admiral Chamorro, the man who had been Vildoza's immediate superior. In South Africa, as in London, the old boys from the extermination camp enjoyed full diplomatic privileges while they set about buying arms.

The French government was also interested in the Escuela. Two French nuns had been kidnapped and taken there, one from the church of Santa Cruz in a Buenos Aires suburb, the other from her residence. Sisters Léonie Duquet and Alice Domon came from provincial French towns and were members of the Institut des Missions Etrangères based in Toulouse. The Argentine government had officially told the Organisation of American States that it had "no record" of the nuns' whereabouts. The ex-prisoners did. One of them told us that she had seen Alice after she had been tortured. "She looked terrible, she had all the colour drained out of her body . . . she kept asking for the others . . ." The nuns had been helping to place advertisements in Buenos Aires newspapers by people seeking information about their missing relatives. Vildoza's men assumed that the money for such notices must have come from secret guerrilla sources.

In the Spanish Foreign Ministry in Madrid we were shown a large filing cabinet devoted entirely to dossiers relating to the Escuela. King Juan Carlos had recently visited Argentina. While there he talked about human rights. Just as he was about to address the Argentine nation on television the screens mysteriously went blank. The Spanish officials were not surprised. Rather they felt that their point had been made.

174

But what about the British? Hadn't Argentina become the UK's main arms customer in Latin America? Hadn't Cecil Parkinson, as Minister of Trade, flown to Buenos Aires within weeks of Margaret Thatcher's election with a covey of executives eager for business? Hadn't Vickers at Barrow-in-Furness provided the Argentine navy with a brand new Type 42 guided missile destroyer, the *Hercules*, whose sister ship, the *Santissima Trinidad*, built in Argentina under licence from Vickers, was then steaming towards Portsmouth for sea trials? The Argentine navy had patterned even its uniforms and table service on Royal Navy designs. With relations as snug as that it seemed inconceivable that Her Majesty's Government was ignorant of the Escuela and the backgrounds of the three naval personnel posted to Vauxhall Bridge Road. But could we be sure? That was a journalistic question and as such relatively straight-forward. Whether Her Majesty's Government cared or not was an entirely different affair.

At least one man within the British Ministry of Defence took a rather dim view of what had happened at the Escuela. He told us so over lunch.

"Nasty place," he said. "The things they did to people there." He chewed another forkful of steak Bernaise. "They were a pretty barbaric crowd."

He knew, because he had been posted to Buenos Aires at the time of the coup. Frequently he used to drive past the Escuela. Sometimes he saw the Ford Falcons going towards the main gate. At cocktail parties and receptions he had heard about and met some of the navy officers who worked there.

Interrogation, of course, is the bread and butter of "counter-insurgency," used to telling effect in Northern Ireland for example, in the early 1970s against suspected members of the IRA. I wanted to know how the goings-on at the Escuela differed from what had transpired in the British Holywood Barracks just outside Belfast. The MoD man took the question in his stride.

"There's a difference between standing a man against a wall for hours and playing loud music, and attaching electrodes to his genitals. Certainly you can see that."

Yes, I could. On the other hand there sometimes seems to be but a fine line between ostensibly civilised and obviously not so civilised ways of making people so uncomfortable that they blurt out betrayals of their friends and colleagues. He continued to make his point.

"There's a difference, obviously, when you start tying their heads in plastic bags, or dunking their heads in pails of slops. That's called 'El Submarino' you know."

Yes, I had heard.

"In Northern Ireland we were doing interrogations in depth. It's a dirty business. And sometimes it worked. But we weren't pushing electrodes up people's private parts. Or killing them."

"And were they at the Escuela?"

"I'm afraid so," he replied.

The MoD man was now sitting behind a desk in Whitehall. He'd heard rumours that "a few of them" from the Escuela had turned up in town. If he had heard as much, someone else in the government must have known.

The Foreign Office was not enthusiastic about the thrust of our endeavours. The press officer made little pretence that he was at all interested, amused, or flattered that it had fallen to him to deal with our enquiries. It wasn't the sort of situation to which they could reply with a simple "no comment", or an off-the-record briefing which would guarantee our discretion. The Foreign Office is responsible for recommending that diplomatic status be granted to foreign dignitaries in Britain, and therefore holds some responsibility for having vouched for Vildoza and his friends' good character. The system, which is based on reciprocity, is obviously a bit of a charade, but then so much is in diplomacy. And like all charades, it works as long as the identity of the guests is not questioned too closely, especially by people who decidedly haven't been invited to the party.

On the other hand we were preparing our own little party, with the British television-viewing audience as freely invited guests. And as we saw it, it was up to them to decide for themselves whether the three fine fellows from Argentina now shunting between Harrods and British arms firms were fit and proper persons to remain in the country.

The Foreign Office was not much taken with our point of view. If they were officially to acknowledge that the three Argentinians were indeed known to be from a secret extermination camp, then questions would immediately be raised as to why they had been allowed into the United Kingdom in the first place. More to the point, such an admission would have amounted to a public condemnation of the Argentine junta by one of its staunchest Western supporters, let alone arms suppliers. From the Foreign Office's point of view that was pregnant with undesirable consequences.

Nonetheless we were assured that enquiries would be made. Could we provide the Foreign Office with information about the gentlemen? Nothing could be easier. How much did they want? We sent biographies, personal details, aliases, addresses and documents running, all told, into hundreds of pages. And then waited. And waited. For weeks.

The minister, it was said, would need more time to consider the matter, as one of the documents was quite long and written in Spanish. So we waited. Then we were told that the matter had to be referred to the British embassy in Buenos Aires bearing in mind the seriousness of the allegations being made. So we waited some more. What came next was hardly surprising. No telex, we were informed, had as yet been received from Buenos Aires which meant, of course, that London was in no position to comment . . .

The Foreign Office's little game was becoming pathetic. Yet the press officer's humble efforts may well have been judged a success by his Whitehall colleagues as he managed to prevaricate until after the programme had been transmitted. From our point of view it didn't really matter that Her Majesty's Government had its eyes officially closed. El Capitán Vildoza and his chums had been involved in an exercise which no amount of temporising by either the Argentine military or their official British friends could hide.

★ ★ ★

There are difficulties which all mass murderers face. Relatives, for one, have an unnerving habit of persisting in wanting to know what has happened to their loved ones. Also, short of using gas chambers, dead bodies, despite precautions taken, somehow keep turning up. The Argentine navy tried to master both problems. Nevertheless they too have been cheated of the perfect crime.

In Argentina it's called the "Nuremberg Syndrome". "Captain Whamond said to me, he said, you know, in the end we will kill you. We will have to kill you. You can't be allowed to survive. We can't afford to have another Nuremberg." The speaker is another of the women held in the Escuela, Ana Marie Martí, a young woman whose husband "disappeared" before she herself was kidnapped as a member of a guerrilla organisation. At the Escuela she too was tortured with the electric prod, doused with cold water. After the torture sessions she, as with the other prisoners, was returned under guard to the attic of the Escuela where under the eaves they lay chained ankle and wrist, capuchas over their heads, lying on the floor. If they talked they were kicked.

Wednesdays were bitten with fear.

Pedro Morrón, the man you call Cardó, would come into the attic—we called it the capucha because we had to wear the hoods there—and he would read out a list of numbers. We all had numbers, nobody was referred to by name. Everyone was very tense, the guards were very nervous. We just sat there frozen with the hoods over our heads. The guards would go around picking those whose numbers had been called up off the floor. Then we heard the noise of the shackles dragging along the floor and the noise of the door opening and closing as they were taken to the basement. Afterwards it became dead still, quiet, as if some deep calm had been restored. People sobbed. The guards hit them. We never saw them again. We were told they had been 'transferred'.

Where did they go? Captain Vildoza had been faced with a serious organisational problem from almost the first day Gonzalez and the other junior officers began kidnapping "suspects" off the streets. The kidnappings were done incognito. Police stations would be rung up before a swoop and told to stay clear of a neighbourhood. The naval officers wore plain clothes and always drove unmarked cars. The scheme neatly did away with the usual and often cumbersome police procedures of formally charging suspects, bringing them before a judge, holding them in prison and finally standing trial. But in abrogating the law Vildoza's unit and others like it created another problem for themselves. If people had not been formally arrested, then neither the navy, army nor air force for that matter could formally acknowledge that they were holding them without also publicly admitting to operating outside the legal system. And the law, of course, was one of the very keystones of that precious civilisation which the armed forces were ostensibly set to defend. Secrecy was the solution.

But that didn't particularly help Captain Vildoza. He had to run a torture centre with only an attic in which to store his suspects. A few hundred at most could be crowded in. Yet his men kidnapped over 4,000 victims. The answer was to dispose of them.

At first, we were told, people were strangled after they were tortured. Then some were shot. The bodies were dumped into the river. But soon they began to wash ashore. There was another problem. Some of the women were pregnant. The women themselves may have been guilty in Vildoza's men's eyes, but their unborn children were sinless. To kill them was to murder in the eyes of the church, and many of the naval officers at the Escuela were practising Catholics. So Vildoza set up a nursery in the Escuela. After the babies were born they were taken from mothers and farmed out for adoption to childless military couples through the notice board at the naval hospital. Their mothers were then disposed of, dragged across the capucha floor on Wednesdays.

But where to? The ex-inmates spoke of a man named Tincho. He was the only one to have been dragged away and returned. He told them. Downstairs, in the corridor where the torture cells were, the prisoners were blindfolded and given injections. Some struggled. But soon they became drowsy and stumbled and fell as they were pushed into the backs of lorries and driven to the nearby military airport. There they were loaded on to the Argentine navy's Dutch made Fokker "Friendship" aeroplanes. But Tincho heard his name being called out. One of the officers recognised him. A friend from the past. Tincho was called back. And returned to the Escuela for a few days. Then his turn came again and he too was "transferred".

The prisoners were flown out over the South Atlantic and dumped into the ocean. Those in the attic of the Escuela heard the Fokker "Friendships" as they flew overhead. One of them told us Vildoza's officers occasionally talked about the airdrops.

> They found a current in the Atlantic that, according to them goes round the Falkland Islands and across the South Atlantic to the Indian Ocean. They said it was not a painful death because they said that people died during the fall. If they didn't die then, they drowned. They were very proud of what they called a naval solution to the problem of the bodies.

Any suggestion that this constituted or would be judged as tantamount to Nazi war crimes could be safely left to the sharks.

★ ★ ★

So how were the men at the Argentine Naval Commission on Vauxhall Bridge Road coping with life in London? One of the survivors from the Escuela, a young woman, agreed to come to London and confront the men on their way to work. Gonzalez, as usual, was arriving from the Victoria Station underground just a little bit late, and as usual well dressed. The woman walked up to him and simply said, "Do you recognise me?" Apparently so. The brave lieutenant covered his face with his newspaper and sprinted the 50 yards down the sidewalk to the safety of the Naval Commission front door. It was a useful incident to have filmed.

After the programme was transmitted Gonzalez went overseas for a few days. Later he skulked back to his home in Richmond to pack his belongings and quit Britain with his wife and child. The neighbours were horrified, phoning us asking whether everything about the Escuela that they had seen in the film was really true. In news kiosks, pubs and restaurants near the Naval Commission the Argentinians began to be snubbed. Captain Vildoza walked into his office the day after the programme went out and said, "I understand I'm famous now." The comment didn't go down well.

The Foreign Office continued "to make enquiries". It simply was not prepared officially to kick the men out of Britain. The business of selling them arms was too important to be allowed to become hostage to such political embarrassments. Vildoza eventually left Britain and the Argentine Naval Commission continued to stock up for what turned out to be the Falklands War. Captain Astiz led the Argentine landing party on South Georgia Island.

★ ★ ★

Such are the men who made the coup in Argentina in 1976, "to protect the Free World and Christian civilisation . . .", who hosted the World Cup in 1978, who invaded the Falklands and who ran up a $30 billion foreign debt. The military's much-touted efficiency turned into shambles once it took upon itself the self-ordained task of running a country, Henry Kissinger's blandishments notwithstanding. Inflation in Argentina ran regularly at several hundred per cent annually. Much of the workforce was unemployed. The military has been replaced by a civilian government since the war. Many senior officers, such as Admiral Massera, have been under arrest. Yet women have continued to parade silently outside the Presidential Palace in the Plaza de Mayo, wearing scarves on which they embroidered the names of their missing children and husbands. Hundreds of bodies have been disinterred from secret graveyards.

Captain Vildoza and his cronies were not only sadists. They were fools. Apparently at Admiral Massera's insistence a few score of the prisoners at the Escuela were kept alive. Some for sexual favours. But more crucially, the politically important ones, Montonero leaders, their wives and friends. Hostages are useful in war, even in a clandestine one carried out at night while honest citizens best kept to their beds, asked no questions and slept. The Montoneros were fabled to have a secret multimillion dollar war chest, and the navy wanted that. Massera also seems misguidedly to have believed they could be instrumental in delivering to him much of the Peronist vote should he take part in Argentina's return to civilian rule.

So just under 100 of the 4,000 inmates of the Escuela were politically "rehabilitated" and eventually released. Some of them work for Argentine naval intelligence today, at home and overseas. Others, having promised to remain silent, spoke out once they were safely on foreign soil. Sometimes they have nightmares of Wednesdays in the capucha and people being dragged away in chains.

The British Foreign Office knew the calibre of the men to whom they were selling arms on Vauxhall Bridge Road, just as some

180

British government officials knew about the Argentine navy's secret extermination camp, the Escuela Mecánica de la Armada. And yet they chose to do nothing about it, as with so much else concerning Argentina, until they could no longer ignore their own blindness and Britain was embroiled in the Falklands War.

11
Home Truths about Foreign News

IT IS OFTEN said that journalists jump too quickly into bed with politicians, do fair bidding for corporate executives and cultivate civil servants as they would exotic plants. People then complain that journalists are not independent, as if independence is a quality journalists alone must exemplify. To which one can only ask, independence from what?

Here are a few lines from a book recently written by a friend of mine. Before he goes overseas he says he drops into the Foreign Office for an off-the-record briefing. "When back in London I meet British and foreign diplomats socially; I go to their parties and receptions. Some become close personal friends and naturally we pick each other's brains. These are the essential tools of the journalist's trade."

So, too, are the handshakes, expense account lunches and afternoon hangovers. I wish he'd said something about them too, just to give a fairer picture. Yet no sooner had that book appeared than a senior journalist writing for one of London's more sedate Sunday newspapers sputtered back, "Nothing in my experience as a journalist over a period of 46 years would support the suggestion of a cosy collusion between the Establishment and the prestige press." An experienced man ought not to feign surprise on reading of such a time honoured *modus operandi*. The public is not completely asleep.

Yet for that journalist, as for most, there is an important issue at stake—pride. No journalists like to be told they are bent or can be bought, any more than do policemen or MPs. Press and television executives must also be careful. In Western democracies, to retain readers' and viewers' confidence, it is crucial for their companies to be seen as independent of government. The public doesn't expect to watch ministerial spokesmen in mufti reading the television news or pay good money for rewritten official handouts at newsstands and corner shops. That my friend implied, as much by example as by argument, that government and press often go hand in hand tarnished the myth of the media's much trumpeted independence from official influence. This civic myth is as important for governments to foster as it is for the press.

What neither of these journalists concede is that the press' greatest power often lies not in its ability to comment, inform and reveal, but in its largely unquestioned and at times awesome propensity to misinform and suppress. Decisions not to publish are taken in the very same newspaper offices and television studios as all decisions to go ahead. The difference is that the former don't get into print. The public is told of the media's courage to publish; it is seldom aware of the way news is censored out of existence.

Say this in a Fleet Street bar and most hacks will yawn and order another pint. They've had too many stories spiked too often to feel bruised. And after all, someone will undoubtedly chip in, we don't live in Eastern Europe where journalists foolish enough to write hardhitting stories are likely to be gaoled, even if they are no longer shot. Not so here in the West, my colleagues and I are reminded. Here we have freedom of the press. Just so. But what exactly does that mean?

It's editors' privilege to decide what is printed or broadcast. By and large they are decent people; and they share with the powers that be decent values, more or less. The trouble is that among the congeries who rule the country are men and women who aren't happy to see their more unsavoury qualities and squalid deals—which often really matter—discussed in public. And often they aren't, partly—but only partly—because of legal and other deterrents available to them. Commercial confidentiality, official secrecy and the threat of expensive litigation when combined with such ruses as dissimulation, flummery and outright lying can effectively thwart most hacks claiming to be snooping in the public interest.

Yet there are also the velvet muzzles—the rewards to be had for keeping the media, as the society, on an even keel. Today, an editor who quietly promotes the country's supposed virtues, spicing them up from time to time with a bit of scandal, a whiff of intrigue, can reasonably look forward to a mention in the honours list. Many editors are sensitive to these polite, unspoken inducements. A journalist who survives in harness for 40 years should receive a comfortable pension, and probably private health insurance, not just a gold watch, in return for a modicum of "good judgment". The result, much of the time, is a lively complacency, occasionally laced with sensationalism—as good a recipe as any for success today in much of broadcasting and Fleet Street.

Point out the more obvious frauds, journalists are enjoined. Expose charlatans, philanderers and outright crooks, even if this entails long hauls through the libel courts. But when it comes to questioning those self-same values espoused by both government and newspapers, well . . . think again. It won't often be done; partly because the commerce of day to day news gathering is biased so strongly against it.

The press depends on information; government and business have it to give, not just in press handouts, but in off-the-record briefings, over lunches, at dinner parties, and in plain brown envelopes. Journalists and politicians, civil servants and corporate executives need to understand each other. They need to know whom to trust, to respect confidentialities, or so the thinking runs. That confidentiality is worth having is not at issue. Speaking "off the record" makes it possible for people to provide news without risking their jobs, safety or reputations.

But another side to confidentiality, that has nothing to do with protecting individuals' rights, is when it is used to ensure the anonymity of people who should be publicly accountable. A bond of trust then becomes a gagging contract. In Britain this convention emanates from the very top: the Prime Minister's press secretary's briefings to the parliamentary reporters, the lobby.

It's a curious ritual. Every day the Downing Street press secretary talks to a group of journalists who have agreed, as accredited lobby correspondents, not to quote him directly. "The government feels," they may write the next day. "It is believed in senior government circles. . . ." "On the highest authority we understand. . . ." The Prime Minister's press secretary is there in flesh and blood, delivering morsels of hard information, gossip, trailing the occasional red herring. But as these comments are unattributable the lobby reporters are obliged to clothe them in circumlocutions; they have even agreed not to say "Downing Street sources say". In exchange for these dubious civilities the journalists are guaranteed a few pearls which appear on the front pages of the next day's press. That's the deal. Its supporters say that at least the system has the virtue of guaranteeing that the entire press, not just the government's favoured papers, are privy to some of its private thoughts. This is another way of saying that as the press will never agree collectively, individual newspapers act at their peril if they summon the courage to challenge the Prime Minister's office.

And yet this ostensible evenhandedness, this neutered gentility, also applies to top level briefings throughout the government, at the Ministry of Defence, the Treasury, the Metropolitan Police. "Whitehall sources say . . ." In Britain today newspapers and television are shot through with the hollow voices of the country's rulers. In the United States, universities even teach budding journalists how to drape their country's leaders in the anonymity of "official sources". This humbling deference may be the price journalists pay to gain access to their society's hallowed chambers. It's also profoundly undemocratic. It stunts lively, informed debate because the public never knows for sure who's really talking. And it intimidates and bewilders, especially ordinary people who believe they have a right to know what's going on in their government but don't have a hot line to Henry Kissinger, a brother in the Treasury or, for that matter, a job on a national newspaper.

We all know that no one can scream as loudly as editors when something happens about which they feel they should have been informed. In the same way employees, especially civil servants, also tend to cry "foul" when their bosses become particularly mendacious. When governments demand of their bureaucrats political partiality beyond trying to do a reasonable job, or ask that policies be systematically covered up, or lie to Congress or the House of Commons, civil servants have an attractive habit of posting plain brown envelopes to journalists. The journalists, of course, are extremely grateful because then it's the government's turn to shout, claiming it has been subverted to cover evidence of its highhandedness. And this, of course, is news. Recently, particularly in Britain, the government has gone one further, claiming that national security has been at stake. Not once has it convincingly proved its case.

Most of the time, however, many journalists, public servants and politicians share a collusive relationship, involving mutual confidentiality that goes far beyond a simple matter of trust. The British press lobby is only the most well known, and so in a sense the most innocuous manifestation of the bargain struck between the press and the powers that be within government, finance and industry.

Roughly it is the government which acts while the fourth estate keeps its fingers on the pulse. Occasionally it quickens the tempo; just as often it acts as a damp sponge, carefully absorbing the implications of policies, squeezing them out before offering up stories to a public thirsty for news. Sometimes what's left over is interesting and worthwhile; at others it's dross. And the impression conveyed? Despite the wonders of communications technology the news often seems little more than folklore, a steady stream of nursery tales for adults.

★ ★ ★

With a press like that, what is to be expected of reporting from overseas? Some very strong and consistent journalism, but also a tendency to project on to foreigners a good deal of mawkish conventional wisdom and dubious ideological humbug. At times the entire press seems awash with cliché as journalists pay obeisance to the "Big Lies", those acceptable illusions about the state of the world which bind together the political life of their country. Truth is drowned.

For evidence one need look no further than much of what passes for reporting of Mikhail Gorbachev's proposals for nuclear arms reductions. The chances are that the reporting is likely to be about Western distrust of Soviet intentions. A ruthless coup installing a pro-Western military regime is often described—and so justified—as a firm response to an unstable situation provoked by irresponsible agitators. Terrorist outrages have come to be blamed as a matter of course on leftists and Arab zealots, though culprits have often turned out to be *agents provocateurs* and fascists on Interpol's index.

Common to these occasionally petty, though pervasive, distortions is not just a healthy scepticism towards hostile foreigners' intentions. The underlying emotions are more visceral, reaffirming a commitment to a coherent world view in step with a country's conventional wisdom. We decry this process in Eastern Europe; yet the Western press is also steeped in Cold War sentiments, to say nothing of its ethics.

Journalists who stray far from such assumptions know they are unlikely to see their work screened or published. Like it or not, most have a bit of the state lodged in their brains competing with their wit and sagacity. The rules of the game and the boundaries of tolerance are fairly clearly defined; one can but accept them or not. Simply put, a double standard is at work today in the Western press. Most journalists know it, live with it, and will admit it. To pretend otherwise is utterly disingenuous.

★ ★ ★

Consider the type of substantiation and supporting material needed to corroborate different stories, particularly those from unpleasant countries overseas, compared to what would be written were the same standards of evidence and "judgment" insisted upon as are used at home. Here's an undignified example.

On 27 March 1983 the *Sunday Times* led with the following "exclusive". "Starving babies' food sold for Soviet Arms", was the

186

front page headline above a large photograph of a crying, naked, emaciated child. "There is mounting evidence", wrote the reporter, Simon Winchester, "that food sent from the West to drought-stricken northern Ethiopia is being diverted by the Ethiopian military regime to its army—and also, to an increasing extent, to the Soviet Union to help meet the regime's huge arms bill . . ."

But where was the proof? Winchester cited an anonymous Ethiopian official who had defected and a few people in Britain, some of them known critics of the Ethiopian regime. The piece mentioned a European Parliament emergency hearing scheduled for 5 April, "at which testimony of those who are convinced that aid is being diverted will be presented".

A telephone call to the European Parliament elicited no record of this hearing, but there was a debate on emergency aid to Ethiopia on 14 April in nearby Strasbourg. How, given the considerably greater distances and difficulties involved, could Soviet duplicity be detected in far off Ethiopia? The answer is it couldn't.

One searched in vain through the following weeks' *Sunday Times* for more information about the horrific Soviet-arms-for-food-aid-barter-scandal. Instead Oxfam, Canadian and other officials administering aid programmes in Ethiopia insisted that food was getting through. On 3 April, in a small piece on page two, Winchester talked of "the possibility that aid is being diverted". The Soviet connection had silently vanished. Instead the *Sunday Times* was now quoting Christopher Jackson, Conservative member of the European Parliament.

Four months previously the same Mr Jackson had tabled an amendment in the European Parliament to stop further aid to Ethiopia until allegations of misappropriation and human rights violations were investigated and reported on. So why wasn't he mentioned in the original front page story?

Why also didn't the *Sunday Times* report the debate in the European Parliament which followed its story, during which EEC commissioners replied in detail to the original allegations? The text is freely available in the Official Journal of the European Communities.

The threads of the unfolding of this dreary episode are readily apparent. Without the suggestion of Soviet arms the original story may not have survived as a small news item. But fabricate a nefarious Soviet connection and it becomes a Cold War cracker-jack. Add a shocking headline and a powerful photograph and the story could disguise the absence of any amount of hard news. It's not hard to do. After all, there's no cheaper shot than trashing communists, whether under the bed or abroad. But what about readers who paid 40 pence for their Sunday paper in the vague hope of finding out what was going on in the world? And what about the Ethiopians who went without food?

Could the same sort of front page report have been printed about, say, allegations of low wages paid by a British firm overseas, based entirely on the testimony of a resentful ex-employee who insisted his firm was secretly siphoning the payroll to a foreign power? That's a good story. But it would never be printed until it had been combed over by a newspaper's lawyers, the firm had been approached for comment, and hard, corroborative evidence had been found. High journalistic standards would have been maintained largely, one suspects, because editors know British firms are quick to call their lawyers. Ethiopians are unlikely to sue.

Take another, slightly different example about what can and cannot be filmed. When making the programme about the kidnapping and subsequent murder of René Machón, the head of El Salvador's coffee board, we filmed an eye-witness to his kidnapping. This involved us in some danger and she frankly risked her life in doing so.

But what about filming the London warehouse where coffee from El Salvador is stored? Nothing could be easier. Yet we were instructed to ask the company for permission. It refused. To have done so surreptitiously would have been trespass, a matter on which we would have had to take a legally informed view. And what about filming coffee from El Salvador on sale in Marks and Spencers? Not on your life. The management told us that to do so would be a diversion from their elaborate security precautions. So both firms' names were kept out of the programme.

All journalists know that even to ask some questions is treated as impertinence. Some questions will never be answered. And even if journalists find interesting answers to others they will never be published, particularly at home.

That's when journalists cry "foul", when they begin to argue that their right to investigate is synonymous with the public interest and right to know.

It is hardly surprising that when covering places such as Czechoslovakia, Western journalists are sometimes surprised to find a strong and compelling expression of a state of affairs they know themselves. Czechoslovakia may be, as Neville Chamberlain said, having just given it to Hitler, a faraway place. It is also a state of mind, an old but unwanted friend who drops by uninvited from time to time. We call it censorship. Its effect on foreign reporting can be disastrous.

Consider coverage of Iran under the Shah: a widely discussed case
study. Throughout the 1970s most papers had only good things to
say about the self-appointed heir to the Peacock Throne. They said
the Shah was a force of modernity, enlightenment, a strong anti-
communist influence, key to that chimera—"stability" throughout the Near East.

In 1971, scores of press men and women flew to Iran, expenses
paid, to cover the Shahanshah's multi-million pound bean feast in
Persepolis to celebrate the almost entirely specious 2,500th anni-
versary of the Peacock Throne. Official guests from Britain
included the Duke of Edinburgh, Princess Anne, Lord Thomson
(owner of Times Newspapers), Vere Harmsworth (Chairman of
Associated Newspapers), Lord and Lady Shawcross and the Leader
of the Liberal Party, Jeremy Thorpe. The banquet, according to a
front page report in *The Times*, "consisted of quails eggs stuffed
with golden imperial caviar (Champagne and Château de Saran);
mousse of crayfish tails (Haut Brion Blanc, 1964); roast saddle of
lamb with truffles (Château Lafite Rothschild, 1945); sorbet of
Moët et Chandon, 1911; fifty peacocks with tail feathers restored,
encompassed by roasted quails and served with nut and truffle
salad (Musigny Conte de Vogue, 1945); fresh figs and cream in
raspberries and port wine (Dom Perignon, 1959, reserve vintage);
coffee and cognac Prince Eugene."

Understandably it came as something of a surprise to several
Western editors and television executives, not to say their friends in
Washington and Whitehall, when seven years later the Shah was
unceremoniously overthrown. "Khomeini who?" many of them
asked. How could so many commentators, who had been so well-
fed, be so ill-informed about the growing dissent in Iran? How
could such a ground swell of public protest emerge as if from
nowhere?

Soon after the Shah's fall droves of Western editors were wearing
metaphorical hair-shirts, indulging in ritual and conspicuous self-
criticism, making sure the public took note. "We were wrong
about Iran. We made mistakes," they said. But there were few
mistakes.

With few exceptions, stories about torture by SAVAK, the Shah's
secret police, were not printed; neither were stories about labour
unrest on British and other Western firms' construction sites.
Accounts of growing food shortages in Tehran's southern slums
were consigned to the wastebin. Many editors tended not to look
critically on the man who kept offering his journalists "freebies",
all-expenses paid tours of the exotic Persian hinterland. Nor did

many challenge the basic judgment behind overseas contracts earning some of Britain's leading construction firms several hundred million pounds. They didn't question extravagant weapons sales. Richard Nixon is said to have told the Shah he could have any American weapons short of nuclear bombs. The Shah's order for over 2,000 Chieftain tanks was worth over one billion pounds. Many editors succumbed to this commercial patriotism, eagerly concurring when Henry Kissinger provided the intellectual trappings of *realpolitik* and the moral legitimacy of anti-communism.

But more than that, they stopped listening: to the stories about torture, about corruption, about the inappropriateness of so much of the new business in Iran to ordinary Iranians' lives. In a word they stopped being well informed; consequently they perpetrated on to their readers and viewers a picture of Iran which, along with several of those contracts and the Shah himself, came hideously undone.

Among the newspapers most outspoken in support of the Shah was *The Times*. For years Lord Alun Chalfont wrote pieces in the paper so steadfastly congratulatory that they were held in particularly high regard by the Iranian ambassador to London, Parvis Radji. Articles with titles such as "The Double Standard of Human Rights", "Exporting British Insults to Iran", and "Who is Behind the Violent Unrest in Iran" left readers of *The Times* in no doubt that, but for the mindless rantings of what Chalfont called "the fascist left", the Shah would be seen as he truly was, selfless and forward-looking, interested only in the best for his country.

It was a misconception and a dangerous one. For when the troubles really began in late 1978, *The Times* was hopelessly unprepared. "What is clear beyond doubt is that someone outside Iran is closely involved in the organisation of civil disturbances," Chalfont wrote in August 1978. "There is no doubt in the minds of most Iranian leaders that agents of the Soviet Union are losing no opportunity to exploit the situation . . . The mullahs, whatever may be the sincerity of their religious preoccupations are being manipulated by extremists."

He couldn't have been more wrong. Charles Douglas-Home's brother, David, a director of Morgan Grenfell Ltd, a merchant bank with considerable interests in Iran, went to look for himself, especially after the British embassy had been set alight by a rampaging mob.

He was appalled by what he found. "The question is not whether he is personally corrupt," *The Times* leader thundered on 13 November. "The question is whether the corruption, inadequacy, even beastliness (since the former head of the secret police is now officially charged with torture) of the regime can be officially admitted . . ." A week later another leader spelled out the extent to which British interests and the Shah's now differed. "In Teheran with the Shah on the throne it is hard to visualise a glad confident morning again . . . He should be coaxed into seeing that it is unwise to persist with the illusion that his own wishes for his country and himself are indivisible . . . He should be helped now to reach this decision and to start preparing for the moment of departure; for the good of himself and for Iran."

In effect, the Shah was being unceremoniously ditched by the British, much as his father had been. *The Times* readers were treated to a rare dose of candour. They may have been confused, as, undoubtedly, was the Shah. Unfortunately, within days of those editorials, *The Times* closed due to an industrial dispute which lasted over a year.

Since reopening, the paper's coverage of Iran has been more soundly based on reports from within the country. The Western establishment is critically disposed to the Shah's successor as it never was to him. So today readers of *The Times* can be in no doubt that Khomeini is a high priest of death sending the flower of a generation to the killing grounds and wounding the spirit of two entire nations. The carnage in his prisons and on the battlefields with Iraq attest to that. But trade must go on, and British firms, as ever, play an active role. Where has *The Times*' reporting of that been?

British arms firms were supplying Khomeini's regime several years before Oliver North began the covert shipments which caused so much distress in the US. *The Times* has said little about that. Margaret Thatcher has been as resolutely outspoken in her opposition to terrorism as Ronald Reagan, yet the Iranian weapons procurement office is in London, within sight of the House of Commons. *The Times* never seems to have taxed the Prime Minister to explain whether she saw any contradiction.

And how fares British business in Iran's civil sector? What, if anything, are Earl Jellicoe's firm, Tate and Lyle, and others doing? In the Shah's time Tate and Lyle provided sugar for Persian housewives. Other firms were trying to sell Iran hospitals complete with nurses and nightlites, and at a pretty hefty price. And now? *The Times* could enquire. Readers might also be interested in how relations stand between Khomeini's regime and Morgan Grenfell, David Douglas-Home's bank.

★ ★ ★

If there is anything to be drawn from the experiences recounted in this book it would seem to be this. Journalists are sent off to all sorts of catastrophes and political feuds overseas and told to file tight, comprehensible copy, and quickly. Those who don't, don't go overseas next time. To function like this journalists have to have fairly durable, well-stocked kit bags, not just with a few clean shirts or blouses, but of attitudes and recognisable perspectives as well. Whatever and however razor-sharp their guile and wits may be, in the end what's going to be printed has to make sense in terms editors believe their readers will understand. And so it should.

The trouble comes when situations begin to look at first strangely, and then remarkably, different on the ground from what editors are prepared to imagine, and what readers and viewers have been led to assume. So a difficult, but useful process of re-education has to be entered into. This is, of course, one of the main roles journalists are employed to perform, and which most of the rest of society is prepared to allow and to see them do.

It is also where the problems begin. There are obviously occasionally gross and blatant disparities between what is seen, filed and reported and what editors are prepared to hear. Some journalists simply fail to see a hidden Soviet or American or Vatican conspiracy behind every disturbance whether at home or abroad. So they cannot report with a clear conscience what their boss has told them he desperately hopes they will find. At the end of the day they either have no story or it is consigned to the passing news.

Journalists to whom this happens are not usually at fault, though they may be made to feel they are. They've learned from experience that the world has a curious habit of turning out to be more interesting than much-loved conspiracy theories and Cold War epithets allow.

But sometimes editors don't care. Hurling abuse at society's stock bogeymen and revealing dark conspiracies is a proven way to sell newspapers. It's also cheap; and the public knows what to expect. So the press' dog-eared lexicon of conspiracies thwarted and justices done is dragged out to fend nobly in the cause of the Free World.

The opposite of such editorial cudgellings is when journalists "go native" to the extent that they are so deeply and personally involved as to file copy which is utterly incomprehensible in terms of what concerns their readers and their bosses. This can be as professionally suicidal as it was for colonial administrators years ago. It's possible to "go native" in Whitehall, but journalists who do usually end up writing fiction or public relations handouts.

The redeeming quality of the others—editors obsessed with proving that the world is flat and reporters who simply refuse to see other points of view besides those of their chums—is that they eventually make fools of themselves. They lose credibility. In his memoirs the Shah's ambassador to London recounts how a friendly journalist explained to him that this is known as "The Chalfont Syndrome".

This book has not really been concerned with the press' levy of lunatics and hardened ideologues. It is more about the day to day work of hacks and their bosses trying to do their best simply at understanding the world. Here is where, ultimately, the most significant lapses occur.

How is this possible? A reporter flies into a coup, say in a country such as Chad. His news desk is waiting and he files a story about who is fighting whom, where some of their weapons come from, making sure the names are spelled reasonably correctly and trying to prop up his report with an interview with a well-informed person on the spot, such as the French ambassador, who both his editor and readers are likely to find interesting, and possibly believe. He does a competent job, perhaps illustrated with a few photographs. The public at home learn about yet another war in Africa, that it's a complicated affair in which their government possibly plays a role, and on which they might or might not be expected to have a view. Many readers will probably be bored.

What they are unlikely to learn is that that coup, as any coup, revolution, war or natural disaster, has a shape of its own. In Chad it was a struggle between groups living next to each other fought in the streets of their own homes. That gave it its own special qualities. What if you had a son out on the street and his enemies broke into your house to set up a rocket launcher to fire at his friends from your front room? What do you do? Possibly more importantly, what would you expect them to do? The problem may seem farfetched in Philadelphia and Bristol, less so in Belfast.

Yet to most who even bothered to read about it, the coup in Chad must have seemed but another crooked piece in an ever changing African political jigsaw puzzle. They were unlikely to have discovered that at its core was a fragile moment when so-called civilised warfare spills over into massacre. In Chad there were forces which acted in the person of the local Imam, the French military advisers, the women, lack of ammunition and threat of retaliation that kept everyone within reach from literally having their throats cut. We came across one man who suffered that terrible fate. We saw others. And there were hundreds. But why not thousands? After all that was a real possibility.

193

What I'm suggesting is that the way in which that coup didn't turn into wholesale massacre is a significant part of the story, and possibly worth recounting in view of the likelihood of other coups and potential massacres elsewhere. Yet to have portrayed it as such would have been at odds with the entirely legitimate conventional pressures under which most journalists had to report. But once this significance became apparent it was too late; copy had already been filed, the coup had quietened down, and editors had sent other journalists elsewhere for fresh news. Many editors probably asked themselves if it had been worth sending a reporter at all.

Yet look at Chad again. Who was doing the fighting? Among those I met, many had been to university in Cairo, Moscow and Paris. Others had worked on the Renault assembly line just outside Paris in Billancourt. They spoke several languages, and still ate sitting on the ground in their families' mud enclosures. The meagreness of their surroundings is disarming. Their sophistication in many cases far exceeded that of the French army conscripts, previously unemployed boys billetted in one of Chad's few Europeanised hotels, drinking beer every night.

Throughout Africa there are now tens of thousands of men such as the Chad combatants. Men who, by their mid-20s, have fought in at least a few very real and very nasty wars, who have travelled overseas, and who know something of the political dealings on which their support and, they believe, their futures depend. These are a new generation who have a fairly shrewd idea, rough as it may appear and may well be, of what they expect from their governments and, given that their families are seldom immune to the consequences of warfare, have a good idea of what they are fighting for.

And yet one suspects that most Americans and Europeans have little idea of who these young men are; partly because Africa is a long way from home, partly because they have been ill-served by the media. For people who like to read novels, countries such as Chad tend to be packaged as fairly tasteless bad jokes. Professional travellers write in literary reviews about the lack of basic amenities and the fading Europeanised hotels. Aid agencies and international charities portray whole continents as a little kid with a swollen belly and a begging bowl. It is this pot-pourri of stock caricatures that most people are encouraged to turn when they have time to think about what's going on elsewhere, particularly in what's called the Third World.

Journalists, by and large, have neither the time nor the interest to lay these descriptions to rest, especially if they are in a hurry to get to the Foreign Office or State Department for a briefing

194

before catching a plane. So it's hardly surprising that stories should occasionally but regularly appear as if out of nowhere which, to put it mildly, come as a shock. Shocks are news. They are also "crises". And crises for editors are inevitably matters of retaining readers' trust in their professional competence. They have to find coherent explanations of what's happening. They also have to explain their failure to have reported adequately on developments which led to the "crisis" in the first place. And fast.

This is not simply a question of being right or wrong about a particular course of events. No editor or journalist can be expected to predict the future. It has to do with the terms within which the whole description of the newsworthy situation is cast. Some crises are easily managed: the quality press prints page after page of expert opinion to explain their way out of these epistemological knots; the tabloids quickly bury their dreadful coverage under bingo, football and pinups. Others are more difficult to reconcile with what readers have been led to expect, such as the fall of the Shah.

It would be wrong to think the press intentionally misinforms the public. The rot is more benign. The world is a fast changing place, and some newspapers and television companies are just lagging comfortably behind. If there is some compensation it must be that popular culture serves the public much worse.

Warfare in Africa has grown up. It is not yet comparable to the great tank battles of the Middle East and the Second World War, but it is mechanised and commanded by trained professional officers. No longer are battles a matter of a handful of European mercenaries with a few thousand pounds' worth of arms tying down the presidential palace until United Nations forces arrive to bail them out.

And yet pick up a thriller set in the Third World, particularly Africa, off any newsstand. As likely as not it's still going to be the same old white-man-mercenary-killer-hero stuff. How Bart Throb and a small band of carefully chosen adventurers wipe out a terrorist threat and restore order knee deep in the locals' blood. The only adventurers I knew of languished in an Angolan gaol for several years—those who weren't shot.

Here are a few lines taken from book jackets at a newsstand at London's King's Cross railway station recently. Two of the books were written by journalists.

Total brutality was the creed by which they lived...and died...They killed, they raped, they destroyed—nothing was beyond the reach of their cruelty . . . The blood-soaked novel of a band of brutal Congo mercenaries.

195

Ex-para, SAS man ... joins the mercenaries in Angola ... written with inside knowledge of the harsh realities of mercenary life—its violence, its cynicism, its strange code . . .

He was in love, he was in desparate danger, and he was in the middle of the biggest story in Africa . . . A brutally exciting novel of personal courage and international power politics.

Such are today's adventure comics, bloodthirsty little fantasies for adolescent would-be conquistadors, roaming beyond the limits of their daily lives, even if that means sitting on the underground with no job in a country at the end of its empire confronted by a world in which adversaries now have modern arms with which to retaliate. These modest palliatives in the absence of an overseas national purpose are strikingly sexist, racist and anti-communist. Perhaps this is just the medicine their elders want for them: every boy a Popeye vanquishing the enemy whether in the jungle or Moscow's back streets in league with the secret agencies of the British establishment—a nation of closet heros weaned on video nasties and killer comics. The pity is that these thrillers are hardly more than political wet dreams, a form of moral impotence reserved largely for the millions of kids and their fathers who quit secondary schools with no qualifications. For them Eton is a cruel joke. The thrillers—their primers in armpit patriotism, and a real step down from the Victorian creed of muscular Christianity.

People who read the stuff probably won't be interested in the political ramifications of yet another coup in yet another Third World country, or even a change in the Soviet leadership. But what about reporters who carry such thrillers in their cases and hip pockets and aspire to write them? Are they going to appreciate what's going on around them? Or are they going to file crackpot copy, some typed in the taxi from the airport, sketching in a deft hero's role for themselves? Perhaps the tropics, not to say the entire Cold War, should be left to the fevered imaginations of young boys and hacks getting off on verbal steroids, hard men with the moral sense of Daffy Duck.

The trouble is that too many of my colleagues have recently had to spend too much time stepping over bodies to find much amusement in that. They're getting fed-up writing biographies of the dead found lying only a short drive from air-conditioned bars of five-star hotels, a few hours' flying time from Miami and Rome. On the other hand they now have a reasonably good idea as to why people will take up arms and fight just to stay alive, why women are today joining guerrillas to keep their children from being shot.

It should be apparent that this is now happening across much of the world where people see little choice of doing otherwise.

★ ★ ★

On Saturday night, 3 April 1982, I was in Portsmouth with British squaddies and sailors drinking last pints, squeezing girls before embarking for the Falkland Islands. They hadn't seen their country carved up by greed-crazed politicians bent on graft and bribery, nor learned how to talk aid agency personnel into relinquishing a few sacks of grain, nor been to party indoctrination school, nor fought in a war. They knew more about the dole, Paddy-bashing and nuclear games in NATO. They were open, frank and a bit concerned. They were also kids.

Soon they learned a few cold and windswept truths in the South Atlantic. Much of the fighting in the Falklands was a bloody close match. There was little doubt that Britain would win. But at what cost? A lot of men who returned are more genuinely confident now. They're also more sober, the realisation coming to them under fire that the "Argies" aren't Spanish-speaking idiots, that most of the Argentine forces had good weapons, adequate clothing, some fine air support and at times fought fiercely and well. Without American Sidewinder missiles the air war could have been very different. Without American satellite communications British tactics could well have floundered. It seems as if General Galtieri's forces have been the historic instrument to drive home the high price of keeping Britain's already much diminished sovereignty overseas intact. Newsstand thrillers and the "Gotcha!" press hadn't prepared squaddies for that.

Now they know. The question today is whether their parents and the rest of the British public will ever find out.

Behind the razzamataz, bunting and drum thumping victory speeches the Falklands affair was an unedifying sight. The British government had been caught with its pants down, and before they were hoiked up again a couple of billion pounds had been dumped into the South Atlantic and several hundred men were dead.

Before that happens again it might be a good idea if several more journalists and their editors quietly ditched their tired lies and fawning mimicry. They don't have to go the whole hog and begin prowling the offices of Third World revolutionary movements, interviewing men on the run in chintzy bed-and-breakfast hotels, working the other side of the street as it's called. But they might just once give the Foreign Office a miss, and just once skip those off-the-record briefings and chats with their school chums. They might just try to think for themselves. Isn't that, after all, what independence of the press is all about?

197

Index

199